Trademark Law
A Practitioner's Guide

Trademark Law
A Practitioner's Guide

Siegrun D. Kane

Date of Publication: June 1987

G1-1004
Practising Law Institute
New York City

Library of Congress Catalog Card Number: 86-83354

To David H.T. Kane, my partner twice over,
and our most important issues:
David D. and Brendon

With grateful appreciation to
Barbara A. Larsen
my partner and in-house editor
who made an impossible task possible

Table of Chapters

Table of Contents

Table of Contents

1

Introduction

The Basics

What Is a Trademark?

A common synonym for trademark is brand name. COKE and 7-UP are well known trademarks (brand names) for soft drinks. CHRYSLER and CHEVROLET are trademarks (brand names) for automobiles. Trademarks or brand names identify the product as coming from a particular company. Consumers may not know the name of the company, but they do know that products bearing the same brand originate from a single company.

While a brand name is always a trademark, a trademark is not always a brand name. Trademarks can consist of a variety of symbols:

A design can be a trademark. For example, the Ralston Purina Checkerboard Square and the Gucci Red and Green Stripes are trademarks.

A product shape can be a trademark. The shape of the COCA-COLA bottle is exclusively associated with the makers of COCA-COLA.

A number can be a trademark. "4711" is a trademark identifying the cologne of a German manufacturer.

A slogan can be a trademark. "COLOR SO NATURAL ONLY HER HAIRDRESSER KNOWS FOR SURE" identifies the hair coloring made by Clairol.

The critical element in all these trademarks, be they words, designs, shapes, numbers, or slogans, is that they identify and distinguish one company's products from another's.

The Trademark Act of 1946 (known as the Lanham Act) defines a trademark this way:

> The term "trademark" includes any word, name, symbol, or device or any combination thereof adopted and used by a manufacturer or merchant to identify and distinguish his goods, including a unique product, from those manufactured or sold by others and to indicate the source of the goods, even if that source is unknown.[1]

Trademark Versus Service Mark

A service mark is to services what a trademark is to products. A service mark identifies and distinguishes the services of one company from another. Again, the Lanham Act provides a straightforward definition.

> The term "service mark" means a mark used in the sale or advertising of services to identify and distinguish the services of one person, including a unique service, from the services of others and to indicate the source of the services, even if that source is unknown.[2]

Typical service marks are retail department store names (SAKS and MACY'S), bank names (CITIBANK), and restaurant names (MAXIM'S, LUTECE). The same name can be a trademark and a service mark. SAKS is a service mark for department store services and SAKS is a trademark for clothing sold under the SAKS label.

Trademark Versus Trade Name

A trade name is a name used to identify a business. The Lanham Act gives a trade name the same definition as commercial name:

> The terms "trade name" and "commercial name" include individual names and surnames, firm names and trade names used by

1. 15 U.S.C. § 1127.
2. *Id.*

> manufacturers, industrialists, merchants, agriculturists, and others to identify their businesses, vocations, or occupations; the names or titles lawfully adopted and used by persons, firms, associations, corporations, companies, unions, and any manufacturing, industrial, commercial, agricultural, or other organizations engaged in trade or commerce and capable of suing and being sued in a court of law.[3]

A trade name may also be used as a trademark to identify products—and a trade name may be used as a service mark to identify services. Thus the IBM company uses IBM in its company name, it uses IBM to identify its computer products, and it uses IBM to identify its computer leasing services.

To summarize: Trademarks identify products.
Service marks identify services.
Trade names identify businesses.

Certification and Collective Marks

The picture gets more complicated when we move on to certification and collective marks. The definition of certification and collective marks ties in with their titles. Certification marks "certify" product characteristics such as regional origin or production by union members. In addition, the certification mark is used on products that are not owned or sold by the owner of the certification mark.

Some examples should help: The UNION LABEL on clothing certifies that the clothing was worked on by members of the garment union. But the clothing bearing the label is not sold or owned by the union. The GOOD HOUSEKEEPING SEAL OF APPROVAL certifies that products meet certain standards. But the products bearing the Seal are not sold or owned by the GOOD HOUSEKEEPING people.

The Lanham Act definition for certification mark is a mouthful. It is easier to digest if you keep in mind the principle that

---

3. *Id.*

certification marks certify characteristics of products not belonging to the certifier.

> The term "certification mark" means a mark used upon or in connection with the products or services of one or more persons other than the owner of the mark to certify regional or other origin, material, mode of manufacture, quality, accuracy or other characteristics of such goods or services or that the work or labor on the goods and services was performed by members of a union or other organization.[4]

A collective mark also ties in with its name. A collective mark is used to indicate membership in a collective or group. A 4H CLUB member uses the 4H CLUB symbol to indicate membership in the 4H CLUB. Thus speaks the Lanham Act:

> The term "collective mark" means a trademark or service mark used by the members of a cooperative, an association or other collective group or organization and includes marks used to indicate membership in a union, an association or other organization.[5]

If you're not too sure what kind of mark you are dealing with, the term "mark" should cover the situation. The Lanham Act defines "mark" this way:

> The term "mark" includes any trademark, service mark, collective mark, or certification mark entitled to registration under this chapter whether registered or not.[6]

For purposes of simplicity, this book will use the word trademark as a synonym for mark, unless otherwise indicated. Now that we have the basics down, let's see how trademarks fit into the legal framework.

---

4. *Id.*
5. *Id.*
6. *Id.*

Relation Between Trademarks and Other Intellectual Property Rights

Trademarks and Unfair Competition

Trademark law is part of the broader law of unfair competition. Trademark infringement is one kind of unfair competition.

Unfair competition law also protects against a variety of other unfair commercial acts. Examples of unfair competition include trade name infringement (use of a business name likely to cause confusion with an established business), false advertising, copying of trade dress (packaging, labeling, and/or product appearance), and misappropriation (unfairly benefitting from another's investment).

Trademarks are often lumped together and confused with other "intellectual property" rights. Chief among these rights are patents and copyrights. The source of patent and copyright law is the U.S. Constitution. The Constitution authorizes the "securing for Limited Time to Authors and Inventors the exclusive rights to their respective Writings and Discoveries. . . ."[7] A brief description of the different kinds of exclusive rights preserved under the patent and copyright law follows.

Patents

Patents are granted for new, useful, and nonobvious inventions. A patent is issued by the U.S. Patent and Trademark Office after a patent application has been examined and determined to meet the statutory criteria.

The patent owner is entitled to exclude others from practicing his invention for a term of seventeen years from the date the patent is issued. Design patents, which are granted for new, ornamental, and nonobvious designs, have a more limited life (maximum of fourteen years).

---

7. U.S. CONST. art. I, § 8 cl. 8.

Patent rights are delineated by the federal Patent Act of 1952.[8] There is no state patent protection. Indeed, the states may not enact laws that conflict with the rights or limits specified by the federal Patent Act.[9]

Copyrights

Copyright law protects the original writings of an author. The word "writings" has broad application, extending to any fixed, tangible expression. "Writings" include not only books, but jewelry, fabric designs, phonorecords, plays, television broadcasts, etc.

Copyright law does not protect abstract ideas, but only the tangible expression of an idea.

To secure copyright protection, a proper copyright notice should be affixed at first publication. Generally, the notice includes the symbol ©, the author's name, and year of publication.

Copyright registration is obtained by submitting an application and two copies of the work to the Register of Copyrights. The application is examined and if the work is determined to be copyrightable, a registration is issued. The owner of a copyright registration may bring suit in federal court.

Under the Copyright Law of 1976, the time period of exclusive use runs for the life of the author plus fifty years. Where the author is a corporation, the limit is seventy-five years from first publication or one hundred years from first creation, whichever expires first.

Copyrights, like patents, are exclusively governed by federal statute and states are prohibited from granting protection that conflicts with the federal law.

8. 35 U.S.C. § 1 *et seq.*
9. Sears, Roebuck & Co. v. Stiffel Co., 376 U.S. 225 (1964).

Trademarks, Patents, and Copyrights Compared

Trademarks, patents, and copyrights are independent rights and the claiming of one does not preclude the claiming of any other. All these rights may apply to a single product.

Take your new personal computer for example. The interior mechanism may be protected by patent. During the seventeen-year patent term, anyone who makes, uses, or sells the computer's patented mechanism or its equivalent is liable for patent infringement.

The computer's instruction manual and software programs may be protected by copyright. During the author's life plus fifty years, anyone who makes a copy "substantially similar" to the copyrighted work is liable for copyright infringement.[10]

The name of the computer may be protected by trademark. The shape of the computer may also be protected by trademark, as well as by design patent law.[11] Trademark law, unlike patent and copyright law, confers a perpetual monopoly. So long as the trademark continues to identify a single source, anyone who uses a confusingly similar mark is liable for trademark infringement.

Use as Essential to Trademark Protection: Use It or Lose It

"Use it or lose it" should be a guiding principle for trademark owners. Use is not only essential to establishing trademark rights, continued use is essential to preserving trademark rights. Over sixty years ago the Supreme Court recognized this critical distinction between trademarks on the one hand and patents and copyrights on the other. The Court warned against:

> [T]he fundamental error of supposing that a trademark right is a right in gross or at large, like a statutory copyright or a patent for an invention, to either of which, in truth, it has little or no analogy.

10. Soptra Fabrics Corp. v. Stafford Knitting Mills, Inc., 490 F.2d 1092, 1093 (2d Cir. 1974).
11. *In re* Mogen David Wine Corp., 328 F.2d 925, 929 (C.C.P.A. 1964).

> *Delaware & H Canal Co. v. Clark*, 13 Wall. 311, 322, 20 L. ed. 581, 583; *McLean v. Fleming*, 96 U.S. 245, 254, 24 L. ed. 828, 832. There is no such thing as property in a trademark except as a right appurtenant to an established business or trade in connection with which the mark is employed. The law of trademarks is but a part of the broader law of unfair competition; the right to a particular mark grows out of its use, not its mere adoption; its function is simply to designate the goods as the product of a particular trader and to protect his good will against the sale of another's product as his; and it is not the subject of property except in connection with an existing business.[12]

Overview of Trademark Law

Purpose of Trademarks

Identify Origin

The Supreme Court back in 1916 described the primary purpose of a trademark "to identify the origin or ownership of the article to which it is affixed."[13] This purpose is at the heart of the Lanham Act definition of trademark: "to identify and distinguish" one manufacturer's or merchant's products from another's. As one court put it:

> Trademarks help consumers to select goods. By identifying the source of the goods, they convey valuable information to consumers at lower costs. Easily identified trademarks reduce the costs consumers incur in searching for what they desire, and the lower the costs of search the more competitive the market.[14]

12. United Drug Co. v. Theodore Rectanus Co., 248 U.S. 90, 97 (1918).
13. Hanover Star Milling Co. v. Metcalf, 240 U.S. 403, 412 (1916).
14. Scandia Down Corp. v. Euroquilt, Inc., 772 F.2d 1423, 1429 (7th Cir. 1985), *cert. denied*, 106 S. Ct. 1801 (1986).

It is not necessary, however, that consumers know the name of the source.[15] Not many people know that CREST toothpaste is made by Procter & Gamble.

It is also not necessary that the trademark belong to the manufacturer of the product. The source or origin identified by the mark may be a merchant (*e.g.*, Sears), whose goods are manufactured for him.

> The use of a trademark, however, does not necessarily and as a matter of law impart that the articles on which it is used are manufactured by its user. It is enough that they are manufactured for him, that he controls their production, or that they pass through his hands in the course of trade and that he gives to them the benefit of his reputation or his name and business style.[16]

Quality Assurance

Trademarks are symbols of quality. The familiar STANLEY trademark on tools assures the consumer that each STANLEY tool he buys is of the same high quality as the last STANLEY tool he bought. This quality assurance function requires the trademark owner to maintain consistent quality standards so that the consumer gets what he expects.

> A trademark also may induce the supplier of goods to make higher quality products and to adhere to a consistent level of quality. The trademark is a valuable asset, part of the "goodwill" of a business. If the seller provides an inconsistent level of quality, or reduces quality below what consumers expect from earlier experience, that reduces the value of the trademark. The value of a tradmark is in a sense a "hostage" of consumers; if the seller

15. Warner Bros., Inc. v. Gay Toys, Inc., 724 F.2d 327, 333-34 (2d Cir. 1983).
16. Victor Tool & Mach. Corp. v. Sun Control Awnings, Inc., 299 F. Supp. 868, 874 (E.D. Mich. 1968), *aff'd*, 411 F.2d 792 (6th Cir. 1969).

> disappoints the consumers, they respond by devaluing the trademark. The existence of this hostage gives the seller another incentive to afford consumers the quality of goods they prefer and expect.[17]

If quality control is not maintained, the consumer is deceived and the trademark owner stands to lose his trademark.[18]

Symbols of Goodwill

Trademarks are symbols of goodwill. The value of this goodwill increases with length of use, advertising, and sales. Trademarks used for a long time on successful, highly-advertised products have developed tremendous goodwill. The universal goodwill for such famous marks as PEPSI and 7-UP is priceless.

Over forty years ago, the Supreme Court recognized the role of trademark law in protecting the goodwill symbolized by a well-known mark. The Court described this goodwill as "commercial magnetism" and warned that poachers would be prosecuted.

> The protection of trade-marks is the law's recognition of the psychological function of symbols. If it is true that we live by symbols, it is no less true that we purchase goods by them. A trademark is a merchandising short-cut which induces a purchaser to select what he wants, or what he has been led to believe he wants. The owner of a mark exploits this human propensity by making every effort to impregnate the atmosphere of the market with the drawing power of a congenial symbol. Whatever the means employed, the aim is the same—to convey through the mark, in the minds of potential customers, the desirability of the commodity

17. Scandia Down Corp. v. Euroquilt, Inc., 772 F.2d 1423, 1429-30 (7th Cir. 1985), *cert. denied,* 106 S. Ct. 1801 (1986).
18. The Lanham Act provides that acts of commission or omission by the trademark owner can cause a mark "to lose its significance as an indication of origin." *See* 15 U.S.C. § 1127(b). The failure to exercise quality control has been recognized as the kind of act that can result in loss of trademark rights in a number of cases. *See* Kentucky Fried Chicken Corp. v. Diversified Packaging Corp., 549 F.2d 368, 387 (5th Cir. 1977); United States Jaycees v. Philadelphia Jaycees, 639 F.2d 134, 140 (3d Cir. 1981). *See* chapter 15, *infra*, on trademark licensing.

upon which it appears. Once this is attained, the trade-mark owner has something of value. If another poaches upon the commercial magnetism of the symbol he has created, the owner can obtain legal redress.[19]

Down through the years, the Supreme Court teaching has been applied to enjoin the second user who "comes as close as he dares" to the well-known mark.[20]

The Legal Framework

A network of federal and state statutory and common law insures that a trademark does serve to identify origin, assure quality, and symbolize goodwill. The Trademark Act of 1946 (the Lanham Act) is the federal statute governing trademark rights.[21] The states also have their own trademark statutes. In addtion to statutes providing for state registration, a number of states have Deceptive Trade Practice Acts and Anti-dilution Statutes (statutes designed to protect a distinctive mark from being "diluted."

Trademarks are acquired in this country only by use, under common law principles. The Lanham Act provides for *registration* of marks already owned; it does not *create* trademarks, which must exist before they *can* be registered. They must also have been used in interstate or foreign commerce since the Lanham Act is a federal statute, which rests on the Commerce Clause of the Constitution.

Consumer Protection: The Likelihood of Confusion Standard

The Lanham Act is intended to secure to the owner of the mark the goodwill of his business and to protect the ability of consumers

19. Mishawaka Mfg. Co. v. Kresge Co., 316 U.S. 203, 205 (1942).
20. A.T. Cross Co. v. Jonathan Bradley Pens, Inc., 470 F.2d 689, 692 (2d Cir. 1972); Q-Tips, Inc. v. Johnson & Johnson, Inc., 206 F.2d 144, 146 (3d Cir. 1953).
21. 15 U.S.C. § 1051 *et seq.*

to distinguish among competing products.[22] The Lanham Act accomplishes this intent by providing that the user of a mark likely to cause confusion, mistake, or deception shall be liable in a civil action.[23]

Likelihood of confusion is also the test for common law trademark infringement and unfair competition claims.[24]

Kinds of Confusion

"Confusion" is not limited to confusion of source. "Confusion" includes confusion between products as well as confusion as to endorsement, sponsorship, or any connection with the trademark owner.[25]

Originally the Lanham Act required a showing that the infringer's use "is likely to cause confusion or to cause mistake, or to deceive *purchasers as to the source of origin of such goods or services*" (emphasis supplied).[26] However, the section was amended in 1962 to delete the italicized language. The purpose of this amendment was:

> to outlaw the use of trademarks which are likely to cause confusion, mistake, or deception of any kind, not merely of purchasers nor simply as to source of origin.[27]

"Confusion of any kind" includes psychological subliminal confusion as well as confusion before and after purchase.[28]

22. 15 U.S.C. § 1127. Park 'N Fly, Inc. v. Dollar Park & Fly, Inc. 469 U.S. 189, 198 (1985).
23. 15 U.S.C. § 1114.
24. Geisel v. Poynter Prods., Inc., 283 F. Supp. 261 (S.D.N.Y. 1968).
25. Standard & Poor's Corp. v. Commodity Exch., Inc., 683 F.2d 704, 708 (2d Cir. 1982); Shakey's Inc. v. Covalt, 704 F.2d 426, 631 (9th Cir. 1983); Amstar Corp. v. Domino's Pizza, Inc., 615 F.2d 252, 258 (5th Cir.), *cert. denied*, 449 U.S. 899 (1980).
26. 15 U.S.C. § 1114(1).
27. Syntex Laboratories, Inc. v. Norwich Pharmacal Co., 437 F.2d 566, 568 (2d Cir. 1971).
28. Ortho Pharmaceutical Corp. v. American Cyanamid Co., 361 F. Supp. 1032, 1044 (D.N.J. 1973); Playboy Enters., Inc. v. Chuckleberry Pub., Inc., 486 F. Supp. 414, 419 (S.D.N.Y. 1980), *aff'd*, 687 F.2d 563 (2d Cir. 1982);

In the *Steinway* piano case, the Court pointed to the "subliminal confusion" surrounding the relationship between the corporate entities and their piano products sold under the name STEINWAY.[29] The Court recognized the damage that resulted from "initial confusion" where defendant's name "attracts potential customers" based on plaintiff's reputation. Even if no one actually buys defendant's product thinking it is plaintiff's or guaranteed by plaintiff, misleading potential buyers "into an initial interest" works an injury.[30]

Confusion of nonpurchasers has also been recognized as an injury:

> Even before the 1962 amendment Judge Learned Hand deemed the potential confusion of nonpurchasers to be legally material. In *G.H. Mumm Champagne* v. *Eastern Wine Corp.*, 142 F.2d 499 (2d Cir.), *cert. denied*, 323 U.S. 715, 65 S. Ct. 41, 89 L. Ed. 575 (1944), he found defendant's deceptively labeled champagne could be substituted for plaintiff's champagne and mislead nonpurchasers. In *Mastercrafters Clock & Radio Company* v. *Vacheron and Constantin-Le Coultre Watches, Inc.*, 221 F.2d 464 (2d Cir.), *cert. denied*, 350 U.S. 832, 76 S. Ct. 67, 100 L. Ed. 743 (1955), *reh. denied*, 350 U.S. 897, 76 S. Ct. 149, 100 L. Ed. 789 (1955), the purchasers of defendant's cheap imitation of plaintiff's distinctive clock knew exactly what they were buying. But the court regarded it as wrongful that guests in the homes of those purchasers might be led to believe that the imitation displayed by their host was, in fact, the prestigious timepiece. Although the findings cited above were made under theories of unfair competition, they certainly were part of the legal context in which Congress acted in adopting the 1962 amendment.[31]

Grotrian, Helfferich, Schulz, Th. Steinweg Nachf. v. Steinway & Sons, 523 F.2d 1331 (2d Cir. 1975); Lois Sportswear, U.S.A., Inc. v. Levi Strauss & Co., 799 F.2d 867 (2d Cir. 1986).

29. Grotrian, Helfferich, Schulz, Th. Steinweg Nachf. v. Steinway & Sons, 523 F.2d 1331, 1341 (2d Cir. 1975).

30. *Id.* at 1340-42.

31. Koppers Co. v. Krupp-Koppers GmbH, 517 F. Supp. 836, 843-44 (W.D. Pa. 1981). For other decisions noting that confusion is not restricted to purchasers see AMP, Inc. v. Foy, 540 F.2d 1181, 1183 (4th Cir. 1976); Grotrian, Helfferich, Schulz, Th. Steinweg Nachf. v. Steinway & Sons, 523

While confusion may occur before, during, or after purchase, the parties confused must fall within the general category of prospective purchasers. Moreover, the strongest evidence of confusion is confusion that actually affects a purchase.[32]

The Average Purchaser

Likelihood of confusion is confusion by an appreciable number of average purchasers of the products in issue.[33] If the product is sold only to skilled technicians, then the average purchaser is the skilled technician. If the product is sold to the general public, the average purchaser is the general public. The general public, however, is not all stamped from the same mold. Rather, the public is:

> that vast multitude which includes the ignorant, the unthinking and the credulous, who, in making purchases, do not stop to analyze, but are governed by appearances and general impressions.[34]

The care exercised by the general public is a function of the type and price of the product. Less care is involved in the purchase of chewing gum than the purchase of automobiles or pianos:

> The relevant cases not only authorize but instruct the trial courts, in making a determination as to likelihood of confusion, to consider the level of sophistication of the relevant purchasers.... The greater the value of an article the more careful the typical consumer can be expected to be; the average purchaser of an automobile will no doubt devote more attention to examining different products than will the average purchaser of a ball of twine.... In some cases, of course, as where the products are identical and the marks are identical, the sophistication of buyers cannot be relied on to prevent confusion.[35]

F.2d 1331, 1342 (2d Cir. 1975); Rolls-Royce Motors, Ltd. v. A & A Fiberglass, Inc., 428 F. Supp. 689, 694 n.10 (N.D. Ga. 1976); Levi Strauss & Co. v. Blue Bell, Inc., 632 F.2d 817, 822 (9th Cir. 1980).

32. ITT Corp. v. XTRA Corp., 225 U.S.P.Q. 723, 729 (D. Mass. 1985).
33. Maternally Yours, Inc. v. Your Maternity Shop, Inc., 234 F.2d 538, 542 (2d Cir. 1956).
34. Florence Mfg. Co. v. J.C. Dowd & Co., 178 F. 73, 75 (2d Cir. 1910).
35. McGregor-Doniger, Inc. v. Drizzle, Inc., 599 F.2d 1126, 1137 (2d Cir. 1979).

As careful or careless as the average purchaser may be, the law does not expect the average purchaser to:

1. make detailed side-by-side comparisons; or
2. have perfect recall.[36]

These principles are important to emphasize to an adversary or judge who may view plaintiff's and defendant's products from the unrealistic perspective of side-by-side comparison.

Beyond Confusion: Protection of Trademark Owner's Goodwill from Dilution

Case after case echoes the importance of protecting the goodwill symbolized by a trademark. Trading on that goodwill is uniformly deplored. But the Lanham Act and common law trademark infringement go only so far in protecting that goodwill. The boundary is drawn, as noted above, at the not always clear cut line of likely confusion.

What about the situation where a well known trademark is used on goods completely unrelated to the famous mark. Suppose, for example, that famous BRAND X was used on steam shovels, and the infringer comes along with the identical BRAND X on butter. It may be difficult to persuade a court that purchasers are likely to confuse BRAND X steam shovels with BRAND X butter. But BRAND X has another avenue of attack: the dilution claim.

State anti-dilution statutes prohibit use of a distinctive mark "notwithstanding the absence of competition between the parties or the absence of confusion as to the source of goods or services."[37]

Initially courts were reluctant to enforce the literal wording of state anti-dilution statutes. However, there is a growing body of

36. Union Carbide Corp. v. Ever-Ready, Inc., 531 F.2d 366, 382, 385 (7th Cir. 1976).

37. N.Y. Gen. Bus. Law, § 368-d. As of 1986, some twenty-three states had enacted anti-dilution statutes.

case law holding that it is not necessary to show confusion or competition to obtain an injuction under these statutes.[38]

The Equitable Nature of Trademark Rights: Bad Guys Finish Last

In assessing the chance of protecting your trademark in court, remember the court sits in equity. Trademark cases do not turn on the cut and dried application of legal principles. Rather, they turn on equitable considerations.

Any time defendant can be pictured as the bad guy, *e.g.*, through evidence of copying, plaintiff's chance of success improves. By the same token, a plaintiff who engages in misrepresentations to the court or other non-good-guy behavior had better be thinking of settlement.

Defendant's case will also be stronger where he has a large investment in the mark. Courts bend over backwards to permit continued use of even identical marks where the second user has made a substantial investment in good faith.[39] The key phrase here is good faith. A substantial investment in bad faith will get defendant little sympathy.

In the final analysis, it is the court's perception of the equities, *i.e.*, the relative harm to each party and the public interest in protection from confusion that will determine which party is the winner in a trademark action.

---

38. Allied Maintenance Corp. v. Allied Mechanical Trades, Inc., 198 U.S.P.Q. 418, 422 (N.Y. Ct. App. 1977); Dallas Cowboys Cheerleaders, Inc. v. Pussycat Cinema, Ltd., 604 F.2d 200, 204 (2d Cir. 1979); Sally Gee, Inc. v. Myra Hogan, Inc., 699 F.2d 621, 624 (2d Cir. 1983). See chapter 7, pp. 140-47, *infra*, for discussion of dilution.
39. Mushroom Makers, Inc. v. R.G. Barry Corp., 580 F.2d 44 (2d Cir. 1978); Vitarroz Corp. v. Borden, Inc., 644 F.2d 960 (2d Cir. 1981).

2

Selecting a Trademark

Trademark Categories

Some trademarks are stronger and easier to protect from the outset than others. Some terms claimed as trademarks turn out to be not protectable at all. Some terms—not protectable at first—after some period of use and advertising, gain protection.

In assessing trademark strength, courts recognize four basic categories.[1]

Generic	The common name for the kind of product —can never be a trademark.
Descriptive	A term that describes something about the product—can only be a trademark after some period of exclusive use.
Suggestive	A term that subtly suggests something about the product—can be a trademark immediately upon use.
Arbitrary/ Fanciful	A term that bears little or no relationship to the product—the strongest of trademarks.

This chapter will discuss the guidelines used to classify trademarks in the four basic categories. These guidelines should give you a feel for the protectability of your proposed mark and how it will fare in court.

---

1. Abercrombie & Fitch Co. v. Hunting World, Inc., 537 F.2d 4, 9 (2d Cir. 1976).

Generic Terms

A generic term is the common name for a type of product made by many companies, *e.g.*, automobile; cat food. A generic term can never be a trademark.

To bestow a monopoly on a generic term would be contrary to the public interest in promoting competition. Terms or symbols that are needed by competitors to describe their goods should be freely available for use.

> To allow trademark protection for generic terms, i.e., names which describe the genus of goods being sold, even when these have become identified with a first user, would grant the owner of the mark a monopoly, since a competitor could not describe his goods as what they are.[2]

Examples of terms found to be generic include: LITE for low calorie beer,[3] SURGICENTER for surgical center,[4] SUPER GLUE for strong bonding, rapid setting glue,[5] CONSUMER ELECTRONICS for magazine title,[6] SAFARI for hunting expedition, hats, and boots,[7] and SOFTSOAP for liquid hand soap.[8]

A term that is generic for one product can be "arbitrary" and hence a strong mark when applied to a different product. Spoon is generic for a certain kind of eating utensil we all know, but "Spoon" has no meaning (is arbitrary) as applied to cigarettes.

Terms that are not initially generic can become generic. A trademark that comes to be understood by the public as the

---

2. CES Publishing Corp. v. St. Regis Publications, Inc., 531 F.2d 11, 13 (2d Cir. 1975).
3. Miller Brewing Co. v. Heileman Brewing Co., 561 F.2d 75 (7th Cir. 1977).
4. Surgicenters of America, Inc. v. Medical Dental Surgeries Co., 601 F.2d 1011 (9th Cir. 1979).
5. Loctite Corp. v. National Starch & Chem. Corp., 516 F. Supp. 190 (S.D.N.Y. 1981).
6. CES Publishing Corp. v. St. Regis Publications, Inc., 531 F.2d 11 (2d Cir. 1975).
7. Abercrombie & Fitch Co. v. Hunting World, Inc., 537 F.2d 4 (2d Cir. 1976).
8. *In re* Minnetonka, Inc., 212 U.S.P.Q. 772 (T.T.A.B. 1981).

generic (common) name for a type of product will no longer be protected. "Cellophane" and "aspirin" are prime examples of trademarks that became generic and freely available for use.[9]

Descriptive Terms

A descriptive term tells something about the product. It describes some characteristic, quality, purpose, component, or other property of the product. A frequently cited test for descriptiveness is:

> A mark is descriptive if it forthwith conveys an immediate idea of the ingredients, qualities or characteristics of the goods.[10]

Examples of marks found to be descriptive are:

MARK	GOODS	CITATION
HONEY-BAKED HAM	hams	*Schmidt v. Honeysweet Hams, Inc.*, 609 F. Supp. 227 (E.D. Mich. 1985)
HOMEMAKERS	family housekeeping services	*Homemakers Home & Health Care Services, Inc.* v. *Chicago Home for the Friendless*, 484 F.2d 625 (7th Cir. 1973)
TENDER VITTLES	cat food	*Ralston Purina Co.* v. *Thomas J. Lipton, Inc.*, 341 F. Supp. 129 (S.D.N.Y. 1972)
QUIK PRINT	fast printing and duplicating services	*In re Application of Quik-Print Copy Shops, Inc.*, 616 F.2d 523 (C.C.P.A. 1980)
TRIM	manicuring implements	*W.E. Bassett Co.* v. *Revlon, Inc.*, 435 F.2d 656 (2d Cir. 1970)

9. Bayer Co. v. United Drug Co., 272 F. 505 (D.C.N.Y. 1921); DuPont Cellophane Co. v. Waxed Prods. Co., 85 F.2d 75 (2d Cir. 1936), *cert. denied*, 299 U.S. 601, *cert. denied*, 304 U.S. 575, *reh'g denied*, 305 U.S. 672 (1938). *See* chapter 8, *infra*, on the generic defense.

10. Stix Prods. Inc. v. United Merchants & Mfrs., Inc., 295 F. Supp. 479, 487-88 (S.D.N.Y. 1968).

MARK	GOODS	CITATION
VISION CENTER	optical clinics	*Vision Center* v. *Opticks, Inc.*, 596 F.2d 111 (5th Cir. 1979)
AUTO PAGE	automatic dialing device	*Gimix, Inc.* v. *JS&A Group, Inc.*, 699 F.2d 901 (7th Cir. 1983).

Secondary Meaning

Secondary Meaning Required to Protect Descriptive Marks: Because descriptive terms initially describe, rather than identify the source of a product, they are not protectable until the consumer learns to associate them with a single source. This learned association is called "secondary meaning." A descriptive mark is protected only when secondary meaning is shown.[11]

The term "secondary" comes from the fact that this meaning of source association occurs second in time to the primary descriptive meaning. The primary meaning is the ordinary English language meaning conveyed by the term. For example, the primary meaning of "EXTRA STRENGTH PAIN RELIEVER" is a strong analgesic. The secondary meaning of "EXTRA STRENGTH PAIN RELIEVER," developed second in time to the primary meaning, is the EXCEDRIN product made by Bristol-Myers.

Secondary meaning is established by some period of use, sales, and advertising:

> [B]y secondary meaning we mean that romance readers associate the Harlequin Presents cover with a particular series and publisher * * * Harlequin's extensive national advertising, its phenomenal sales success, and the results of a consumer survey indicate that romance readers correlate the Harlequin Presents cover with Harlequin and the Harlequin Presents Series.[12]

11. Vision Center v. Opticks, Inc., 596 F.2d 111, 115 (5th Cir. 1979), *cert. denied*, 444 U.S. 1016 (1980); Miss Universe, Inc. v. Patricelli, 408 F.2d 506, 509 (2d Cir. 1969).
12. Harlequin Enters., Ltd. v. Gulf & Western Corp., 644 F.2d 946, 949-50 (2d Cir. 1981).

It is not necessary that purchasers know the name of the manufacturer to establish secondary meaning. The true inquiry is whether purchasers associate the mark with a single source.[13]

Another term for secondary meaning is distinctiveness. A descriptive mark can be registered under Section 2(f) of the Lanham Act upon proof of "distinctiveness."[14]

Secondary Meaning in the Making: There is also a doctrine known as "secondary meaning in the making," which affords protection to marks that are copied before secondary meaning has attached.[15] Secondary meaning in the making has had a checkered career. The doctrine has been accepted by some courts[16] and rejected by others.[17]

Suggestive Terms

Suggestive terms are protected without secondary meaning. They identify source immediately upon use. Suggestive marks suggest something about the goods but "require imagination, thought, and perception to reach a conclusion as to the nature of the goods."[18]

The following marks have been held to be suggestive:

---

13. Warner Bros., Inc. v. Gay Toys, Inc., 724 F.2d 327, 333-34 (2d Cir. 1983).
14. 15 U.S.C. § 1052(f). *See* chapter 5, pp. 92-93, *infra*, on Section 2(f).
15. National Lampoon, Inc. v. American Broadcasting Co., 497 F.2d 1343 (2d Cir. 1974).
16. Metro Kane Imports, Ltd. v. Federated Dep't Stores, Inc., 625 F. Supp. 313, 316-317 (S.D.N.Y. 1985), *aff'd*, No. 86-7104, slip op. (2d Cir. Mar. 22, 1986).
17. A.J. Canfield Co. v. Concord Beverage Co., 629 F. Supp. 200, 211-12 (E.D. Pa. 1985), *aff'd*, 808 F.2d 291 (3rd Cir. 1986); Autry Indus., Inc. v. Chesapeake Shoe Co. of Cal., Inc., 230 U.S.P.Q. 552, 554 (N.D. Cal. 1986).
18. Stix Prods., Inc. v. United Merchants & Mfrs., Inc., 295 F. Supp. 479, 488 (S.D.N.Y. 1968).

MARK	GOODS	CITATION
CONTACT	self-adhesive shelf paper	*Stix Prods., Inc.* v. *United Merchants & Mfrs., Inc.*, 295 F. Supp. 497 (S.D.N.Y. 1968)
HABITAT	home furnishings	*Habitat Design Holdings, Ltd.* v. *Habitat, Inc.*, 436 F. Supp. 327 (S.D.N.Y. 1977)
ORANGE CRUSH	orange-flavored beverage	*Orange Crush Co.* v. *California Crushed Fruit Co.*, 297 F. 892 (D.C. Cir. 1924)
PLAYBOY	magazine	*Playboy Enters., Inc.* v. *Chuckleberry Publishing, Inc.*, 486 F. Supp. 414 (S.D.N.Y. 1980), *aff'd*, 687 F.2d 563 (2d Cir. 1982)
PSYCHOCALISTHENICS	physical and mental exercises	*West & Co., Inc.* v. *Arica Inst., Inc.*, 557 F.2d 338 (2d Cir. 1977)
SKINVISIBLE	transparent medical adhesive tape	*Minnesota Mining & Mfg. Co.* v. *Johnson & Johnson*, 454 F.2d 1179 (C.C.P.A. 1972)
SPRAY 'N VAC	aerosol rug cleaner	*Glamorene Prods. Corp.* v. *Boyle-Midway, Inc.*, 188 U.S.P.Q. 145 (S.D.N.Y. 1974)
UNCOLA	non-cola soft drink	*Coca-Cola Co.* v. *Seven-Up Co.*, 497 F.2d 1351 (C.C.P.A. 1974).

Arbitrary/Fanciful Marks

Arbitrary marks are common words applied in an unfamiliar way. As stated in the McCarthy treatise:

> "Arbitrary" means that the ordinary meaning of the word mark is applied to these goods in a totally arbitrary and non-descriptive sense. . . . [T]he fact that a word is found in a dictionary does not derogate from that word's trademark significance, unless the dictionary meaning of the word is descriptive of the goods in connection with which the word is used.[19]

Examples of arbitrary marks are CAMELS for cigarettes, IVORY for soap,[20] and JELLIBEANS for a roller skating rink.[21]

Fanciful marks are coined (made up) terms with no dictionary meaning. EXXON, KODAK, and ROLEX are fanciful marks. These marks were coined to identify the trademark owner's goods.

Arbitrary and fanciful marks are inherently distinctive. Like suggestive marks, they are protected without the need for proving secondary meaning.

The trademark owner who selects an arbitrary or fanciful mark is at a distinct advantage. He is much less likely to encounter conflicts in the searching process and will find it a lot easier to protect his mark after adoption.

Drawing the Line Between Trademark Categories

A good deal of trademark litigation is devoted to drawing the line between generic/descriptive and descriptive/suggestive marks. This line is drawn from the perspective of the average purchaser.

---

19. 1 MCCARTHY, TRADEMARKS AND UNFAIR COMPETITION, § 11.4, at 440 (2d ed. 1984).
20. Abercrombie & Fitch, Co. v. Hunting World, Inc., 537 F.2d 4, 9 n.6 (2d Cir. 1976).
21. Jellibeans, Inc. v. Skating Clubs, Inc., 716 F.2d 833, 835 (11th Cir. 1983).

Generic Versus Descriptive Marks

To determine if a particular term is generic, the question is: What does this term mean to the prospective purchaser of the goods?[22]

To answer this question, courts look to:

1. dictionary definitions for the term as the common name for a kind of goods;
2. use of the term by third parties as the common name for their goods;
3. use of the term by the trademark owner as the common name for his goods;
4. use of the term in texts, patents, newspapers, and other literature as the common name for the goods;
5. the availability of other terms as the common name for the goods;
6. survey evidence.

An interesting case history in the generic/descriptive area is the Eastern Airlines "shuttle" decision.[23] Shuttle was used by Eastern for twenty-two years for its guaranteed seat/no reservation required service. Eastern's exclusive rights to shuttle were challenged by New York Air's directly competitive "shuttle service."

The major difficulty with Eastern's position was the commonly understood meaning for shuttle as evidenced by dictionary definitions and other sources. Shuttle was defined in the *American Heritage Dictionary of the English Language* as:

---

22. 15 U.S.C. § 1064(c); Bayer Co. v. United Drug Co., 272 F. 505, 509 (S.D.N.Y. 1921); H. Marvin Ginn Corp. v. Int'l Ass'n of Fire Chiefs, 782 F.2d 987 (Fed. Cir. 1986). The Third Circuit has adopted a special test to determine genericness when the product is considered its own class, *i.e.*, the competitor's need to use it. A.J. Canfield Co. v. Honickman, 808 F.2d 291, 305-06 (3rd Cir. 1986) holding chocolate fudge generic for diet soda.
23. Eastern Air Lines, Inc. v. New York Air Lines, Inc., 559 F. Supp. 1270 (S.D.N.Y. 1983).

a train, bus or plane making short, frequent trips between two points.

The term shuttle had a history of use for various modes of transportation:

Shuttle was used for a subway service in New York (between Times Square and Grand Central).

Shuttle bus was applied to short distance bus trips.

Air shuttle was listed in Roget's International Thesauraus as a synonym for air travel.

Nor was Eastern helped by survey evidence. Eastern's survey showed that only 10 percent of the respondents associated shuttle with Eastern. The survey was discounted, not only because of the low association figure, but because the survey question did not go to the generic issue. As the Court pointed out, even a high association between shuttle and Eastern would not prove that consumers recognize shuttle as a trademark. A high association between shuttle and Eastern might exist merely because Eastern was the only company or the best known company offering a shuttle service.[24]

While the Court refused to protect shuttle as a trademark, it did recognize that shuttle had come to mean a particular kind of air service. Because of Eastern's long use and advertising, shuttle as applied to air transportation had come to mean a guaranteed seat/no reservation service. Since New York Air's shuttle service did not provide a guaranteed seat/no reservation service, the Court enjoined New York Air's use of shuttle as misleading.

Here we see that, even when a mark is found generic, the court will impose limits on its use if necessary to protect the public from confusion.

---

24. For a survey going squarely to the generic issue, see the Dupont TEFLON case discussed in chapter 4, pp. 73-74, *infra*.

Descriptive Versus Suggestive Marks

Line drawing between the descriptive/suggestive category is a very subjective process. A mark that immediately describes the goods to one person may only subtly suggest something about the goods to another.

The problem in predicting the outcome of descriptive/suggestive battles is illustrated by these cases reversed on appeal:

MARK	GOODS	LOWER COURT	APPEAL COURT
POLY PITCHER	polyethylene pitcher	descriptive	suggestive[25]
COZY WARM ENERGY SAVERS	women's pajamas	suggestive	descriptive[26]
SKINVISIBLE	transparent bandage	descriptive	suggestive[27]

Moreover, a mark that is suggestive at one point in time, may become descriptive at another. This is what happened in the COZY WARM ENERGY SAVERS case. Plaintiff adopted COZY WARM ENERGY SAVERS for women's pajamas at the height of the energy crisis. The District Court found the mark to be suggestive. In reversing, the Second Circuit Court of Appeals noted:

> The district court mischaracterized the mark because it failed to consider how the meaning of the words "Cozy Warm ENERGY-SAVERS" had changed over time. The court assumed that a step of the imagination is needed to connect the concept of energy saving to women's pajamas and concluded that the mark is "suggestive" rather than "descriptive." And it may be true that such a step would have been needed, say, in 1973 or 1975. But by 1981, the

25. Blisscraft of Hollywood v. United Plastics Co., 294 F.2d 694 (2d Cir. 1961).
26. 20th Century Wear, Inc. v. Sanmark-Stardust, Inc., 747 F.2d 81 (2d Cir. 1984), *cert. denied*, 105 S. Ct. 1755 (1985).
27. Minnesota Mining & Mfg. Co. v. Johnson & Johnson, Inc., 454 F.2d 1179 (C.C.P.A. 1972).

connection between "Cozy Warm ENERGY-SAVERS" and the warming quality of plaintiff's pajama no longer required imagination, since many people were using this kind of language to describe clothing.[28]

While court determinations of descriptive/suggestive categories are hard to predict, suggestiveness may be signaled where:

1. The term is an unusual combination, *e.g.*, UNCOLA was coined by Seven-Up contrary to ordinary English language construction.[29]
2. The term is so general or nebulous that the purchaser will not know the precise nature of the goods.

> While "psychocalisthenics" . . . bears some relationship to the physical exercises conducted by Arica, this would be expected of any suggestive mark, and, in fact, would be one of the purposes of the mark. But we cannot say that "psychocalisthenics" merely describes "a combination of various yoga systems, dance and calisthenics" which require continual motion and are designed to produce specific mental, emotional and spiritual results.[30]

3. The descriptive nature of the term is not known to the general purchasing public. POLY in POLY PITCHER was known in the trade as an abbreviation for polypropylene, the plastic composition of the pitcher. But this abbreviation was not commonly known to the public.[31]
4. The term is incongruous or fanciful in the sense that it evokes an absurd image. ROACH MOTEL is incongruous for roach traps because motels are not built for roaches.[32]

---

28. 20th Century Wear, Inc. v. Sanmark-Stardust, Inc., 747 F.2d 81, 87-88 (2d Cir. 1984), *cert. denied,* 105 S. Ct. 1755 (1985).
29. Coca-Cola Co. v. Seven-Up Co., 497 F.2d 1351, 1355 (C.C.P.A. 1974).
30. West & Co. v. Arica Inst., Inc., 194 U.S.P.Q. 32, 35 (S.D.N.Y. 1976), *aff'd,* 557 F.2d 338, 343 (2d Cir. 1977).
31. Blisscraft of Hollywood v. United Plastics Co., 294 F.2d 694, 699 (2d Cir. 1961).
32. American Home Prods. Corp. v. Johnson Chem. Co., 589 F.2d 103, 106 (2d Cir. 1978).

One helpful tip in avoiding a descriptiveness finding: Do not use the trademark to describe the product. ORIGINAL BLEND, a claimed trademark for catfood, began its life as a tag line ORIGINAL BLEND OF FISH MEAT AND MILK FLAVORS. This usage weighed heavily in the finding that ORIGINAL BLEND was merely descriptive.[33]

Avoiding descriptive uses of the mark in the trademark owner's literature is easier said than done. Advertising copy writers love to play on the trademark and its relation to the product. Just remember that the more descriptive the mark, the more important it is to avoid its use in the ordinary descriptive sense.

Personal Names and Geographic Terms as Trademarks

Trademark use of a merchant's personal name and his geographic location is frequently equated with trademark use of a descriptive word. A surname, like a descriptive term, has an original nontrademark meaning. A geographic term also has an original nontrademark meaning. Just as the law gives all merchants the right to use ordinary descriptive terminology, it gives merchants the right to use their own name or the name of their geographic location.

This right, however, is limited. Just as descriptive marks are protected when secondary meaning is proven, so are personal names and geographic terms.

> Personal names used as trademarks are generally regarded as descriptive terms, not arbitrary or fanciful terms; they are thus protected only if, through usage, they have acquired distinctiveness and secondary meaning. See 3A R. Callmann, *The Law of Unfair Competition, Trademarks and Monopolies* § 21.36, at 145-46 (L. Altman 4th Ed. 1984) ("An individual name is rather similar to a

33. General Foods Corp. v. Ralston Purina Co., 220 U.S.,P.Q. 990, 994 (T.T.A.B. 1984).

descriptive word, in the sense that it might properly be regarded as a convenient description of the fact that the named individual is or was affiliated with the firm."); 1 J. McCarthy, *Trademarks and Unfair Competition* § 13.2, at 578.[34]

Personal Names

Personal name cases frequently involve battles among family members. If the court perceives that the second user has developed his own reputation in the business, it will bend over backwards to permit his use with certain restrictions.

Types of Injunctive Relief

Injunctions issued in personal name cases may permit the second comer's use with certain restrictions. Common restrictions include required use of the second comer's full name, disclaimers of connection with the more established firm, and limitations on the size of the second comer's name.[35]

A case in point is *Joseph Scott Co.* v. *Scott Swimming Pools, Inc.*[36] There were two brothers in the Scott swimming pools business: James and Joseph Jr. Joseph Jr. left in 1972 and formed his own firm, Scott AquaScapes. For over ten years the brothers operated under an agency agreement. Joseph sold pools on behalf of Scott Pools while his AquaScapes company provided landscaping and pool servicing. During this period, Joseph had acquired his own reputation as a pool designer. In 1983, Joseph terminated his agreement with Scott Pools Company and changed his name to Joseph Scott Co.

The District Court enjoined the use of Joseph Scott as Joseph's company name because it caused considerable confusion with Scott Pools. The Court permitted use of the name Joseph Scott along with another company name provided that: 1) Joseph Scott was no larger than one-quarter the size of the company name; and

---

34. Abraham Zion Corp. v. Lebow, 761 F.2d 93, 104 (2d Cir. 1985).
35. Taylor Wine Co. v. Bully Hill Vineyards, Inc., 569 F.2d 731 (2d Cir. 1978).
36. 764 F.2d 62 (2d Cir. 1985).

2) Joseph Scott appeared in direct conjunction with a disclaimer stating "Not connected with Scott Swimming Pools, Inc." The Court of Appeals modified the District Court injunction to: 1) permit use of the full name Joseph M. Scott, Jr. on pool signage and advertising materials in size as large as the company name; and 2) require use of the disclaimer of association with Scott Pools in the same size as the name Joseph M. Scott, Jr.

The Appeal Court's decision reflects the balancing process typical of trademark cases in general and personal name cases in particular:

> By its very nature, a preliminary injunction is a specific equitable remedy and, thus, must be framed in such a way as to strike a delicate balance between competing interests. By necessity, the scope of the injunction must be drawn by reference to the facts of the individual case, reflecting a careful balancing of the equities. Where, as in the instant case, a decree serves to limit an individual's use of his own name in a business that he has nurtured, a court must be particularly cautious to enjoin only those uses that are likely to create appreciable confusion, and no more. See *Waterman Co. v. Modern Pen Co.*, 235 U.S. 88, 35 S. Ct. 91, 59 L. Ed. 142 (1914). The ultimate aim is to frame an injunction that will avoid confusion in the marketplace, protect a prior company's property interest in its name, and permit an individual to exploit his own identity and reputation in a legitimate manner.[37]

Where a defendant has no established reputation under his surname, or otherwise appears to be trading on the goodwill of the first user, the courts have no trouble issuing an absolute injunction.[38] Just because your name is MAX FACTOR, don't think you can use MAX FACTOR as a trademark.[39]

---

37. *Id.* at 67.

38. Champion Spark Plug Co. v. Champion, 23 F. Supp. 638, 641 (D.C. Mich. 1938).

39. Max Factor & Co. v. Factor, 226 F. Supp. 120 (S.D. Cal. 1963) (MAX FACTOR for women's hosiery enjoined because of likely confusion with MAX FACTOR cosmetics).

And, if the first user has sold the rights to his name, he should not expect to continue use of his name as a trademark.[40]

Primarily Merely a Surname

Not all surnames are descriptive to start with. To be descriptive under the Lanham Act, the primary meaning of the term has to be that of a surname.[41] Many surnames have more than one meaning; they are first names, they are geographic locations and/or they have an ordinary English language meaning. BIRD, for example, is a surname, but it is also a well-known name for our fine feathered friend. Therefore, BIRD is not primarily a surname.[42]

Evidence that a name is not primarily a surname includes presence of the term in dictionaries, in geographic references, and use as a first name.

Evidence that a name is primarily a surname includes frequent phonebook listings and use as a surname by the trademark owner.

Geographical Terms

Not all geographical terms are descriptive *ab initio*. The trademark NANTUCKET for shirts is not descriptive because the shirts do not emanate from Nantucket and Nantucket is not noted for shirts.[43]

However, where a merchant uses the name of his geographical location to identify his wares, the mark is usually descriptive. In this case, secondary meaning is required to obtain protection.[44]

---

40. Levitt Corp. v. Levitt, 593 F.2d 463, 468 (2d Cir. 1979).
41. The Lanham Act prohibits registration of a trademark that "is primarily merely a surname" on the Principal Register. 15 U.S.C. § 1052(e)(3).
42. Fisher Radio Corp. v. Bird Elec. Corp. 162 U.S.P.Q. 265, 266 (T.T.A.B. 1969).
43. *In re* Nantucket, Inc. 677 F.2d 95, 99 (C.C.P.A. 1982).
44. Marwood v. Hubbard, 228 U.S.P.Q. 702 (Mont. S. Ct. 1985).

Primarily Geographically Descriptive Terms

As is the case with personal names, geographic terms are not registrable on the Principal Register if they are primarily geographically descriptive.[45] A term may not be primarily geographically descriptive where:

1. The term identifies several different geographic locations, *e.g.*, LAUDERDALE;[46]
2. The term is also a surname, *e.g.*, WALDRON is a town located in Arkansas as well as a surname;[47]
3. The term does not impart information about the geographical origin of the goods, *e.g.*, ALASKA for bananas.

Deceptively Misdescriptive Versus Deceptive

The Lanham Act also prohibits registration of primarily geographically deceptively misdescriptive marks.[48] If the public makes a goods-place association, *i.e.*, if the public is likely to believe the mark identifies the place from which the goods originate, but the goods do not in fact come from the place named, the mark is primarily geographically deceptively misdescriptive.[49]

This does not mean, however, that the mark is deceptive. Does it matter? Yes, because the deceptively misdescriptive mark can be registered with proof of distinctiveness under Section 2(f). A deceptive mark cannot be registered at all.[50]

The difference between primarily geographically deceptively misdescriptive and deceptive hinges on the materiality of the geographic association to the purchaser. The following formulation of the materiality test is helpful:

---

45. 15 U.S.C. § 1052(e)(2). See chapter 5, pp. 77-79, *infra*, on the difference between Principal and Supplemental Registers.
46. *In re* Consolidated Foods Corp., 218 U.S.P.Q. 184, 186-87 (T.T.A.B. 1983).
47. *In re* Waldron Furniture Mfg. Corp., 149 U.S.P.Q. 460, 461 (T.T.A.B. 1966).
48. 15 U.S.C. § 1052(e)(2).
49. *In re* Loew's Theaters, Inc., 769 F.2d 764, 757-68 (Fed. Cir. 1985).
50. 15 U.S.C., § 1052(a) prohibits registration of deceptive marks.

> Are purchasers likely to care whether or not the product comes from the place or region which the mark identifies? If the answer is in the negative, the mark is "deceptively misdescriptive" but if the affirmative, it is "deceptive" and unregistrable under another provision of the Act. This is to say that if a locality identified by a geographical name or term is known or noted for the production of goods in the category [sic] of applicant's or for components of such goods, and purchasers are moved by the geographical name to buy the goods in the belief that they originate in the locality name, the geographical name or term is "deceptive" as applied to the goods. Leeds, "Trademarks—The Rationale of Registrability," 26 GEO. WASH. L. REV. 653, 622-63.[51]

An example of a misdescriptive, but not deceptive geographic mark is SWEDEN for artificial kidney units not made in Sweden. The public was likely to believe that the goods came from Sweden but would not be moved to purchase the goods because of their supposed Swedish origin.[52]

The Fair Use Defense

The Lanham Act specifically sanctions the defense of "fair use" of a party's individual name in his own business. "Fair use" also protects use of a geographical term to describe the geographical origin of the goods.[53]

Thus, even where a surname or geographic location has acquired secondary meaning and is a valid trademark for one merchant, another merchant can still use his own name or his geographic location in a nontrademark sense.

---

51. Quoted with approval in *In re* House of Windsor, Inc., 221 U.S.P.Q. 53, 57 (T.T.A.B. 1983).
52. *In re* Sweden Freezer Mfg. Co., 159 U.S.P.Q. 246, 248 (T.T.A.B. 1968).
53. 15 U.S.C. § 1115 (b)(4). For more detailed discussion of fair use, see chapter 8, pp. 172-79, *infra*.

Slogans as Trademarks

A slogan, like a single word, functions as a trademark if it identifies and distinguishes one company's goods from those of others.[54]

However, slogans present some peculiar difficulties and will not be protected where:

1. The slogan does not create a commercial impression separate and apart from the other material on the labels.[55]
2. The slogan is viewed not as a trademark but merely as an explanatory, instructional, or informational statement.[56]
3. The slogan is a familiar expression with an ordinary non-trademark meaning.[57]
4. The slogan is part of a phrase or slogan conveying an advertising message.[58]

Slogans that have survived these obstacles and been granted trademark registration include:

YOUR FINANCIAL SECURITY IS OUR BUSINESS;[59]
QUALITY THROUGH CRAFTSMANSHIP;[60]
DEDICATED TO ACHIEVING THE HIGHEST LEVEL OF PROFESSIONALISM.[61]

---

54. *In re* National Training Center of Lie Detection, Inc., 226 U.S.P.Q. 798, 799 (T.T.A.B. 1985).
55. *In re* Morganroth, 208 U.S.P.Q. 284, 287 (T.T.A.B. 1980).
56. *In re* Illinois Bronze Powder & Paint Co., 188 U.S.P.Q. 459, 463 (T.T.A.B. 1975) (GO AHEAD—TRY AND FINGERNAIL THIS!).
57. *In re* European-American Bank & Trust Co., 201 U.S.P.Q. 788, 790 (T.T.A.B. 1979) (THINK ABOUT IT).
58. *In re* Morganroth, 208 U.S.P.Q. 284, 287 (T.T.A.B. 1980) (where NATUR-ALL-IZE YOUR HAIR COLORING was used only in the full slogan NATUR-ALL-IZE YOUR HAIR COLORING WITH ANOTHER NEW SERVICE).
59. *In re* Sottile, 156 U.S.P.Q. 655 (T.T.A.B. 1986).
60. *In re* Hallicrafters Co., 153 U.S.P.Q. 376 (T.T.A.B. 1967).
61. *In re* National Training Center of Lie Detection, Inc., 226 U.S.P.Q. 798 (T.T.A.B. 1985).

Slogans that are descriptive, like single word marks, may also be protected upon proof of secondary meaning.[62]

Letters and Numbers as Trademarks

Letters and numbers can function as trademarks just like ordinary words. They do not require proof of secondary meaning unless they are descriptive of the goods.

Letter Trademarks

Letters are strong trademarks where they have no recognizable, descriptive meaning. The absence of a recognizable meaning makes it hard to distinguish between similar letter combinations. Thus, the second user's change in just one letter or the rearrangement of letters may not be enough to avoid confusion.[63]

Radio call letters are a good example of letter combinations that have no recognizable meaning. The call letters "WMCZ" were held likely to cause confusion with "WMEE," particularly because of the similarity in sound.[64]

Letter trademarks are descriptive if they are recognizable abbreviations for descriptive terms. Descriptive letter marks, like descriptive word marks, will be protected upon proof of secondary meaning. Generic letter marks, like generic word marks, are not capable of trademark protection. For example, "PVP", a recognizable abbreviation for the generic term polyvinylpyrolidone, was held generic and incapable of becoming a trademark.[65]

---

62. Roux Laboratories, Inc. v. Clairol, Inc., 427 F.2d 823, 829 (C.C.P.A. 1970).
63. *In re* Standard Kollsman Indus., Inc., 156 U.S.P.Q. 346 (T.T.A.B. 1967) (SKI held confusing to series of SK marks: SK-97, SK-98, etc.); Cluett Peabody & Co. v. J.H. Bonck Co., 390 F.2d 754 (C.C.P.A. 1968) (TTM confusing with TMT).
64. Pathfinder Communications Corp. v. Midwest Communications Co., 593 F. Supp. 281 (N.D. Ind. 1984).
65. *In re* General Aniline & Film Corp., 136 U.S.P.Q. 306 (T.T.A.B. 1962).

Number Trademarks

Numbers, like letters, are strong trademarks where they have no recognizable, descriptive meaning. "4711" is a strong trademark for cologne because the numbers have no recognizable meaning.

Numbers, like letters, are descriptive if they are recognizable abbreviations for descriptive terms. Descriptive number marks, like descriptive letter marks, will be protected upon proof of secondary meaning. For example, 7-ELEVEN supermarkets, arguably descriptive of stores open from 7 A.M. to 11 P.M., was able to enjoin another use of 7-ELEVEN because of established secondary meaning.[66] A number used to indicate size, model, style, or grade will also be protected where secondary meaning is established.[67]

Number and letter marks, like word marks, do not require secondary meaning if they are suggestive rather than descriptive.[68] For example, "8.48" was found suggestive for computers with eight storage registers and a forty-eight-step memory.[69]

Designs as Trademarks

The marketplace abounds with designs used on products and packages—sneakers bearing stripes, cookware bearing flowers, outline designs surrounding word trademarks, alligators on T-shirts. Some of these designs are clearly trademarks. They identify and distinguish one merchant's products from another's. But some of these designs will not be protected as trademarks, either because the purchaser regards them as ornamental decorations rather than symbols of origin—or, because they are so common

---

66. Southland Corp. v. Schubert, 297 F. Supp. 477, 479-80 (C.D. Cal. 1968).
67. Textron, Inc. v. Omark Indus., Inc., 208 U.S.P.Q. 524, 528 (T.T.A.B. 1980); Ideal Indus., Inc. v. Gardner Bender, Inc., 612 F.2d 1018, 1022 (7th Cir. 1979).
68. See this chapter, p. 26-28, *supra*, for discussion of suggestive versus descriptive marks.
69. *In re* Barry Wright Corp., 155 U.S.P.Q. 671 (T.T.A.B. 1967).

that public policy prohibits their exclusive appropriation absent proof of secondary meaning.

General Rules

A design will not qualify for trademark protection where:

1. The design is merely ornamental and hence not used as a trademark;[70]
2. The design is merely background material that merges with the word trademark and does not create a separate commercial impression;[71]
3. The design consists of ordinary geometric shapes, *e.g.*, common circles, squares, etc. that cannot be protected without proof of secondary meaning;[72]

Even an inherently distinctive design may have to overcome objection on grounds that it is merely ornamentation or background, *i.e.*, nontrademark material. Now, let's look at those general rules more closely.

Ornamentation Versus Trademark Significance

Designs particularly vulnerable to the ornamental objection are designs that cover the entire surface of an article. For example, a series of black and white stripes covering a battery,[73] and the phrase "Santa Claus Was Here"[74] randomly printed on Christmas wrapping paper were found merely ornamental.

---

70. *In re* Burgess Battery Co., 112 F.2d 820, 821-22 (C.C.P.A. 1940); *In re* Paramount Pictures Corp., 213 U.S.P.Q. 1111, 1113 (T.T.A.B. 1982).
71. *In re* E.J. Brach & Sons, 256 F.2d 325, 327 (C.C.P.A. 1958).
72. *In re* Raytheon, 202 U.S.P.Q. 317, 319 (T.T.A.B. 1979); Wiley v. American Greetings Corp., 762 F.2d 139, 141-42 (1st Cir. 1985) (red heart design on teddy bear not "inherently distinctive").
73. *In re* Burgess Battery Co., 112 F.2d 820 (C.C.P.A. 1940).
74. *In re* Lynes, 122 U.S.P.Q. 614 (T.T.A.B. 1959).

There is, however, no per se rule that precludes trademark protection for a repeating overall pattern covering the entire surface of an article.[75]

In determining whether a design is merely ornamental or is perceived as a symbol of origin, we turn again to the average purchaser. Evidence bearing on the ornamental issue is similar to evidence submitted in support of a claim to distinctiveness. However, strictly speaking, distinctiveness is not the issue.[76] That is, even a distinctive design is subject to the ornamental objection.

Particularly useful in overcoming the ornamental objection is evidence that the owner has promoted the design as a trademark. "Look for the polka dot label" teaches consumers that the polka dot design is not just decoration—rather it identifies a single source.[77]

Separate Commercial Impression Versus Mere Background

The question of separate commercial impression arises where the design serves as a background for a word mark. If the background design blends into and is part of the impression created by the word mark, the design does not serve to identify source. If the design stands by itself to create a commercial impression separate from the word mark, the design serves as a trademark.

Evidence that the design creates a separate commercial impression includes use of the design without the word mark, the seller's promotion of the design as a trademark, and consumer surveys.

The separate commercial impression test is, like many areas of trademark law, a subjective judgment. The trier of fact must ask: would a purchaser identify this design with a single source if he saw it without the word mark? Surveys can be persuasive evidence

75. Vuitton et Fils S.A. v. J. Young Enters., Inc., 644 F.2d 769, 775 (9th Cir. 1981) (LV and Fleur de Lis repeating pattern held valid trademark).

76. *In re* Owens-Corning Fiberglas Corp., 221 U.S.P.Q. 1195, 1198 n.3 (T.T.A.B. 1984).

77. *In re* Swift & Co., 223 F.2d 950, 953 (C.C.P.A. 1955).

on this point. For example, if purchasers are shown the design by itself and associate the design with a single company, this is evidence that the design per se is recognized as a trademark.

Inherently Distinctive Versus Ordinary

A common, ordinary design cannot be protected unless it has acquired secondary meaning. An uncommon, "inherently distinctive" design can be protected without proof of secondary meaning.

The difficulty in protecting common, ordinary designs is illustrated by the *Wiley* teddy bear case.[78] Plaintiff sold stuffed teddy bears featuring a red heart affixed to the bear's left breast. The heart shape was also used by other manufacturers on toys, including teddy bears.

The First Circuit concluded that a red heart, universally regarded as denoting love and affection and occupying its usual anatomical position, could not be regarded as an "inherently distinctive mark." Absent proof of secondary meaning, the red heart could not be protected.

The same result was reached in the *Brooks Shoe* case. Plaintiff's simple geometric "V" design for sneakers was not protected in the absence of secondary meaning.[79]

Designs that are "inherently distinctive" are unusual designs unrelated to the product's use. For example, a combination of colored stripes for an insecticide package, a package shaped like an ice-cream cone for baby pants, and a cone shaped parking meter have been found "inherently distinctive."[80]

78. Wiley v. American Greetings Corp., 762 F.2d 139 (1st Cir. 1985).
79. Brooks Shoe Mfg. Co. v. Suave Shoe Corp., 716 F.2d 854, 857-58 (11th Cir. 1983).
80. Chevron Chem. Co. v. Voluntary Purchasing Groups, 659 F.2d 695, 702 (5th Cir. 1981); *In re* Playtex Int'l Corp., 153 U.S.P.Q. 377 (T.T.A.B. 1967); Time Mechanisms, Inc. v. Qonaar Corp., 422 F. Supp. 905 (D.N.J. 1976).

Colors as Trademarks

General Rules

The general rule is that a combination of colors in connection with some definite, arbitrary design may be a valid trademark.[81] Until recently, another rule was that a single color applied to the entire article could not be a trademark.[82] This rule was based on the color depletion theory. Since there are only seven basic colors, the available colors would soon be exhausted if competitors were allowed to monopolize individual colors.[83]

The Owens-Corning "pink" insulation case may have lifted the ban against single color trademarks.[84] The Court of Appeals for the Federal Circuit found nothing in the Lanham Act to bar registration of the overall color of the goods. In holding that pink for fibrous glass insulation was registrable based on secondary meaning, the majority stated:

> [P]ink has no utilitarian purpose, does not deprive competitors of any reasonable right or competitive need and is not barred from registration on the basis of functionality.[85]

The dissent adhered to the traditional view that trademark protection should not be extended to a single color per se.

It remains to be seen whether *Owens-Corning* signals an unequivocal departure from the traditional rule against single color trademarks. *Owens-Corning* does not, however, alter the rules denying trademark protection to colors where:

---

81. Campbell Soup Co. v. Armour & Co., 175 F.2d 795, 798 (3d Cir. 1949); Chevron Chem. Co. v. Voluntary Purchasing Groups, 659 F.2d 695, 702-703 (5th Cir. 1981).
82. Norwich Pharmacal Co. v. Sterling Drug, Inc., 271 F.2d 569, 572 (2d Cir. 1959).
83. Campbell Soup Co. v. Armour & Co., 175 F.2d 795, 798 (3d Cir. 1949).
84. *In re* Owens-Corning Fiberglas Corp., 774 F.2d 1116, 1122-23 (Fed. Cir. 1985).
85. *Id.* at 1122.

1. The colors are merely decorative background or ornamentation.[86]
2. The colors merely define a commonplace design such as a circle, square, heart, etc.[87]
3. The colors serve a functional purpose or identify a kind of product and hence are generic.[88]

Where the color scheme is mere ornamentation, evidence showing that the design functions as a trademark is required.[89] Where the design is commonplace, secondary meaning is required.[90] Where the colors are functional or generic, no amount of secondary meaning will gain trademark rights.

Colors Serving Functional Purpose

There are two types of functionality objections:

1. The color is a necessary element in the use of the product. [Utilitarian Functionality]
2. The color is aesthetically pleasing and helps to improve the saleability of the product. [Aesthetic Functionality]

A good example of utilitarian functionality is the "blue dot" flashbulb case.[91] The blue in the blue dot was the color of a chemical that turned pink when air leaked into the bulb causing it to malfunction. The continued presence of the blue dot showed the bulb was in good working order. Accordingly, there was a need for competitors to use blue dots for the same functional purpose.

---

86. Vitarroz Corp. v. River Brand Rice Mills, Inc., 266 F. Supp. 981, 985 (S.D.N.Y. 1967).
87. Wiley v. American Greetings Corp., 762 F.2d 139, 141-42 (1st Cir. 1985).
88. William R. Warner & Co. v. Eli Lilly & Co., 265 U.S. 526, 531 (1924).
89. *In re* American Home Prods. Corp., 226 U.S.P.Q. 327, 330-31 (T.T.A.B. 1985).
90. American Basketball Ass'n v. AMF Voit, Inc., 358 F. Supp. 981, 986-87 (S.D.N.Y. 1973), *aff'd without opinion*, 487 F.2d 1393 (2d Cir. 1973).
91. Sylvania Elec. Prods., Inc. v. Dura Elec. Lamp Co., 247 F.2d 730 (3d Cir. 1957).

On the other hand, the color scheme for the movable squares on the RUBIK's CUBE puzzle was found nonfunctional.[92] The Court noted that symbols instead of colors, or different color combinations, would work just as well as the specific color sequence used for the RUBIK's puzzle. Colors for pharmaceutical capsules have also been found nonfunctional.[93]

The aesthetic functionality argument has had its ups and downs and seems now to be on the wane.[94] An early application of the doctrine to trademark color claims involved the pink color of the Pepto-Bismol stomach medicine.[95] The Court referred to the pink color of the medicine as having a pleasing appearance to the disordered stomach. It is questionable, however, whether pink is any more soothing than white or ivory or cream.

In any event, under more recent authority, the aesthetic appeal of a particular color should not be the basis for denying trademark protection so long as the color primarily serves a trademark purpose.[96]

Generic Colors Incapable of Trademark Protection

Where a color or color combination has become identified with a type of product, it is a generic designation and cannot be a trademark. For example, a black-gold label for spool thread was held generic for a type of thread quality.[97]

---

92. Ideal Toy Corp. v. Plawner Toy Mfg. Corp., 685 F.2d 78, 81 (3d Cir. 1982).
93. Ciba-Geigy Corp. v. Bolar Pharmaceutical Corp., 747 F.2d 844, 851 (3d Cir. 1984).
94. *See* this chapter, pp. 47-49, *infra*.
95. Norwich Pharmacal Co. v. Sterling Drug, Inc., 271 F.2d 569, 572 (2d Cir. 1959).
96. *See* this chapter, pp. 47-49, *infra*.
97. Coats v. Merrick Thread Co., 149 U.S. 562, 570-71 (1893).

Trade Dress and Product Design as Trademarks

Definition

The trade dress of a product "involves the total image of a product and may include features such as size, shape, color or color combinations, texture [or] graphics."[98]

Traditionally, trade dress infringement actions involved product packaging or labeling.[99] More recently, courts have come to recognize that the design or appearance of a product may itself function to identify and distinguish it from other products.[100] Product design as well as product packaging and labeling are now all referred to as trade dress.

Trade Dress Protection Under Section 43(a)

In many trade dress infringement actions, plaintiff's packaging or product design is not a registered trademark. In this situation, plaintiff may bring suit under Section 43(a) of the Lanham Act. This Section affords federal statutory protection for unregistered marks used in commerce.[101]

---

98. John H. Harland Co. v. Clarke Checks, Inc., 711 F.2d 966, 980 (11th Cir. 1983).
99. 1 McCarthy, Trademarks and Unfair Competition § 8:1, at 282 (2d ed. 1984).
100. *See, e.g.*, Warner Bros, Inc. v. Gay Toys, Inc., 658 F.2d 76 (2d Cir. 1981) (distinctive color and symbols on toy car); Harlequin Enters. Ltd. v. Gulf & Western Corp., 644 F.2d 946 (2d Cir. 1981) (cover of romance novel).
101. Section 43(a), 15 U.S.C. § 1125(a) provides:

> Any person who shall affix, apply, or annex, or use in connection with any goods or services, or any container or containers for goods, a false designation of origin, or any false description or representation, including words or other symbols tending falsely to describe or represent the same, and shall cause such goods or services to enter into commerce, and any person who shall with knowledge of the falsity of such designation of origin or description or representation cause or procure the same to be transported or used in commerce or deliver the same to any carrier to be transported or used, shall be liable to a civil action by any person doing business in the locality

Product design protection under Section 43(a) developed as a reaction to the companion Supreme Court cases known as *Sears-Compco.*[102] *Sears-Compco* refused to enjoin product imitation under state law where the products were unprotected by federal patent or copyright law. The Supreme Court reasoned that "to forbid copying under state unfair competition law would interfere with the federal policy . . . of allowing free access to copy whatever the federal patent and copyright laws leave in the public domain".

Litigants unhappy with the *Sears-Compco* result found a way around the decisions by claiming product appearance as a trademark under Section 43(a) of the Lanham Act.[103] They argued that *Sears-Compco* did not apply where product design protection was afforded by a federal statute. The argument was fortified by the very language of the Supreme Court in *Compco*: "If the design is not entitled to a design patent *or other federal statutory protection*, then it can be copied at will." It follows that if the design is entitled to federal statutory protection under Section 43(a), it cannot be copied at will. As one court put it, "Sears and Compco did not purport to redefine the permissible scope of trademark protection."[104]

Under current law, the physical details and design of a product may be protected under the Lanham Act if these features are: 1) "non-functional;" and 2) have acquired secondary meaning.[105]

---

falsely indicated as that of origin or in the region in which said locality is situated, or by any person who believes that he is or is likely to be damaged by the use of any such false description or representation.

102. Sears, Roebuck & Co. v. Stiffel Co., 376 U.S. 225 (1964); Compco Corp. v. Day-Brite Lighting, Inc., 376 U.S. 234 (1964).

103. *See* Boston Professional Hockey Ass'n v. Dallas Cap & Emblem Mfg., Inc., 510 F.2d 1004 (5th Cir. 1975); Truck Equip. Serv. Co. v. Freuhauf Corp. 536 F.2d 1210 (8th Cir. 1976).

104. Rolls-Royce Motors Ltd. v. A & A Fiberglass, Inc., 428 F. Supp. 689, 692 (N.D. Ga. 1977).

105. Vuitton et Fils S.A. v. J. Young Enters., Inc., 644 F.2d 769, 722 (9th Cir. 1981); LeSportsac, Inc. v. K Mart Corp., 754 F.2d 71, 75 (2d Cir. 1985).

Trade Dress Protection Under Unfair Competition: The New York Rule

Under New York state's unfair competition law, protection against confusion of trade dress may even be accorded in the absence of secondary meaning.[106]

Functionality

Utilitarian Functionality

Functional design features, like generic terms, cannot be protected even where the public associates the feature with a single source.

The rationale for this doctrine is the public interest in preventing a monopoly that will deprive others of advances in useful design features and substantially hinder them in competition.[107]

> [A]s to some . . . shapes the courts will never apply the "secondary meaning" doctrine so as to create monopoly rights. The true basis of such holdings is not that they cannot or do not indicate source to the purchasing public, but that there is an overriding public policy preventing their monopolization, of preserving the public right to copy. A certain amount of customer confusion may even be tolerated in order to give the public the advantages of free competition.[108]

The definition of "functional" has given rise to persistent controversy. Certain basic principles, however, have emerged.

Essential to Purpose: Where the design is essential to the utility of the item, it is "functional." The Supreme Court has defined functional as follows:

---

106. Perfect Fit Indus., Inc. v. Acme Quilting Co., 618 F.2d 950, 952-53 (2d Cir. 1980), *cert. denied*, 459 U.S. 832 (1982); Morex S.p.A. v. Design Inst. of Am., 779 F.2d 799, 802 (2d Cir. 1985).
107. Keene Corp. v. Paraflex Indus., Inc., 653 F.2d 822, 824 (3d Cir. 1981); Warner Bros., Inc. v. Gay Toys, Inc., 724 F.2d 327, 331 (2d Cir. 1983).
108. *In re* Deister Concentrator Co., 289 F.2d 496, 504 (C.C.P.A. 1961).

In general terms a product feature is functional if it is essential to the use or purpose of the article or if it affects the cost or quality of the article.[109]

Availability of Alternative Designs: The overall composite design of a product is not functional when the same functions can be equally performed by a variety of other designs. In the leading *Morton-Norwich* case, the court stated:

> The evidence, consisting of competitor's molded plastic bottles for similar products, demonstrates that the same functions can be performed by a variety of other shapes with no sacrifice of any functional advantage. There is no necessity to copy appellant's trade dress to enjoy any of the functions of a spray-top container. . . .
>
> The pictures of the competition's spray bottles further illustrate that no particular housing design is necessary to have a pump-type sprayer. Appellant's spray top, seen from the side, is rhomboidal, roughly speaking, a design which bears no relation to the shape of the pump mechanism housed within it and is an arbitrary decoration—no more de jure functional than is the grille of an automobile with respect to its under-the-hood power plant. The evidence shows that even the shapes of pump triggers can and do vary while performing the same function.[110]

The Court in *Morton-Norwich* concluded that the overall composite design of the FANTASTIK spray container was not dictated by the functions performed and did not result in a functionally or economically superior design.

Useful Purpose Does Not Equal Functionality: Just because the product design also serves a useful purpose does not deprive it of trademark status.

> Where a shape or feature of construction is in its concept arbitrary, it may be or become a legally recognizable trademark because there is no public interest to be protected. In such a case

---

109. Inwood Laboratories, Inc. v. Ives Laboratories, Inc., 456 U.S. 844, 850 n.10 (1982).

110. *In re* Morton-Norwich Prods., Inc., 671 F.2d 1332, 1342 (C.C.P.A. 1982).

protection would not be lost merely because the shape or feature also serves a useful purpose.[111]

Design as a Whole Should Be Considered: The determination of whether an overall design is functional should be based on the superiority of the design as a whole, rather than on whether each individual feature is useful.[112] The presence of an insignificant functional element in the design does not render the overall design functional.[113]

Relevant Factors: Factors bearing on the functionality issue include:

1. the existence of a utility patent that discloses the utilitarian advantage of the design sought to be registered as a trademark;
2. advertising by the design owner touting the design's utilitarian advantages;
3. the lack of alternative designs; and
4. the comparative simplicity or cost saving resulting from the method of manufacturing the article.[114]

Aesthetic Functionality: The Rise and Fall of the "Important Ingredient" Test

A number of cases have found a design functional because it was an important ingredient in the commercial success of the product. This test has its roots in the *Pagliero* china case. The aesthetic appeal of the china pattern was an important ingredient in its commercial success. Hence the term "aesthetic" functionality.

> "Functional" . . . might be said to connote other than a trademark purpose. If the particular feature is an important ingredient

111. Vuitton et Fils S.A. v. J. Young Enters., Inc., 644 F.2d 769, 774 (9th Cir. 1981).
112. *In re* Teledyne, Inc., 696 F.2d 968, 971 (Fed. Cir. 1982).
113. Textron, Inc. v. United States Int'l Trade Comm'n, 753 F.2d 1019, 1026 (Fed. Cir. 1985).
114. *In re* Morton-Norwich Prods., Inc., 671 F.2d 1332, 1341 (C.C.P.A. 1982).

> in the commercial success of the product, the interest in free competition permits its imitation in the absence of a patent or copyright. On the other hand, where the feature or, more aptly, design, is a mere arbitrary embellishment, a form of dress for the goods primarily adopted for purposes of identification and individuality and, hence, unrelated to basic consumer demands in connection with the product, imitation may be forbidden where the requisite showing of secondary meaning is made. Under such circumstances, since effective competition may be undertaken without imitation, the law grants protection. . . .[115]

More recently courts have noted the difficulty with the "important ingredient" test: the trade dress of a popular product will "almost always" be an important ingredient in the sale of the product:

> This formulation, which appears in earlier cases as well, see, e.g. *Ives Laboratories, supra*, 601 F.2d at 643 [quoting *Pagliero v. Wallace China Co.*, 198 F.2d 339, 343 (9th Cir. 1952)], has also been criticized for over-inclusiveness. See, e.g., *Keene Corp. v. Paraflex Industries*, 653 F.2d 822, 824-25 (3d Cir. 1981); *Vuitton et Fils, supra*, 644 F.2d at 773. Trade dress associated with a product that has accumulated goodwill, such as the LeSportsac line, will almost always be "an important ingredient" in the "saleability" of the product. A related difficulty with the "important ingredient" formulation, read literally, is that "it provides a disincentive for development of imaginative and attractive design. The more appealing the design, the less protection it would receive." *Keene Corp., supra*, 653 F.2d at 825. The *Inwood Laboratories-Warner II* formulation, in which a feature must be "essential to the use or purpose of the article" or must affect "the cost or quality of the article," *Warner II, supra*, 724 F.2d at 331, provides no such disincentive and is less susceptible to confusion or an overly broad interpretation.[116]

Thus, aesthetic functionality should not be a bar where the design primarily serves a trademark purpose. Even though the attractiveness of the design is an "important ingredient" in the

115. Pagliero v. Wallace China Co., 198 F.2d 339, 343 (9th Cir. 1952).
116. LeSportsac, Inc. v. K Mart Corp., 754 F.2d 71, 77 (2d Cir. 1985).

product's commercial success or buyers find the design pleasing, the design can still serve as a trademark.[117]

Burden of Proof

There is some doubt as to whether plaintiff or defendant has the burden of proof on the issue of functionality. In January 1985, the Second Circuit, recognizing the prior unclear state of the law, placed the burden squarely on defendant on the grounds that functionality was a "defense".[118]

Coincidentally, on the very same day, the Court of Appeals for the Federal Circuit adopted the formulation of a shifting burden of proof. Where defendant makes out a prima facie case of functionality, the burden shifts to plaintiff to prove the design is nonfunctional.[119]

In the Seventh Circuit, it appears that plaintiff has the burden of proving nonfunctionality.[120]

Wherever the burden is officially placed, the court may have an initial reluctance to grant rights in product designs. The best way to overcome this reluctance is to show the court alternative designs that function as well and cost as little to produce as plaintiff's design.

Secondary Meaning

The trade dress of a product, just like a descriptive word mark, attains secondary meaning when the purchasing public associates the dress with a single source. Proof of secondary meaning includes:

long use;
sales success;

117. *See* W.T. Rogers Co. v. Keene, 778 F.2d 334, 343 (7th Cir. 1985).
118. LeSportsac, Inc. v. K Mart Corp., 754 F.2d 71, 76 (2d Cir. 1985).
119. Textron, Inc. v. United States Int'l Trade Comm'n, 753 F.2d 1019, 1025 (Fed. Cir. 1985).
120. W.T. Rogers Co. v. Keene, 778 F.2d 334, 341 (7th Cir. 1985).

substantial advertising expenditures;
advertising stressing the design feature;
unsolicited media coverage;
requests from third parties to license the design;
intentional copying of the trade dress by defendant and other competitors; and
survey evidence.[121]

Some courts hold that copying establishes a presumption of secondary meaning.[122] Others treat copying as just one factor in determining secondary meaning.[123]

Survey evidence has gained increased judicial recognition. Although there is no requirement that survey evidence be introduced, you can expect a court and your adversary to take note of its absence.[124]

Inherently Distinctive Designs

Some decisions have held that where the design is inherently distinctive, it can be protected without proof of secondary meaning. Take for example an ice cream cone package design for baby pants:

> The subject matter sought to be registered gives the appearance of an ice-cream cone. It is unique as a packaging for baby pants and the design is inherently distinctive. No proof of secondary meaning is necessary under the circumstances.[125]

---

121. LeSportsac, Inc. v. K Mart Corp., 754 F.2d 71, 78 (2d Cir. 1985).
122. Audio Fidelity, Inc. v. High Fidelity Recordings, Inc., 283 F.2d 551, 558 (9th Cir. 1960); Clairol v. Cosway Co., 184 U.S.P.Q. 583, 586 (C.D. Cal. 1974).
123. Brooks Shoe Mfg. Co. v. Suave Shoe Corp., 716 F.2d 854, 860 (11th Cir. 1983).
124. LeSportsac, Inc. v. K Mart Corp., 754 F.2d 71, 78 (2d Cir. 1985). See chapter 12, pp. 237-39, 242-50, *infra*, for more detailed discussion of secondary meaning and surveys.
125. *In re* Playtex Int'l Corp., 153 U.S.P.Q. 377, 378 (T.T.A.B. 1967); *See also In re* Days-Ease Home Prods. Corp., 197 U.S.P.Q. 566, 567 (T.T.A.B. 1977).

At least one opinion, however, has confined this principle to container designs, as opposed to product designs:

> A product design or representation of a product is manifestly equivalent to words which describe its appearance and must be given the same treatment as inherently descriptive words.[126]

Summary

This fundamental principle runs through most trademark decisions: If there is a need for others to use the claimed mark to effectively compete, the mark will not be protected. This principle applies to every form of mark, be it word, design, color, or product shape. The more unique the mark, the more unrelated it is to the product, the less the need for a competitor to use the mark and the easier it will be to protect.

By applying this principle early in the selection process to screen out candidates incapable or difficult of protection, trademark owners will have deprived their adversaries of a substantial defense.

126. *In re* DC Comics, Inc., 689 F.2d 1042, 1051 (C.C.P.A. 1982) (Judge Nies specially concurring).

3

Searching a Trademark

Purpose of Search

Once a proposed mark is selected, it is prudent practice to run a trademark search. A search helps to ferret out potential conflicts (*i.e.*, prior users claiming rights to a similar mark).

A search also gives you an idea of the protectability of the mark. If there are numerous references to similar marks for similar goods, the proposed mark may be considered "weak" and the scope of protection narrow.[1]

Foregoing a search can be risky business. Defendant's failure to make a search may constitute "carelessness" and weigh in favor of plaintiff's right to injunctive relief.[2] Defendant's conduct of a search may also be evidence of good faith where he is sued by a prior user who was not disclosed in the search.[3]

How and What to Search

Scope of Search

The scope of the search varies widely. It can include one or all of the following:

- U.S. Trademark Register;

---

1. See chapter 7, pp. 119-22, *infra*, for discussion of "weak" vs "strong" marks.
2. Chips 'N Twigs, Inc. v. Chip-Chip, Ltd., 414 F. Supp. 1003, 1015 (E.D. Pa. 1976); *compare* Pizzazz Pizza & Restaurant v. Taco Bell Corp., 642 F. Supp. 84, 94 (N.D. Ohio 1986) ("no duty to conduct trademark search").
3. Vitarroz Corp. v. Borden, Inc., 644 F.2d 960, 963 (2d Cir. 1981).

- U.S. pending trademark applications;
- state registrations;
- market directories;
- phonebooks (major cities);
- trade name listings; and
- reported decisions.

Generally it is advisable to do a "full search" that covers all of the above. More in-depth searches, *e.g.*, expanded phonebook coverage, are also available and may be appropriate for searching a new company name.

Timetable for Search

Searches usually take from one to two weeks. For a premium price, twenty-four-hour and forty-eight-hour service is available. It is desirable to search well in advance so that if the mark is not clear there will be ample time to select and search alternatives. In addition, you need time to evaluate the search, including time to investigate pertinent references.

Goods to Cover in Search

A description of goods for the proposed mark must be furnished in arranging for a search. It is important that this description be accurate because the search will focus on similar marks for similar goods as well as identical marks for unrelated goods.

Searching Shortcuts

There are some searching short cuts that may quickly turn up "knock out" marks, thus saving you the time and expense of a full search. For example, you can consult major trade references to see if a direct competitor is claiming rights in your proposed mark. You should, of course, submit the marks that survive this initial check to the "full search" treatment.

One shortcut to avoid is a single search on several different terms with the same prefix. If the mark searched is GRAND FANTASY for amusement park services and the client suddenly decides to go with GRAND ADVENTURE, a new search is needed. The term GREAT ADVENTURE may not be disclosed in the first search for GRAND FANTASY, although it should be disclosed in the search for GRAND ADVENTURE.

Analyzing a Search

The search should be analyzed from two perspectives: 1) availability of the mark for use; and 2) protectability of the mark from infringing use by others.

Availability

Clearing a mark for use is one of the most difficult aspects of trademark practice. First, you must spot potential conflicts. Next, you must evaluate whether the prior user has grounds for protest. Finally, if grounds for protest exist, you must assess the risk of injunctive and/or monetary relief should suit be filed.

Spotting Potential Conflicts

Trademark conflicts most often occur between similar marks on competitive or closely related goods. Where a competitor owns a mark similar to your proposed mark for goods similar to your proposed goods, watch out! Your competitor has a natural interest in protecting his own turf. The chances that your competitor will challenge your proposed use are especially strong if there is no one else around using a similar mark on similar goods.

On the other hand, if your competitor already co-exists with similar marks on competitive goods owned by different companies, he is less likely to single out your use for attack.

Other clues to whether your proposed mark will draw fire are contained in the opposition and cancellation actions recorded in the search and *Shepard's Citations*. Reported decisions involving the mark may tell you if a prior user was successful in protesting a use similar to yours—or if the prior mark was held to be "weak" or descriptive.

Of course, you must also consider possible conflicts with marks for goods that are not directly competitive with your goods. But, the further the goods move away from your proposed use, the closer the prior mark must be to your mark to pose a conflict.

Overcoming Conflicts

Investigating References: Sometimes trademarks disclosed in the search that appear to conflict with your proposed mark turn out not to conflict. For example, the conflicting mark might not be in use, though the registration is still on the books. Or the use may be very different from your proposed use. A marketplace investigation may tell you: 1) if and when use of the mark was discontinued; and 2) a lot more about the product than the description in the Patent and Trademark Office registration.

You should also keep in mind that even though a registration has expired, the mark may still be in use. Sometimes a registration expires because of inadvertent failure to file the necessary maintenance documents. Nevertheless, the owner of an expired registration is still entitled to rely on common law rights based on his continued use.

Use of a potentially conflicting mark may be verified by purchase of the product in the marketplace, direct or indirect inquiry to the owner, review of catalogs, D&B reports, annual reports, etc. Sometimes telephone inquiries by office staff or marketing personnel will quickly produce information. There are also investigation agencies that specialize in market investigations.

Another helpful source of information is the trademark registration file on the potentially conflicting mark. Files on pending applications as well as issued registrations are available for public inspection. You should review the file history to see if the trademark owner has distinguished prior registrations on the ground of no confusion. If the prior "nonconfusing" registrations are similar to your mark, the owner may be willing to live with your mark as well. While such assertions of nonconfusion do not estop the owner from acting against your mark,[4] they will cause the court to think twice about enjoining your use.

Seeking Consent: Where a mark appears close to your proposed mark, but there is reason to believe the first user will not object, consider seeking his consent. If, for example, the description of goods on its face is similar, but channels of distribution and purchasers do not overlap, the first user may be willing to agree to your use.

There is, however, one big caveat to the consent approach. Do not ask unless you are ready to abide by the first user's decision. To proceed with use after consent has been denied may be fatal in a later suit by the first user.[5]

Acquiring Conflicts: When the marketing department is wed to a certain mark and a direct conflict exists, consider acquiring the first user's mark. Especially where the prior mark has little commercial value, it may be possible to acquire the mark for a reasonable sum. This not only removes a conflict, but in some cases gives the second user additional rights (*e.g.*, ownership of an existing registration, earlier date of use). Do not count on being able to tack on your predecessor's early use, however, if the goods are of a different type.[6]

4. EZ Loader Boat Trailers, Inc. v. Cox Trailers, Inc., 213 U.S.P.Q. 597, 599 (T.T.A.B. 1982), *aff'd*, 706 F.2d 1213 (Fed. Cir. 1983).
5. Big O Tire Dealers, Inc. v. Goodyear Tire & Rubber Co., 408 F. Supp. 1219, 1232 (D. Col. 1976), *aff'd with modification as to amount*, 561 F.2d 1365 (10th Cir. 1977).
6. PepsiCo, Inc. v. Grapette Co., 416 F.2d 285, 288 (8th Cir. 1969). See chapter 16 on changes in goods by assignee that may invalidate trademark assignment.

Protectability

The search report provides useful information as to the protectability of the mark and the chances of obtaining a registration in the U.S. Patent and Trademark Office.

Suppose the mark is arguably descriptive. If similar marks have been registered on the Principal Register, chances are your mark will also be accepted on the Principal Register.[7] And if the mark you are seeking to register is "disclaimed" in various registrations (because it is considered descriptive), you can expect to have trouble registering the same mark by itself on the Principal Register.[8]

In addition, if there are slews of registrations for the same mark, you can expect a narrow scope of protection—closely confined to your specific goods.

Evaluating the Risks

Suppose investigation of a potential conflict reveals the mark is in use and obtaining consent or acquisition are not viable options. Suppose the marketing people are still wed to their candidate (sometimes it turns out use has even begun). What are the risks?

If the conflicting mark is directly competitive, the worst case scenario is grim. Preliminary injunctive relief could cut the throat of a national advertising campaign. There is also the chance that the infringer will be socked for damages, profits, attorneys fees, corrective advertising, and even product recall.[9]

One well known company lived through just such a nightmare, waking up to a jury verdict of over $19 million for corrective advertising and punitive damages.[10] Even after the reduced ver-

---

7. Marks that are descriptive may not be registered on the Principal Register. See chapter 5, pp. 77-79, *infra*, on differences between the Principal and Supplemental Registers.
8. See chapter 5, pp. 93-94, *infra*, on disclaimers.
9. See chapter 13, *infra*, on remedies available in trademark actions.
10. Big O Tire Dealers, Inc. v. Goodyear Tire & Rubber Co., 408 F. Supp. 1219, 1232 (D. Col. 1976), *aff'd with modification as to amount*, 561 F.2d 1365 (10th Cir. 1977).

dict on appeal, the infringer ended up owing over $4 million. This is not the typical case, but it does caution against appearing to ride roughshod over the rights of others.

A frequent fact pattern involves marks on related but not directly competitive goods. The second user's product is not likely to divert sales from the first user, but may cause confusion as to source. In this situation, the worst case is usually injunctive relief. Frequently, the case can be settled by the second user's change to a new mark after existing stock has been sold. Still, the advertising investment stands to be lost.

Evaluating the risks requires some fine judgment calls by the business people as well as the attorney. The attorney can evaluate what the risks are—but the business people have to decide whether to take them.

4

Using a Trademark

Establishing Priority

First Use, Not First Registration, Controls

Being first to use a mark isn't the only thing—but it is essential to prevail in a dispute with a similar mark. In the United States, unlike many foreign countries, trademark rights stem from use, not from registration. Indeed, a mark cannot be registered by an applicant in the U.S. Patent and Trademark Office unless it is in use in commerce in connection with the goods or services.[1]

Public Use Is Essential

Thinking up a mark does not establish priority. Even writing it down or telling your neighbor won't help. Trademark rights are not secured until the mark is used in connection with the public distribution of goods or services.[2] Actual sales are not required, but public use is:

> Evidence showing, first, adoption, and second, use in a way sufficiently public to identify or distinguish the marked goods in an appropriate segment of the public mind as those of the adopter of the mark, is competent to establish ownership, even without evidence of actual sales.[3]

---

1. A foreign applicant is not required to use a mark prior to filing for registration in the United States where his U.S. application is based on his foreign registration or application. *See* chapter 5, pp. 86-87, *infra*. Use is still required, however, to maintain rights in the mark.
2. Hanover Star Milling Co. v. Metcalf, 240 U.S. 403, 412, 416 (1916).
3. New England Duplicating Co. v. Mendes, 190 F.2d 415, 418 (1st Cir. 1951).

The following uses have been held insufficiently public to establish priority:

- intra company sales;[4]
- shipments from the manufacturer to the trademark owner;[5]
- sales to personal friends and relations;[6]
- display of prototype to prospective distributor;[7]
- use by real estate developer on recorded land plat;[8]
- incorporating name with state.[9]

As one court stated in holding that sales to regional sales managers did not establish priority:

> The sales were not made to customers, but served as an accounting device to charge the salesmen with their cost in case of loss. The fact that some sales managers actively solicited accounts bolsters the good faith of Farah's intended use, but does not meet our essential objection: that the "sales" were not made to the public.[10]

The Effect of De Minimis Use on Priority

There is no set formula as to the quantity of use required to establish trademark rights. On the one hand, trademark rights are not created by sporadic, de minimis use. On the other hand, a

---

4. McQuay-Norris Mfg. Co. v. H-P Tool Mfg. Corp., 141 U.S.P.Q. 405, 406 (T.T.A.B. 1964). But see International Tel. & Tel. Corp. v. International Mobile Machs. Corp., 800 F.2d 1118 (Fed. Cir. 1986) (intra-company shipment to board member who demonstrated product to prospective purchasers held sufficient commercial use to support registration).
5. Avakoff v. Southern Pac. Co., 765 F.2d 1097, 1098 (Fed. Cir. 1985).
6. Merry Hull & Co. v. Hi-Line Co., 243 F. Supp. 45, 56 (S.D.N.Y. 1965).
7. George Washington Mint, Inc. v. Washington Mint, Inc., 349 F. Supp. 255, 260 (S.D.N.Y. 1972).
8. Hovnanian Enters., Inc. v. Covered Bridge Estates, Inc., 195 U.S.P.Q. 658, 662 (T.T.A.B. 1977).
9. Louisiana World Exposition, Inc. v. Logue, 221 U.S.P.Q. 589, 592 (E.D. La. 1983), *aff'd*, 746 F.2d 1033 (5th Cir. 1984).
10. Blue Bell, Inc. v. Farah Mfg. Co., 508 F.2d 1260, 1265 (5th Cir. 1975).

single bona fide shipment coupled with "activities proving a continuous effort or intent" to commercially exploit the mark may be sufficient.[11]

The intent to market on a commercial scale may be easier to establish in a Patent and Trademark Office proceeding (where only the right to register is at stake) than in a court action (where the right to use is at stake).[12] A use that is sufficient to support a registration may be insufficient to enjoin a competitor with a substantial investment in his mark.

In judging whether a use is sufficient to establish trademark rights, some courts frame the issue this way: Is the first user's market penetration at the time of the second user's entry significant enough to pose a real likelihood of confusion?[13] Factors considered in resolving this issue include:

1. the first user's dollar value of sales at the time the second user enters the market;
2. the number of customers of the first user in the area compared to the potential number of customers;
3. the first user's relative and potential growth in sales; and
4. the length of time since the first user achieved significant sales in the area.[14]

These factors were applied in the *Sweetarts* candy case. The Eighth Circuit charted the first user's sales pattern over a twenty-year period in the disputed states.[15] By the time the second user entered the market, the first user's sales had declined to a de

11. Avakoff v. Southern Pac. Co., 765 F.2d 1097, 1098 (Fed. Cir. 1985).
12. La Société Anonyme des Parfums Le Gacion v. Jean Patou, Inc., 495 F.2d 1265, 1271 (2d Cir. 1974)
13. Sweetarts v. Sunline, Inc., 436 F.2d 705, 710 (8th Cir. 1971); Natural Footwear Ltd. v. Hart, Schaffner & Marx, 760 F.2d 1383, 1403 (3d Cir. 1985).
14. Natural Footwear Ltd. v. Hart, Schaffner & Marx, 760 F.2d 1383, 1398-99 (3d Cir. 1985).
15. Sweetarts v. Sunline, Inc., 436 F.2d 705, 708 (8th Cir. 1971).

minimis level in six states. The dollar sales held insufficient to establish priority are set forth below:

	1947-62	1962	1963	1964	1965	1966	1967 6 months
Ida.	$17,487	1,387	1,134	1,876	1,021	1,005	905
Ind.	321	454	151	151	151	151	0
Kan.	5,713	503	711	422	567	151	0
Mont.	19,649	151	0	321	340	340	397
Neb.	471	622	921	0	1,058	302	662
N.Y.	5,054	447	460	404	221	504	334

Continuous Commercial Use

It is not enough for trademark use to be first, to be public, and to be more than de minimis. Continuous commercial use is also required. In the absence of continuous commercial use, the trademark owner will be subject to claims that he is "warehousing" his mark or has abandoned it.

Warehousing is where the owner seeks to preserve rights by making "token" use over some period of time, although he has no present intent to commercially exploit the mark.[16] Abandonment requires proof of discontinued use with the intent not to resume.[17]

A typical warehousing situation occurred in the SNOB perfume case.[18] Sales of only eighty-nine bottles of perfume totaling a gross profit of $100 were made by defendant over a twenty-year period. The court did not believe this "nominal" "token sales" program should serve to bar plaintiff (owner of the mark abroad) from use in the United States.

> [W]e disagree with the district court's conclusion that because of the custom in the perfume industry of "reserving" trade names

16. La Société Anonyme des Parfums Le Galion v. Jean Patou, Inc., 495 F.2d 1265, 1272 (2d Cir. 1974).
17. 15 U.S.C. § 1127(a); see chapter 8, pp. 164-72, *infra*, on abandonment.
18. La Société Anonyme des Parfums Le Galion v. Jean Patou, Inc., 495 F.2d 1265, 1272 (2d Cir. 1974).

and "carrying on trademark maintenance programs," [defendant's] conduct was sufficient to establish rights to the SNOB mark. The token sales program engaged in here is by its very nature inconsistent with a present plan of commercial exploitation.[19]

Following on the heels of SNOB came the SURE case. Although Procter & Gamble made yearly shipments of its SURE tampon, this use was not regarded as "bona fide commercial use."[20]

Procter & Gamble had established a "Minor Brands Program" to protect marks not in active use. The SURE brand for tampons resided in the program for nearly twelve years. Approximately fifty cases were shipped once a year. The court noted that SURE and other minor brands had never been put on the market in any meaningful way and there was no indication of current plans to do so. The court stated:

> "Trademark rights are not created by sporadic, casual, and nominal shipments of goods bearing a mark. There must be a trade in the goods sold under the mark or at least an active and public attempt to establish such a trade" 495 F.2d at 1272-74, citing *Clairol, Inc. v. Holland Hall Products, Inc.*, 165 U.S.P.Q. 214 (Trademark Trial & App.Bd. 1970).
>
> While P&G's annual shipment of 50 cases for periods of nine to twelve years may not be sporadic or casual, it is certainly nominal and does not represent a bona fide attempt to establish a trade in any meaningful way.[21]

Remember the Equities

In determining priority, which may well determine the outcome of the litigation, "the balance of the equities plays an important role." As noted in the SNOB case:

> Determining what constitutes sufficient use for trademark ownership purposes is obviously a case-by-case task. Lest our opinion be taken as cutting more broadly than we intend, it is important to

19. *Id.* at 1273.
20. Procter & Gamble Co. v. Johnson & Johnson, Inc., 485 F. Supp. 1185, 1207 (S.D.N.Y. 1979).
21. *Id.* at 1206.

> note expressly that the balance of the equities plays an important role in deciding whether defendant's use is sufficient to warrant trademark protection, cf. *Chandon Champagne Corp. v. San Marino Wine Corp.*, 335 F.2d 531, 534-535 (2d Cir. 1964). The fact that defendant's conduct has barred a foreign competitor from marketing a well-established product in this country, without promoting any compensating public interest, requires close scrutiny of the propriety of defendant's "use."[22]

The equities will also defeat a first user, who with knowledge of his competitor's plans, beats the competitor to the market.[23]

The equities may even cause the court to place a pox on both houses. Where the well-known mark KIMBERLY was intentionally abandoned and then adopted by two different parties within a day of each other, neither side was awarded exclusive rights.[24]

Use in Anticipation of Commercial Development: Cat Food Is Cat Food

A serious practical problem arises where the trademark owner selects and clears a mark for use in advance of the complete commercial development of the product. By seeking registration in advance of commercial launch, the owner stands a good chance of smoking out prior users and resolving any conflict before undertaking large marketing investments.

To lay the basis for federal registration, use in commerce in connection with the goods is required.[25] But the "goods" may still be undergoing change as development work proceeds. The obvious solution is to make a use on the same type of product, even though it may vary from the product finally developed.

---

22. La Société Anonyme des Parfums Le Galion v. Jean Patou, Inc., 495 F.2d 1265, 1274 n.11 (2d Cir. 1974).
23. Stern Elec., Inc. v. Kaufman, 669 F.2d 852, 857 (2d Cir. 1982).
24. Manhattan Indus., Inc. v. Sweater Bee by Banff, Ltd., 627 F.2d 628 (2d Cir. 1980).
25. 15 U.S.C. § 1127.

The validity of this practice was challenged in the ENCORE cat food case.[26] The Trademark Trial and Appeal Board held in 1983 that the initial use supporting the application had to be on goods "identical" to the goods ultimately developed. Since ENCORE was first used on an existing cat food differing in formula from the cat food intended to bear the mark, the application was declared void.

Trademark owners breathed a collective sigh of relief when the Board was reversed by the Court of Appeals for the Federal Circuit. Recognizing "the realities of the marketplace," the Court rejected the identical goods test in favor of the requirement that "the inherent and identifiable character of the goods remain the same."[27]

Just as "a rose is a rose," cat food, at least for the purposes of first use, is cat food. Sorry, Morris!

Secondary Meaning Required for Priority in Descriptive Marks

While priority attaches immediately upon first use of suggestive and arbitrary marks, this is not so for descriptive marks.

Exclusive rights in descriptive marks require proof of secondary meaning (consumer association with a single source). In order to prevail against a second user, secondary meaning must be established in the descriptive mark before the second user enters the market.[28]

26. On-Cor Frozen Foods, Inc. v. Ralston Purina Co., 220 U.S.P.Q. 567 (T.T.A.B. 1983).
27. Ralston Purina Co. v. On-Cor Frozen Foods, Inc., 746 F.2d 801, 804-05 (Fed. Cir. 1984).
28. Scott Paper Co. v. Scott's Liquid Gold, Inc., 589 F.2d 1225, 1231-32 (3d Cir. 1978).

Use Required for Federal Registration Compared with Use Sufficient for Priority

Before filing a trademark application, applicant must use his mark on goods shipped in commerce, *e.g.*, on labels or containers for the goods or on displays associated with the goods.[29]

Trademark use that does not technically qualify as use on goods shipped in commerce, *e.g.*, use in advertising and pre-sales publicity, will not support a trademark application.[30] This nontechnical use will, however, support a claim of prior rights. The priority issue does not turn on who is the first to make the trademark use necessary for registration. Rather, priority turns on who is the first to "create an association in the mind of the consuming public between the mark and the [goods]."[31]

Summary

Trademark rights depend on use. First use and continuous use are necessary to establish and maintain a mark. The use must be public and more than de minimis. The use must be sufficient to create and perpetuate the consumer's association of the mark with a single source. To that end, the trademark owner will do well to follow the rules of proper trademark use.

Proper Trademark Use

The rules of proper use are designed to emphasize the special status of the mark—a status that is different from a generic or ordinary descriptive term.

---

29. 15 U.S.C. § 1127.
30. See chapter 5, pp. 79-80, *infra*, on use needed to support trademark and service mark applications.
31. Selfway, Inc. *v.* Travelers Petroleum, Inc., 579 F.2d 75, 79 (C.C.P.A. 1978).

The Basic Rules

Trademark to Be Accompanied by Generic Term

To be sure the mark does not become generic, it should be used with a generic term. The more descriptive a mark is, the more frequently the generic term should be coupled with the mark. This consistent reference to the generic term teaches the consumer that the trademark is not the common name for the kind of goods.

With some marks, it may be enough to use the generic term the first time the mark appears, or at least once on each page of literature. With marks that are very descriptive to start with, or in danger of becoming generic, the generic term should be used repeatedly. Frequent use of the word tissue coupled with KLEENEX helps to alert the public to the fact that KLEENEX is a trademark for tissue—not just a common name for a product made by many different companies.

With some very strong well-known marks, the generic use rule need not be strictly followed. It is not really necessary to say CHEVROLET car or COCA-COLA soda. But these famous marks are exceptional cases and they do usually follow the other rules of proper use (see below).

Setting the Trademark Apart

Trademarks should be set off from surrounding text. This special treatment further distinguishes the trademark from ordinary descriptive or generic terms.

Setting off can be accomplished in a number of ways, including:

- large type—all caps or initial caps;
- quotation marks;
- different colors;
- distinctive lettering; and
- use of the word "brand."

Use of "brand" following the mark is especially helpful to combat generic tendencies. Repeated reference to SCOTCH tape as SCOTCH brand cellophane tape helps to remind consumers that SCOTCH is a brand name for tape from a single source.

TM and Registration Notices

The initials TM are a recognized abbreviation for trademark. The TM symbol (usually placed at the end of the mark) indicates the owner claims the term as a trademark. For example:

CRANAPPLE(TM) cranberry apple drink

The TM symbol may be used from the outset. TM does not mean a trademark application has been filed or a registration has issued. TM simply means that the term is claimed as a trademark. SM means that the term is claimed as a service mark.

An alternative to the TM symbol is an asterisk redeemed by a legend (trademark credit line) at the bottom of the text. Typical credit line language is:

CRANAPPLE is a trademark of Ocean Spray Cranberries, Inc.

The TM symbol can also be used with the trademark credit line. The language of the credit line is not carved in stone—more than one mark can be included—words such as "owned by" can be used.

The credit line can also identify the mark as registered:

CRANAPPLE is a registered trademark of Ocean Spray Cranberries, Inc.

If the trademark is registered, it is proper to use any one of the statutory notices:

The letter R enclosed in a circle: ®
Reg. U.S. Pat. & Tm. Off.
or
Registered in U.S. Patent and Trademark Office[32]

Use of a statutory notice is not mandatory. But either a statutory notice, or defendant's actual notice of plaintiff's registration is a prerequisite for recovery of damages and profits in a suit for infringement under the Lanham Act.[33]

A statutory notice should not be used until the registration has issued. If, however, a notice is used inadvertently (good faith mistake), this should not adversely affect the trademark owner's rights.[34]

Claims of Exclusivity

A trademark signifies exclusivity. The trademark owner has the exclusive right to use the mark on the goods. Explicit claims of exclusive use reinforce a term's trademark status. A number of common phrases carry the trademark message:

Only from ______

Exclusively from ______

Made only by ______

Look for (Trademark) your assurance of (Trademark Owner's) quality

Many a successful advertising campaign has focused on the trademark owner's exclusive position. "UNCOLA, the UN and ONLY" effectively broadcast this message for Seven-Up.

---

32. 15 U.S.C. § 1111.
33. *Id.* Nevertheless, damages have been held to be recoverable absent proper notice under section 43(a). Polo Fashions, Inc. v. J & W Enters., 229 U.S.P.Q. 69, 71 (4th Cir. 1986).
34. Shatel Corp. v. Mao Ta Lumber & Yacht Corp., 697 F.2d 1352, 1355 (11th Cir. 1983).

Trademarks and Grammar

To help distinguish trademarks from generic terms, trademark owners are cautioned to follow certain rules of grammar:

1. A trademark should be used as an adjective, not a noun. The adjective (mark) modifies the generic term (noun).
2. A trademark should not be used in the plural.
3. A trademark should not be used in the possessive.

These rules of grammar and other rules of trademark use are not inflexible. There is no law that says absence of the TM symbol will result in forfeiture of rights. But adherence to these rules will foster the public's recognition of the term as a trademark. Trademark owners can only benefit by calling attention to the trademark status of their valued symbols and failure to follow the rules of proper use can have devastating results.

The Consequence of Improper Use

An occasional improper use will not turn a trademark into a generic term.[35] But widespread improper use can cause the mark to lose its exclusive association with a single source and become free for use by all. This fate has befallen a host of former trademarks, including aspirin, yo-yo, and raisin bran.[36]

Improper use by the trademark owner will be a prime factor in deciding if a term should be protected. When the trademark owner uses his mark in a generic manner, a court will be reluctant to enforce trademark rights. The Otis Elevator Company, for

35. Dictaphone Corp. v. Dictamatic Corp., 199 U.S.P.Q. 437, 445 (D. Or. 1978).
36. Bayer Co. v. United Drug Co., 272 F. 505 (S.D.N.Y. 1921); Donald F. Duncan, Inc. v. Royal Tops Mfg. Co., 343 F.2d 655 (7th Cir. 1965); Skinner Mfg. Co. v. Kellogg Sales Co., 143 F.2d 895 (8th Cir. 1944).

example, advertised its "escalator" as "the utmost in safe, efficient, economical elevators and escalator operation."[37] Similarly, Du Pont was guilty of advertising "cellophane" in all small letters.[38] Both marks were found generic.

As to misuse by others, the trademark owner would do well to take affirmative action. Protest letters should be directed to anyone guilty of misuse, including newspapers, dictionaries, trade journals, reference works, and competitors. The trademark owner should also follow up to be sure the misuse is corrected.

Where misuse appears to be a serious problem, an advertising campaign can be an effective antidote. "XEROX® is Spelled with Two Rs" serves as a clever reminder that the second R means XEROX is a registered trademark.

Measuring the Purchaser's Understanding

In the final analysis, the effect of proper and improper use on the ultimate purchaser is what counts. Does the purchaser understand the term as a trademark identifying a single source, or as a generic term (common name) for a kind of goods? In most cases, the purchaser's understanding of a term can be measured by survey evidence. A simple type of survey that has received court acceptance involved the trademark TEFLON.[39] The survey respondent was given a brief definition of trademark and common name (using CHEVROLET versus automobile as an example). The respondent was then presented with a list of trademarks and common names and asked to identify which were trademarks and which were common names.

---

37. Haughton Elevator Co. v. Seeberger (Otis Elevator Co. substituted), 85 U.S.P.Q. 80, 81 (Comr. Pats. 1950).
38. Du Pont Cellophane Co. v. Waxed Prods. Co., 85 F.2d 75, 80 (2d Cir.), *cert. denied*, 299 U.S. 601 (1936).
39. E.I. Du Pont de Nemours & Co. v. Yoshida Int'l, Inc., 393 F. Supp. 502, 526 (E.D.N.Y. 1975).

The survey respondents displayed quite a good understanding of the terms listed:

NAME	Percent Identifying Term as Brandname	Percent Identifying Term as Common Name	Percent Responding Don't Know
STP	90	5	5
THERMOS	51	46	3
MARGARINE	9	91	1
TEFLON	68	31	2
JELL-O	75	25	1
REFRIGERATOR	6	94	-
ASPIRIN	13	86	-
COKE	76	24	-

The sixty-eight percent identification of TEFLON as a brand name was persuasive evidence negating the generic claim.

Discounting Purchaser Motivation: The Monopoly Case

The survey must, of course, ask the correct question. In the infamous MONOPOLY case,[40] the survey focused on the motivation of the buyer, rather than the buyer's understanding of the term. The survey showed that buyers were motivated to buy MONOPOLY primarily because they liked playing the game, rather than because they liked Parker Bros. (the maker's) products. The court held that MONOPOLY was generic.

The dangerous consequences of the motivation theory caused a furor among trademark owners. When asked why they buy a product, most consumers naturally refer to characteristics of the product, rather than their affection for the maker. KODAK cameras are purchased because they take good photographs, not because of some attachment to Eastman Kodak. But this does not mean KODAK lacks recognition as a trademark.

40. Anti-Monopoly, Inc. v. General Mills Fun Group, Inc., 684 F.2d 1316, 1324-26 (9th Cir. 1982), *cert. denied*, 459 U.S. 1227, *reh'g denied*, 460 U.S. 1104 (1983).

Subsequent decisions were quick to point out the fallacy with the motivation rationale:

> The reason the public is motivated to buy the product, whether because of quality, particular features, source, pleasing design, association with other goods, price, durability, taste, or prestige of ownership, is of concern to market researchers but is legally immaterial to the issue of whether a particular designation is generic. . . . [The motivation] rationale ignores the reality that the primary objective of purchasers is to obtain particular goods, not to seek out particular sources or producers, as such. Motivation does not change a descriptive term which has acquired distinctiveness or an arbitrary word, name, symbol or device into a generic designation. The correct inquiry is whether the public no longer associates what was a trademark with that single source.[41]

The motivation test for genericness was finally put to rest by Congressional legislation.[42] In 1984, the Lanham Act was amended to state:

> A registered mark shall not be deemed to be the common descriptive name of goods or services solely because such mark is also used as a name of or to identify a unique product or service. The primary significance of the registered mark to the relevant public rather than purchaser motivation shall be the test for determining whether the registered mark has become the common descriptive name of goods or services in connection with which it has been used.[43]

When Purchaser Association Won't Help: De Facto Secondary Meaning

There are a few situations where proper use, diligent policing, and favorable survey results will not carry the day. Where a term is

41. *In re* DC Comics, 689 F.2d 1042, 1054 (C.C.P.A. 1982).
42. The motivation theory for assessing secondary meaning was also given short shrift in Warner Bros., Inc. v. Gay Toys, Inc., 724 F.2d 327, 333-34 (2d Cir. 1983). The court noted that the Rolls Royce RR symbol was associated with a single source regardless of the reasons people bought Rolls Royce automobiles.
43. 15 U.S.C. § 1064(c).

generic from the outset or the product design is functional, proper use, massive advertising, and consumer association will not produce exclusive rights. This situation is known as "de facto secondary meaning": consumers in fact perceive the symbol as a brand name, but an overriding public policy preserves the right to copy:

> [A]s to some words and shapes the courts will never apply the "secondary meaning" doctrine so as to create monopoly rights. The true basis of such holdings is not that they cannot or do not indicate source to the purchasing public but that there is an overriding public policy of preventing their monopolization, of preserving the public right to copy.[44]

The LITE beer case is an example of de facto secondary meaning.[45] The term LITE, through massive advertising by Miller, had achieved public recognition as a trademark. Nevertheless, LITE was found generic and unprotectable for low calorie, low alcohol beer. This finding was based on dictionary definitions, industry practice, and state statutory references to low alcohol beer as "light." LITE was viewed as the equivalent of LIGHT.

In refusing to protect generic terms or functional shapes that have a de facto secondary meaning, trademark law recognizes that the public interest in protection from confusion may have to give way to the paramount public interest of permitting competitors to inform the public of the nature of their goods.

---

44. *In re* Deister Concentrator Co., 289 F.2d 496, 504 (C.C.P.A. 1961).
45. Miller Brewing Co. v. G. Heileman Brewing Co., 561 F.2d 75 (7th Cir. 1977).

5

Registering a Trademark

The Benefits of Federal Registration

If you have read the chapter on trademark use, you know that trademark rights depend on use, not registration. So why register?

There are a number of evidentiary and substantive advantages to registration (see list below). Beyond these advantages specifically spelled out under the statute and case law, there is the intangible leg up that comes from doing everything necessary to protect your mark. No matter how often a judge is told "trademark rights stem from use," he will still wonder why the trademark owner did not seek registration.[1] Juries and adversaries will also be impressed by the official government stamp of approval symbolized by a registration. And by placing your mark on the register, you may deter a second comer from adopting a similar mark, thus avoiding expensive and time consuming litigation.

The Principal Versus Supplemental Register

There are two Registers in the U.S. Patent and Trademark Office: the Principal Register and the Supplemental Register.

The Principal Register is for arbitrary-fanciful or suggestive marks, or descriptive marks that have acquired secondary meaning (distinctiveness).

1. The failure to seek registration may be particularly troublesome where there is some question whether the claimed symbol is a mark, *e.g.*, in product design cases. *See* Porter v. Farmers Supply Serv., Inc., 617 F. Supp. 1175, 1189 (D. Del. 1985), *aff'd*, 790 F.2d 882 (1986).

The Supplemental Register is for descriptive terms that are capable of becoming trademarks, *i.e.*, acquiring secondary meaning. Generic terms are not eligible for supplemental registration because they are incapable of becoming trademarks. Once a descriptive mark has become distinctive (acquired secondary meaning), it can be transferred to the Principal Register.

Registration on the Principal Register confers the following benefits:

1. prima facie evidence of the validity of the registration, the registrant's ownership of the mark, and the exclusive right to use the mark in commerce.[2]
2. prima facie evidence of continued use since the application filing date.[3]
3. "incontestability" after five years of continuous use. Incontestability precludes an attack against the registration on the basis of prior use or descriptiveness.[4]
4. constructive notice of the registrant's claim of ownership of the mark.[5]
5. nationwide rights (with certain qualifications).[6]
6. right to bring suit in federal court regardless of diversity.[7]
7. statutory remedies such as mandatory treble damages and criminal penalties in counterfeit cases.[8]
8. the ability to bar importation of goods bearing infringing trademarks by depositing the registration with customs.[9]

---

2. 15 U.S.C. § 1057(b).
3. Rolley, Inc. v. Younghusband, 204 F.2d 209, 211 (9th Cir. 1953).
4. 15 U.S.C. § 1065; Park 'N Fly, Inc. v. Dollar Park & Fly, Inc., 469 U.S. 189, (1985).
5. 15 U.S.C. § 1072; see chapter 17, pp. 342-46, *infra*, on effect of registration on territorial disputes.
6. 15 U.S.C. § 1072.
7. 15 U.S.C. § 1121.
8. 15 U.S.C. § 1117; 18 U.S.C. § 2320. Certain of the same remedies, *e.g.*, attorneys' fees, are available in actions to protect unregistered marks under Section 43(a) (15 U.S.C. 1125(a)). *See* chapter 13, p. 262, *infra*.
9. 15 U.S.C. § 1124.

9. rights under the Paris Convention, including Convention Priority Rights on foreign filings and the right to registration abroad based upon registration in the United States.

The presumptions accorded to registrations on the Principal Register do not apply to registrations on the Supplemental Register. This is because the mark on the Supplemental Register is only considered "capable" of becoming a trademark—there has been no determination that it is a trademark.[10]

A main advantage of registration on the Supplemental Register is its presence as a deterrent against use or registration by others. The ® symbol can be used with marks on the Supplemental Register and the registration acts as a bar against registration of marks likely to cause confusion.

In addition, registration on the Supplemental Register permits the owner to register abroad based on his U.S. registration, and to bring suit in federal court.

Federal Versus State Registration

Trademarks can also be registered under state law. If the owner is making purely intrastate use, state registration should be considered. However, if federal registration can be secured, there is usually no advantage to seeking state registration.

Basic Requirements for Federal Registration

To be eligible for federal trademark registration, the mark must be in current use in association with the goods, and the goods must be sold or transported "in commerce," *e.g.*, from one state to another (interstate) or between the United States and some foreign country.

10. See 15 U.S.C. §§ 1091–1096 for statutory provisions as to Supplemental Register.

To be eligible for service mark registration, the mark must be in current use in the sale or advertising of services and the services must be rendered in commerce.[11]

Procedure for Federal Registration: Overview

The procedure for obtaining registration on either the Principal or Supplemental Register includes:

1. filing a trademark application;
2. examination of the application by the Patent and Trademark Office to determine, inter alia:
   a) that the mark acts as a mark, or is capable of becoming a mark; and
   b) that the mark does not conflict with any previously registered mark;
3. publication for opposition as to a mark found registrable on the Principal Register;
4. opposition period for interested parties to oppose or file extension of time to oppose;[12] and
5. issuance to registration—about two to four months after close of the opposition period.

Applications to register marks on the Supplemental Register are not published for opposition. Registrations on the Supplemental Register, however, can be cancelled after they have been issued. Grounds for cancelling a Supplemental registration are similar to grounds for opposing a Principal registration, *e.g.*, likelihood of

11. 15 U.S.C. § 1127. See this chapter pp. 84-85, *infra*, on types of use acceptable for trademark and service mark applications.
12. The initial thirty-day period for filing opposition can usually be extended for an additional period of up to ninety days. After that, extensions will be granted only with applicant's consent.

confusion with a previously used mark. There are, however, some differences.[13]

The Trademark Application: Form and Content

The trademark application is the bedrock of the owner's registration rights. False statements in the application can result in the registration being declared void or unenforceable.

Care in preparing the application not only helps to assure the registration's validity, but also helps to expedite the prosecution process, saving time and money. Remember, the sooner the registration issues, the sooner incontestability is achieved.[14]

The basic elements of the trademark application and the key points as to each element are set forth below.[15]

Identification of the Applicant

- The applicant must be the owner of the mark.
- The applicant can be a natural or juristic person, *e.g.*, individual or joint applicants, joint venture, partnership, or corporation.
- If the owner is a juristic person, *e.g.*, a corporation, the name, state of incorporation, and business address should be recited.
- If the owner is an individual, the country of citizenship, business, and residence address should be set forth.

---

13. See chapter 14, pp. 307-08, *infra*, on cancellation of registrations on Supplemental Register.
14. See chapter 6, pp. 105-11, *infra*, on incontestability.
15. For statutory elements of trademark application, see 15 U.S.C. § 1051. For rules adopted by Patent and Trademark Office, see 37 C.F.R. § 2.33, Trademark Rules of Practice (hereafter T.M.R.P.). See also Appendix 1 for trademark application form.

Description of Goods or Services

- The description of goods or services should be limited to the goods or services currently in use in commerce.
- The description should clearly and briefly identify the goods or services by their common commercial name.
- The description should not be vague, indefinite, or too broad.

Descriptions considered too broad or indefinite are "metallic parts," "beauty products," "etc." and "including."[16] On the other hand, the description should be as broad as possible consistent with applicant's product line. The description "men's shoes" is better than the description "men's leather shoes."

Designation of Class

Goods and services are grouped into various classes under the International Classification System. Applicant must designate the class or classes that cover his goods or services. A helpful guide is *International Classification of Goods and Services* for the purposes of the registration of marks, published by WIPO.[17]

Goods and services falling in more than one class require:

1. a separate filing fee for each class;[18]
2. dates of use to be set forth for each class; and
3. five specimens showing use in each class.

Dates of Use

Applications based on use must include:

- the date of first use of the mark anywhere;

---

16. *In re* Society des Parfums Schiaparelli, 122 U.S.P.Q. 349 (T.T.A.B. 1959); *Exparte* A.C. Gilbert Co., 99 U.S.P.Q. 344 (Comm'r Pat. 1953).
17. World Intellectual Property Organization, Geneva, Switzerland.
18. *See* Appendix 2 (Trademark Fees).

- the date of first use of the mark in commerce and the type of commerce, *e.g.*, interstate or between the United States and a foreign country;[19]
- the specific goods or services to which the date of first use applies, if the date of first use does not apply to all the goods or services in the class;[20]
- the statement that use was by a related company if this was the fact;[21]
- the statement that the mark "is now in use in commerce."

Dates of use do not need to be exact. Phrases such as "at least as early as" or "prior to" are acceptable. Dates can be given as month and year or even just year. If only a month and year is supplied, the effective date assigned by the Patent and Trademark Office will be the last day of the month or, if only the year is given, the last day of the year.

In the event of a battle over priority, applicant is free to prove use before the date alleged in his application, but this proof must be clear and convincing.[22]

Specimens

The application must be accompanied by five specimens.[23] Trademark specimens consist of samples of material bearing the mark used for labeling applicant's goods. Service mark specimens consist of samples of promotional material showing the mark used

19. 15 U.S.C. § 1051(a)(1).
20. T.M.E.P. 806.11 (Trademark Manual of Examining Procedure, published by the U.S. Department of Commerce, Patent and Trademark Office, revised Dec. 1983).
21. T.M.R.P. 2.38. See chapter 15, p. 326, *infra*, for definition of related company.
22. J.C. Hall Co. v. Hallmark Cards, Inc., 340 F.2d 960, 964 (C.C.P.A. 1965).
23. 15 U.S.C. § 1051(a)(3); T.M.R.P. 2.56. See, also, 15 U.S.C. § 1127 and *In re* Ultraflight Inc., 221 U.S.P.Q. 903 (T.T.A.B. 1984) on statutory requirements pertaining to specimens of use.

in the sale or advertising of applicant's services. Some basic rules pertaining to specimens are:

1. The specimens must have been in use on or before the application filing date.
2. Trademark specimens must show use of the mark on the goods or their containers or the displays associated with the goods.
   Acceptable trademark specimens include tags or labels affixed to the goods, printing or stamping on containers for the goods, countercards displayed with the goods, and instruction sheets packaged with the goods.
   Unacceptable trademark specimens include advertising, invoices, price lists, and letterheads.
3. Service mark specimens must show use of the mark in the sale or advertising of services.
   Acceptable service mark specimens include newspaper and magazine advertising, brochures, billboards, and letterheads indicating the type of service.
   Unacceptable service mark specimens include letterheads that do not indicate the type of service, publicity releases, and invoices.
4. The specimens must not exceed 8½ inches wide by 13 inches long and cannot be bulky; *i.e.*, they must fit inside a 9-inch by 14-inch file folder that expands to only one inch. Bulky specimens can be replaced by facsimiles (*e.g.*, photos of the goods bearing the mark).[24]
5. The specimens should not bear the ® symbol. Nevertheless, absent fraudulent intent, improper use of a registration notice will not be a basis for refusal to register.[25]

---

24. T.M.R.P. 2.57.
25. Radiant Mfg. Corp. v. Da-Lite Screen Co., Inc., 128 U.S.P.Q. 132 (T.T.A.B. 1961).

The manner of use of the mark must also be set forth in the application. The manner of use can be recited in specific terms, *e.g.*, "the mark is used by applying it to labels for the goods." Or the manner of use can be recited in broad terms to cover various types of use, *e.g.*, "the mark is used by applying it to the goods, labels, tags, and/or containers for the goods." In any case, the manner of use recited must include the use illustrated by the specimens.

Drawing of the Mark: Less Is More

A drawing showing the mark sought to be registered must accompany the application.[26]

There are two types of drawings: "typed drawings" and "ink drawings." Typed drawings show the word mark in all capital typed letters. Ink drawings show the mark exactly as it appears on the specimens, *e.g.*, the exact style of type.

From the point of view of trademark protection, typed drawings are usually preferable because they are not limited to any particular form. If the style of print is also considered important, two applications, one for the typed drawing and one for the exact style, can be filed.

A typed drawing will not be accepted where the mark appears in a special form that is essential to its commercial impression. If the mark is materially altered by showing it in typewritten form, a typed drawing is not appropriate.

Only material forming part of the mark should be included in the drawing. For example, the generic name of the goods should not appear on the drawing.[27] If the removal of unregistrable matter will change the commercial impression of the mark, however, it may remain on the drawing and be disclaimed.[28] Where color is

26. 15 U.S.C. § 1051(a)(2); T.M.R.P. 2.51(d), 2.52.
27. *In re* Automotive Filters, Inc., 168 U.S.P.Q. 186 (T.T.A.B. 1970) [oil filter removed].
28. See this chapter, pp. 93-94, *infra*, on disclaimers.

a feature of the mark, it can be shown on the drawing by special linings that indicate individual colors.[29]

Verification and Execution by Applicant

The application must include a signed affidavit or declaration and the date of signing. The affidavit or declaration attests to the truth of the statements in the application and to applicant's belief that he is the owner of the mark and that no one else, to the best of his knowledge and belief, has the right to use the mark. The application must be executed by:

- the individual applicant where the applicant is a person;
- all joint applicants or members of a joint venture;
- one general or active partner of a partnership;
- an officer of a corporation or association.

The application must be filed within a reasonable time after execution (eight weeks for domestic applicants and twelve weeks for foreign applicants).[30] If it is not, a verified statement of continued use may be required.

Common mistakes in execution include omission of the date of signing, and execution by a party without the authority to sign. Managers and directors of U.S. corporations are not acceptable, but chairmen of the board are.

Foreign Applicants

The foreign applicant, whose country of origin is party with the United States to a trademark convention or extends reciprocal rights to U.S. nationals, may base his U.S. application on:

1. ownership of a foreign registration;

29. T.M.R.P. 2.52(e).
30. T.M.E.P. 803.04.

2. ownership of a foreign application, if his U.S. application is filed within six months of the filing of his foreign application.

The foreign filing must have taken place in applicant's "country of origin."[31] Some key points for a foreign applicant are:

- The foreign applicant who relies on his foreign filing does not have to use his mark prior to filing in the United States. Accordingly, the foreign applicant need not supply dates of use or specimens.[32] The foreign applicant must, however, use his mark in the United States to maintain his registration.
- The foreign applicant may claim the filing date of his foreign application as his U.S. filing date. In this event, his U.S. application will not be finally allowed until his foreign application issues to registration.
- The foreign applicant may allege use in commerce in addition to reliance on his foreign application. In this event, his U.S. application will be allowed without awaiting issuance of the foreign registration.
- The foreign applicant relying on a foreign registration must furnish a certified copy and translation of the foreign registration.
- Goods or services in the United States application cannot be broader than the goods or services in the foreign registration.
- The foreign applicant must appoint a domestic representative upon which service of process may be made in actions affecting the mark.

---

31. See 15 U.S.C. § 1126(b) *et seq.* for statutory provisions as to foreign applicant. Under Section 1126(c), country of origin includes country where bona fide commercial enterprise is located.
32. Crocker Nat'l Bank v. Canadian Imperial Bank of Commerce, 223 U.S.P.Q. 909 (T.T.A.B. 1984).

Summary

The trademark application filed by an applicant domiciled in the United States requires:

- the trademark owner's full name, state of incorporation, and address;
- dates of first use and use in commerce;
- five specimens showing use in connection with the goods; and
- a description of goods on which the mark is currently used.

The attorney preparing the application should then:

- select the appropriate class or classes of goods;
- consider changes to the description of goods to conform with Patent and Trademark Office requirements and assure the broadest description consistent with use;
- prepare the drawing (including a heading consisting of applicant's name, address, use dates, and identification of goods);
- review specimens for proper trademark use;
- determine the appropriate filing fee;[33]
- prepare the application including the appropriate affidavit or declaration;[34]
- forward the application and supporting materials to the client for review and execution;
- submit the application, specimens, drawing page, and filing fee to the U.S. Patent and Trademark Office within a reasonable time after execution.

---

33. *See* Appendix 2 (Trademark Fees).
34. See Appendix 3 (Declaration of Use form), for trademark application form based on use including declaration.

Overcoming Objections

Procedure

Upon receipt by the Patent and Trademark Office, the application is assigned a serial number and filing date. If a later filed application is considered likely to cause confusion, the earlier filed application will be allowed subject to opposition, even if the second filed application alleges an earlier date of use.

The application is reviewed by an attorney Examiner for defects in form and substance. As of this writing, the Office has targeted a three-month period for the initial examination.

If defects are found, the Examiner issues an Office Action setting forth the basis for rejection. Frequently, the Examiner will suggest how the rejection can be met, *e.g.*, by claiming distinctiveness (secondary meaning), amending the description of goods, etc.

Time for Responding

The applicant has a period of six months from the date of the Office Action to file a response. The response should deal with each basis for rejection set forth in the Office Action. If the applicant fails to file a response within the six-month period, the application will be abandoned.

Final Rejections

When the Examiner is not persuaded by a response to a rejection and does not believe further argument will be useful, he will issue a "Final Rejection."

A Final Rejection means that applicant must comply with the Examiner's request, take an appeal, or abandon the application within the six-month period.

Request for Reconsideration of a Final Rejection will not change the time for complying with a Final Rejection unless it raises new issues or facts.

Grounds for Rejection

Common rejections based on the form of the application are:

- Improper specimens, *e.g.*:

  specimens that contain a name other than applicant;

  specimens that show use on goods not covered by the application;

  specimens that do not show trademark use on the goods, *e.g.*, invoices, price lists;

- drawing that does not conform with mark shown on specimens;
- indefinite description of goods;
- goods falling outside of class identified in application;
- incomplete identification of applicant;
- execution by party without authority;
- omission of dates of use;
- failure to specify type of commerce; and
- failure to include consent of living individual.

Rejections may also be based on the nature of the mark. The statute bars registration of marks that are:

- merely descriptive or deceptively misdescriptive;
- primarily geographically descriptive;
- generic (common descriptive names);
- primarily merely a surname;
- immoral, deceptive, or scandalous or that may disparage or falsely suggest a connection with persons, institutions, beliefs, or national symbols;
- national insignia, *e.g.*, flags, coats of arms;

- names, portraits, or signatures of living individuals or deceased U.S. Presidents during widows' lifetime without written consent;[35] or
- likely to cause confusion with previously registered mark or previously used tradename.[36]

Another ground for rejection is the failure to act as a trademark. This ground is commonly applied to:

- designs that are merely ornamental;
- background designs that do not create a separate commercial impression;
- functional designs, *e.g.*, product shapes that are necessary to the use or efficient manufacture of the product;
- terms that are used as trade names rather than trademarks.

Responses to Rejections

Telephone Interviews

Telephone interviews with the Examiner can often help to overcome the rejection, or at least provide a better understanding of its basis and the chances of successfully meeting it. Sometimes the Examiner will initiate a telephone inquiry, especially where a matter can be easily clarified. If agreed to by applicant, action can be taken by way of an Examiner's Amendment without further filings by applicant. For example, the Examiner may request that applicant confirm and claim ownership of existing registrations for the same mark.

35. 15 U.S.C. § 1052(c).
36. 15 U.S.C. § 1052(d).

Overcoming Descriptiveness Rejections

Descriptiveness is one of the most frequently encountered rejections. Here are some points to pursue in responding to an Examiner's finding that a mark is "merely descriptive."[37]

1. Check for other registrations on the Principal Register that include the allegedly descriptive term. The Office may be persuaded that your mark should be registered in light of past registrations, although sometimes the Office will say it is not bound by past "mistakes."
2. Review and Shepardize the cases cited by the Examiner. There is always a chance that authority he relied on was subsequently reversed.
3. Cite case law analogous to your position. But keep in mind that precedent is most valuable for general principles. It's up to you to persuade the Examiner how these principles apply to support your claim of nondescriptiveness.[38]
4. Consider a Nexis search (computerized database of publications). The absence of a term from published articles supports a finding of nondescriptiveness.[39]

Claiming Distinctiveness Under 2(f)

When all else fails, consider claiming distinctiveness under Section 2(f). If you have five years of use preceding the filing of your application, this may be enough by itself to establish distinctiveness.[40] Five years use is usually sufficient to show distinctiveness for surname and geographical marks.[41]

---

37. 15 U.S.C. § 1052(e).
38. See chapter 2, pp. 26-28, *supra*, for arguments and case law supporting nondescriptiveness.
39. *See* Coca-Cola Co. v. Seven-Up Co., 497 F.2d 1351 (C.C.P.A. 1974).
40. 15 U.S.C. § 1052(f).
41. T.M.E.P. 1211.04.

Typical wording for a distinctiveness claim based on five years use is:

> Applicant believes that the mark has become distinctive, as applied to applicant's goods (or services), by reason of substantially exclusive and continuous use thereof as a mark by applicant in commerce for the five years next preceding the date of the filing of the application.

Additional evidence may be required to support a claim of distinctiveness, including:

- long time use;
- dollar and unit sales;
- advertising dollars; and
- affidavits from retailers and consumers confirming recognition as a mark.

Disclaimers

The Lanham Act specifically provides for the disclaimer of an unregistrable component of a mark.[42] The disclaimer limits the claim to exclusive rights in the disclaimed matter to its precise relation and association with the entire mark appearing in the registration. However, the disclaimer shall not:

> affect the applicant's or registrant's rights then existing or thereafter arising in the disclaimed matter, or his right of registration on another application if the disclaimed matter be or shall have become distinctive of his goods or services.[43]

Disclaimed matter usually consists of descriptive terms or ornamental designs. For example, marks comprising descriptive words displayed in distinctive lettering may be registered with a disclaimer as to the descriptive words.[44]

42. 15 U.S.C. § 1056.
43. 15 U.S.C. § 1056(b).
44. T.M.E.P. 904.03(d).

A disclaimer will not be accepted where the mark is considered a single unitary mark rather than a composite of separate elements.[45] Hyphenated terms are traditionally considered a single unitary mark.

A standardized form for disclaimer language was adopted in 1982. It reads:

> No claim is made to the exclusive right to use . . . , apart from the mark as shown.

The disclaimer does not affect common law rights.[46] It does not mean that the disclaimed material will be ignored in determining likelihood of confusion. Since prospective purchasers will not be aware that a portion of the mark has been disclaimed, the disclaimer is not material in assessing the reaction of the average purchaser.[47]

The disclaimer pretty much means what it says—for the purposes of the subject registration, exclusive rights are not claimed in the disclaimed portion by itself.

Overcoming Prior Registrations

Preliminary Investigations: When a rejection is based on likely confusion with one or more prior registrations, the Examiner will furnish copies of the cited registrations.

First, check the dates of expiration. If a Section 8 affidavit or renewal was recently due, or is due in the next six months, check to be sure the registration has been maintained. Expired or cancelled registrations do not act as a bar. Also, if over five years has gone by and a Section 15 affidavit reciting continuous use has not been filed, this could indicate the mark is not in commercial use.

45. T.M.R.P. 904.03; "X" Laboratories, Inc. v. Odorite Sanitation Serv. of Baltimore, Inc., 106 U.S.P.Q. 327 (Comm'r Pat. 1955).
46. 15 U.S.C. § 1056(b).
47. American Home Prods. Corp. v. B.F. Ascher & Co., Inc., 473 F.2d 903, 904 (C.C.P.A. 1973); *In re* National Data Corp. 753 F.2d 1056 (Fed. Cir. 1985).

Next, consider distinguishing the cited registration on the basis of different goods or channels of distribution. Consult the filewrapper on the cited registration for specimen labeling and other literature on registrant's goods. This information can help you devise a description of goods for your own application that may avoid the cited registration.

You should also check to see if the registrant of the cited mark distinguished his mark from another prior registration. These same arguments may distinguish your pending application from the cited mark.

Where the cited mark is a direct conflict, investigate the marketplace use. If use has been discontinued, the registrant may agree to cancel his registration. If the registrant does not voluntarily cancel his registration, you can file a petition to cancel. Prosecution of your application can be suspended pending determination of the cancellation proceeding.[48]

Remember, What You Say May Be Used Against You: In your effort to overcome a cited registration, you may be tempted to make sweeping arguments of no possible confusion or point to widespread use of similar marks by others. You may also assert that the element your mark has in common with the cited registration is descriptive.

Just remember, what you say may be used against you. Suppose your mark EASY CARRY is rejected on the basis of a prior registration for EASY PACK. Suppose you claim that there is no likely confusion between EASY CARRY and EASY PACK because EASY is descriptive. And then, after you get your registration for EASY CARRY, suppose you want to stop a third party from using EASY TOTE. What is the effect of your statement that EASY is descriptive on your ability to stop EASY TOTE?

While statements made in the prosecution of an application do not estop applicant from acting against another mark, they are

48. T.M.E.P. 1108.01. See chapter 14, pp. 301-08, *infra*, on cancellation proceedings.

admissions and may be considered in evidence.[49] Even if these statements have only an emotional effect on the judge, they may very well turn the tide in a close case. Do not say any more than is necessary to distinguish a prior registration.

Consent Agreements: Sometimes a rejection can be overcome by the consent of the prior registrant. Such a consent is not per se dispositive, but will often be the determining factor.

The ground rules for consent agreements were set forth by the Court of Customs and Patent Appeals in the *Du Pont* RALLY case.[50] The identical mark RALLY was applied to car polish and detergent. The parties agreed to restrict their respective use to the "automobile aftermarket" and the "commercial building or household market." The Board decision denying registration on grounds of likely confusion was reversed. The Court of Customs and Patent Appeals pointed to the consent agreement as substantial evidence of no likely confusion.

Following the *Du Pont* decision, the Board routinely refused to give weight to what it termed "naked" consents. The Board required a "detailed agreement between the parties", *e.g.*, recitation of different marketing channels and differences in goods.[51]

However, the Court of Appeals for the Federal Circuit rejected such "novel and stringent requirements" in the *N.A.D.* case.[52] The Court held that the Board failed to give sufficient weight to the consent in light of other facts. The "other facts" included the differences in the marks, NARCO and NARKOMED, and the sophistication of purchasers of technical medical equipment. The Court stated:

> This consent, moreover, having been given by a competitor well acquainted with the realities of the business suffices to persuade us,

49. EZ Loader Boat Trailers, Inc. v. Cox Trailers, Inc., 213 U.S.P.Q. 597, 599 (T.T.A.B. 1982), *aff'd*, 706 F.2d 1213 (Fed. Cir. 1983).
50. *In re* E.I. Du Pont de Nemours Co., 476 F.2d 1357 (C.C.P.A. 1973).
51. *In re* Loew's Theatres, Inc., 197 U.S.P.Q. 183, 185-86 (T.T.A.B. 1977).
52. *In re* N.A.D. Inc., 754 F.2d 996, 999 (Fed. Cir. 1985).

> when taken together with all of the other facts, that the board and the Examining Attorney were simply wrong in their opinions that there would be likelihood of confusion, and we so hold. "A mere assumption that confusion is likely will rarely prevail against uncontroverted evidence from those on the firing line that it is not." *Du Pont, supra*, 476 F.2d at 1363, 177 USPQ at 568.[53]

Despite the language in *Du Pont* and *N.A.D.*, a naked consent may not carry the day where identical marks are used on closely related goods. For example, after the decision in *N.A.D.*, the Board found confusion between NEWPORTS on shoes and NEWPORT on ladies' outer shirts, despite registrant's consent.[54] The Board noted the marks were identical and the consent agreement contained no restriction as to channels of distribution.

The lesson to be learned here is that the closer the marks and the goods, the more detailed the consent should be. Still, in some cases a "naked" consent may well do the trick.

Review of Examiner Decisions

Review by Appeal to Trademark Trial and Appeal Board

Any final refusal issued by the Examiner, or any second refusal on the same grounds, may be appealed to the Trademark Trial and Appeal Board.[55]

Timing

Appeal must be taken within six months from the date of final refusal. A notice of appeal and appeal fee must be filed within the six-month period.[56] An appeal brief is due sixty days after filing

53. *Id.* at 1000.
54. *In re* Pix of Am., Inc., 225 U.S.P.Q. 691 (T.T.A.B. 1985).
55. T.M.R.P. 2.141.
56. T.M.R.P. 2.142(a).

the appeal.[57] The Examiner will file a responsive brief and applicant has twenty days to file a reply.[58] The Examiner may not raise new grounds for refusal on appeal.

Oral hearing must be requested in a separate notice filed ten days after the reply.[59]

Reconsideration and Appeal from Board Decision

A request for consideration of the decision on appeal must be filed within thirty days of the decision.[60] Further appeal from the Board may be had to the Court of Appeals for the Federal Circuit or review may be sought in federal district court.[61]

Review by Petition to the Commissioner

Generally speaking, nonfinal decisions may be appealed to the Commissioner of Patents and Trademarks by filing a petition and filing fee within sixty days of the Examiner's action.[62]

The category of decisions that may be reviewed by petition to the Commissioner include:

- nonsubstantive requirements of the Examiner;[63]
- reopening an application to introduce new matter;[64]
- refusals to accept Section 8 affidavit or renewal;[65]
- refusals to amend or disclaim portion of registration;[66]
- denial of requests to extend time to oppose;[67]

---

57. T.M.R.P. 2.142(b).
58. *Id.*
59. T.M.R.P. 2.142(e).
60. T.M.R.P. 2.144.
61. 15 U.S.C. § 1071(a), (b). *See* chapter 14, pp. 314-18, *infra.*
62. T.M.R.P. 2.146(d).
63. T.M.R.P. 2.146(a), (b), 2.63(b).
64. T.M.R.P. 2.142(d).
65. T.M.R.P. 2.165(b), 2.146.
66. T.M.R.P. 2.173, 2.176.
67. T.M.R.P. 2.146(e)(1).

- interlocutory decisions that are manifestly erroneous (*e.g.*, the grant or denial of nonfinal motion);[68] and
- waiver of nonstatutory rules in extraordinary circumstances.[69]

The Commissioner's decision is appealable in only two situations:

1. refusal to accept Section 8 affidavit; and
2. refusal to accept renewal.[70]

---

68. *In re* Celotex Corp. 121 U.S.P.Q. 44 (Comm'r Pat. 1959).
69. T.M.R.P. 2.146(a), 2.148.
70. 15 U.S.C. 1071; T.M.R.P. 2.145(a), 2.165, 2.184. See chapter 6, *infra*, on Section 8 affidavit and renewal application required to maintain a registration.

6

Maintaining a Registration

While continued use is required to maintain trademark rights, evidence of use need only be filed with the U.S. Patent and Trademark Office at specified intervals:

1. during the fifth year after the registration issues; and
2. every twenty years after the registration issues.

The required filing within the fifth year is called a Section 8 affidavit of use. The required filing every twenty years is called a renewal.

In addition, a filing may be made attesting to five consecutive years of continuous use anytime after the registration has passed its fifth year. This filing must take place within a year following the five-year period of continuous use. This filing is not mandatory, but will provide the registrant with valuable "incontestable" rights. This filing is called a Section 15 affidavit of incontestability.[1]

The Section 8 affidavit of use, the Section 15 affidavit of incontestability, and the renewal dates are illustrated by this example.

Where the registration issued on January 1, 1970:

- an affidavit of use is required between January 1, 1975 and January 1, 1976;
- an affidavit of incontestability may be filed between January 1, 1975 and January 1, 1976;

1. See this chapter, pp. 105-11, *infra*, on incontestability. The Section 8 and Section 15 filings are commonly referred to as affidavits, although they can be in declaration form. See Appendix 4 for Combined Declaration under Sections 8 and 15.

- renewal is required between July 1, 1989 and January 1, 1990 (or within grace period from January 1–April 1, 1990).

A more detailed explanation as to the procedure involved in filing the necessary maintenance documents follows.

The Section 8 Affidavit of Use

Registrations under both the Principal and Supplemental Registers require the filing of an affidavit of use during the fifth year after issuance of the registration. Section 8(a) of the Lanham Act provides:

> [T]he registration of any mark under the provisions of this Act shall be cancelled by the Commissioner at the end of 6 years following its date, unless within 1 year next preceding the expiration of such 6 years the registrant shall file in the Patent and Trademark Office an affidavit showing that said mark is in use in commerce or showing that its nonuse is due to special circumstances which excuse such nonuse and is not due to any intention to abandon the mark.[2]

Use in Commerce

The affidavit (or declaration)[3] must set forth that the mark is in use in commerce. Prior to 1982, use in commerce was not required for a Section 8 affidavit. Use of any kind, *e.g.*, use abroad, was sufficient. The affidavit must also specify the type of commerce, *e.g.*, interstate or foreign. If the mark is not in use in commerce, the affidavit must explain the reason for the nonuse and state that the nonuse is not the result of intention to abandon.

2. 15 U.S.C. § 1058(a).
3. T.M.R.P. 2.20, 2.162.

Nonuse is excusable if caused by factors beyond the registrant's control, such as use interrupted by war. Excusable nonuse does not mean absence of sales due to lack of demand for the product.[4]

Specimen Showing Current Use

The affidavit reciting use in commerce must be accompanied by a specimen showing current use of the mark. However, it is not necessary that use be made on all the goods recited in the registration or even that the specimen be used on any of the specific goods in the registration.[5]

The mark on the specimen need not be identical to the registered mark, but must create the same commercial impression. If there is a difference merely in type style or background design, the affidavit should be accepted.[6] If the mark has been altered so as to create a different commercial impression, the affidavit will not be accepted. For example, separate registrations for the mark YANKEE and the mark CLIPPER could not be supported by specimens showing the combined term YANKEE CLIPPER.[7]

The specimens should also conform to the requirements for proper specimens submitted with an application, *e.g.*, in the case of a trademark, labels or tags affixed to the goods or containers for the goods—not advertising or price lists.[8]

Non-extendable Deadline

The affidavit of use will not be accepted after the sixth year anniversary. If the registration issued on June 20, 1982, the affidavit of use must be filed by June 20, 1988.

---

4. *In re* Moorman Mfg. Co., 203 U.S.P.Q. 712 (Comm'r Pat. 1979).
5. T.M.E.P. 1603.10.
6. *Ex parte* Petersen & Pegau Baking Co., 100 U.S.P.Q. 20 (Comm'r Pat. 1953).
7. *In re* Continental Distilling Corp., 254 F.2d 139 (C.C.P.A. 1958).
8. See chapter 5, pp. 83-85, *supra*, for discussion of acceptable specimens.

Failure to timely file the Section 8 affidavit results in cancellation of the registration. Should this mistakenly occur, it is advisable to promptly file a new application so the public is advised of registrant's continued claim of rights.

So long as timely filing is timely, lesser defects in the affidavit, *e.g.*, defects in execution,[9] can be corrected after the close of the sixth year.

Meeting the Deadline: Express Mail Certificates and Certificates of Mailing

The "Express Mail" certificate applies to documents that have a statutory deadline, *e.g.*, renewals, affidavits of use, and notices of appeal. The "Express Mail" certificate permits these documents to receive a filing date as of the date deposited as "Express Mail" with the U.S. postal service.[10]

The Certificate of Mailing applies to documents that do not have statutory deadlines, *e.g.*, amendments, notices of oppositions, extensions of time, etc., but must be filed within a set period. The Certificate of Mailing permits these documents to be considered timely if accompanied by a certificate stating that the date of mailing is at or before the final expiration date.[11]

Fraud

Needless to say, the statements made in the affidavit must be accurate. If the mark is not in use on all the goods recited in the registration, do not say it is. Make sure the specimen is one that really is in use in commerce—not just some label whipped up by the art department but never used on any goods.

---

9. 35 U.S.C. Section 26 provides for provisional acceptance of documents filed in the U.S. Patent and Trademark Office despite defective execution where the defect is remedied in the time set by the Commissioner.
10. T.M.R.P. 1.10.
11. T.M.R.P. 1.8.

False statements made in a Section 8 affidavit may constitute fraud. The consequences of the false statements will vary depending on their materiality and the registrant's intent. The false statements could result in cancellation of the registration[12] or inability to rely on it in a subsequent proceeding.[13]

Summary

The Section 8 affidavit must be filed during the fifth year after issuance of registration. The affidavit should contain:

1. identification of the registration including mark, registration number, and date;
2. recitation of ownership by the affiant;
3. recitation of use in commerce, specifying the nature of commerce;

   or

   recitation of circumstances excusing nonuse and absence of intent to abandon;
4. a specimen showing current use in commerce;
5. statements made in affidavit or declaration form;[14]
6. the filing fee for each class.[15]

Section 15 Affidavit of Incontestability

Requirements

The basic requirements for a Section 15 affidavit are:

---

12. Volkswagenwerk Aktiengesellschaft v. Advance Welding & Mfg. Corp., 193 U.S.P.Q. 673 (T.T.A.B. 1976).
13. Duffy-Mott Co. v. Cumberland Packing Co., 424 F.2d 1095 (C.C.P.A. 1970). See chapter 8, pp. 180-83, *infra*, on fraud.
14. For a typical Section 8 form, see Appendix 3 (Declaration of Use under Section 8).
15. *See* Appendix 2 (Trademark Fees).

1. continuous use in commerce on some of the goods specified in the registration for any five consecutive year period after the issuance of the registration;
2. filing the affidavit within one year of completion of said five consecutive year period; and
3. the absence of any final decision adverse to the registrant's claim of ownership or right to register or any pending proceeding involving said rights.

These requirements are set forth in the Lanham Act Section 15 (15 U.S.C. 1065):

> Except on a ground for which application to cancel may be filed at any time under subsections (c) and (3) of section 14 of this Act, and except to the extent, if any, to which the use of a mark registered on the principal register infringes a valid right acquired under the law of any State or Territory by use of a mark or trade name continuing from a date prior to the date of registration under this Act of such registered mark, the right of the registrant to use such registered mark in commerce for goods or services on or in connection with such registered mark has been in continuous use for 5 consecutive years subsequent to the date of such registration and is still in use in commerce, shall be incontestable: Provided that—
>
> (1) there has been no final decision adverse to registrant's claim of ownership of such mark for such goods or services, or to registrant's right to register the same or to keep the same on the register; and
>
> (2) there is no proceeding involving said rights pending in the Patent Office or in a court and not finally disposed of; and
>
> (3) an affidavit is filed with the Commissioner within 1 year after the expiration of any such 5-year period setting forth those goods or services stated in the registration on or in connection with which such mark has been in continuous use for such 5 consecutive years and is still in use in commerce; and the other matters specified in subsections (1) and (2) hereof; and
>
> (4) no incontestable right shall be acquired in a mark which is the common descriptive name of any article or substance, patented or otherwise.

The exceptions to incontestability are discussed in this chapter, below at pages 108-10.

The Benefits of Incontestability

The filing of the Section 15 affidavit confers "incontestable" status on the registered mark. This means that, subject to certain exceptions, the registration is:

1. conclusive evidence of the registrant's ownership and exclusive right to use the mark;
2. immune from attack on the basis of prior use;
3. immune from attack on the basis of descriptiveness.[16]

The Shield Becomes a Sword

For some period of time, there was a split in the circuits as to whether incontestability was strictly a defensive weapon (shield) or could be used offensively (as a sword). Some courts held that plaintiff's incontestable registration could only be used defensively to prevent cancellation of plaintiff's registration. Other courts held that plaintiff's incontestable registration was also an offensive weapon, *i.e.*, it could be relied on by plaintiff in an infringement action to preclude defendant from raising the defense that plaintiff's mark was descriptive. [17]

The conflict in the circuits was settled by the Supreme Court in the *Park 'N Fly* case. The Court held that there was no basis for engrafting an offensive/defensive distinction on the use of an incontestable mark.

> One searches the language of the Lanham Act in vain to find any support for the offensive/defensive distinction applied by the Court of Appeals. The statute nowhere distinguishes between a

---

16. Park 'N Fly v. Dollar Park & Fly, Inc., 469 U.S. 189 (1985).
17. *Compare* Union Carbide Corp. v. Ever-Ready, Inc., 531 F.2d 366 (7th Cir.), *cert. denied*, 429 U.S. 830 (1976) (offensive use sanctioned) *with* Tillamook County Creamery v. Tillamook Cheese & Dairy Ass'n, 345 F.2d 158 (9th Cir.), *cert. denied*, 382 U.S. 903 (1965) (offensive use rejected).

> registrant's offensive and defensive use of an incontestable mark. On the contrary, § 33(b)'s declaration that the registration has an "exclusive right" to use the mark indicates that incontestable status may be used to enjoin infringement by others. A conclusion that such infringement cannot be enjoined renders meaningless the "exclusive right" recognized by the statute. Moreover, the language in three of the defenses enumerated in § 33(b) clearly contemplates the use of incontestability in infringement actions by plaintiffs. See §§ 33 (b)(4)–(6), 15 U.S.C. §§ 1115(b)(4)–(6).[18]

After *Park 'N Fly* resolved the shield versus sword issue, the next question was: could laches be a defense in an infringement action based on an incontestable registration? A few courts have said no. They reason that laches is not one of the seven enumerated defenses to incontestability.[19] Other decisions take the position that laches should be applied in determining infringement and the scope of relief. This view is supported by the Lanham Act provision that injunctive relief should be granted "according to the principles of equity."[20]

Because incontestable status confers valuable rights, it is advisable to file the Section 15 affidavit as soon as the requirements have been met. Normally this is at the beginning of the fifth year after issuance of the registration. Frequently, the Section 8 and Section 15 affidavits are combined.[21]

Exceptions to Incontestability

Incontestability is not quite as good as the name suggests. The following defenses may be specifically asserted against an incontestable registration:

---

18. Park 'N Fly v. Dollar Park & Fly, Inc., 469 U.S. 189 (1985).
19. *See e.g.*, American Automobile Ass'n v. AAA Ins. Agency, Inc., 618 F. Supp. 787 (W.D. Tex. 1985).
20. 15 U.S.C. § 1116. United States Jaycees v. Cedar Rapids Jaycees, 794 F.2d 379 (8th Cir. 1986)
21. T.M.R.P. 2.168. *See* Appendix 4 (for Combined Declaration under Sections 8 and 15).

1. The registration or the incontestable right to use the mark was obtained by fraud;
2. The mark has been abandoned;
3. The mark has been used to misrepresent source;
4. The defendant is making a good faith, fair use, not as a trademark;
5. The defendant adopted the mark without knowledge of registrant's prior use and has made continuous use from a date prior to the registration in a limited geographic area;
6. Defendant's use is pursuant to registration issued prior to plaintiff's; and
7. The mark is being used to violate the antitrust laws.[22]

These are affirmative defenses that must be pleaded and proved by defendant.[23]

There are additional, sometimes overlapping exceptions to incontestability, which are either spelled out in Section 15, or incorporated by reference in Section 15. These exceptions include:

1. The mark becomes generic.[24]
2. The mark violates the statutory bars against registering specified subject matter, including:

    marks containing immoral, deceptive or scandalous matter or marks that suggest a false connection with persons or institutions, national insignia *e.g.*, flags; marks containing the name or portrait of a living individual or a dead President whose widow is still alive absent written consent.[25]

---

22. 15 U.S.C. § 1115(b).
23. *See* Jockey Int'l, Inc. v. Burkard, 185 U.S.P.Q. 201, 206 (S.D. Cal. 1975).
24. 15 U.S.C. § 1064(c).
25. 15 U.S.C. § 1052 (a)–(c).

3. The mark is a collective or certification mark that was improperly obtained or a certification mark that is improperly used.[26]

Fraud

As with other Lanham Act filings, care must be taken to assure accurate statements in the Section 15 affidavit. The affidavit provides important new rights and false statements made in acquiring such rights may result in cancellation or unenforceability.[27]

Particular areas to watch for are the statement of five years' continuous use with respect to all the goods listed in the registration. If continuous use applies only as to some goods, only those goods should be specified.

The requirement of "continuous" use under Section 15 has not received much judicial attention. One court has concluded, in applying another section of the statute, that use interrupted for a year does not qualify as continuous.[28] But suppose token shipments are made each year. Is this the kind of continuous use contemplated by the statute? If the cases criticizing trademark "warehousing" (reserving marks for future use) are any guide, token use may not qualify as continuous use.[29]

Another area to be alert for is litigation involving the mark. An attorney familiar with the company's litigation should review the Section 15 affidavit. Keep in mind that not all proceedings referring to a mark involve the registrant's "claim of ownership or right to register."

---

26. *See* Section 14(c), (d) [15 U.S.C. § 1064 (c), (d)].
27. Duffy-Mott Co. v. Cumberland Packing Co., 424 F.2d 1095 (C.C.P.A. 1970); Volkswagenwerk Aktiengesellschaft v. Advance Welding Mfg. Corp., 184 U.S.P.Q. 367 (T.T.A.B. 1976).
28. Casual Corner Assocs., Inc. v. Casual Stores of Nevada, Inc., 493 F.2d 709, 712 (9th Cir. 1974).
29. *See* chapter 4, pp. 64-65, *supra*, for case law on trademark warehousing.

If a Section 15 affidavit is filed by mistake, corrective steps should be taken. A document should be filed reciting the inadvertent mistake and that registrant makes no claim to the benefits of Section 15.

Summary

The Section 15 affidavit should be considered for filing five years after issuance of the registration. The affidavit should include:

- identification of the mark, registration number, and date;
- claim of ownership;
- statement of those goods in the registration on which the mark has been in continuous use in commerce (specifying the nature of the commerce) for the five years immediately preceding the Section 15 affidavit;
- statement that there has been no final decision adverse to the registrant's claims of ownership or right to register or any pending proceeding involving said right;
- statements made in affidavit or declaration form;[30] and
- a filing fee for each class.[31]

Registration Renewals

Deadline

A registration must be renewed every twenty years after date of registration. The renewal must be filed no earlier than six months before the twenty-year anniversary date. A grace period of three months after the anniversary date is also provided. There is an additional fee for renewing during the grace period.[32]

30. T.M.R.P. 2.167, 2.20.
31. *See* Appendix 2 (Trademark Fees).
32. *See id.*

Requirements

The requirements for renewal applications are similar to those for Section 8 affidavits. The notable difference is that there must be some use on the goods recited in the registration. The Lanham Act Section 9 provides:

> (a) Each registration may be renewed for periods of twenty years from the end of the expiring period upon payment of the prescribed fee and the filing of a verified application therefor, setting forth those goods or services recited in the registration on or in connection with which the mark is still in use in commerce and having attached thereto a specimen or facsimile showing current use of the mark, or showing that any nonuse is due to special circumstances which excuse such nonuse and it is not due to any intention to abandon the mark. Such application may be made at any time within six months before the expiration of the period for which the registration was issued or renewed, or it may be made within three months after such expiration on payment of the additional fee herein prescribed.
>
> (b) If the Commissioner refuses to renew the registration, he shall notify the registrant of his refusal and the reasons therefor.
>
> (c) An applicant for renewal not domiciled in the United States shall be subject to and comply with the provisions of section 1051(d) of this title.[33]

Renewal applications require:

- current use in commerce, specifying the nature of the commerce;
- use on some of the goods recited in the registration; and
- a specimen showing current use.

Alternatively:

- a showing that nonuse is due to special circumstances which excuse the nonuse and not due to any intention to abandon the mark.

---

33. 15 U.S.C. § 1059.

Like affidavits of use, the mark shown on the renewal specimen must present the same commercial impression as the registered mark. Modifications, such as changes in background design, are acceptable so long as they do not constitute a material alteration.[34]

Fraud

Also, like Section 8 and 15 affidavits, false statements may constitute fraud resulting in cancellation[35] or unenforceability. In the *Conwood v. Loew's* case, the fraud consisted of the statement that registrant's mark was in use for cigarette tobacco when, in fact, it was in use for cigarettes and cigars.

Summary

The renewal application must be filed within six months prior to each twentieth anniversary of the registration date or within the following three-month grace period. The application must contain:

1. identification of the registration including registration number and date;
2. recitation of ownership by the applicant;
3. recitation of use in commerce (specifying the nature of the use) on the goods recited in the registration;

   or

   recitation of circumstances excusing nonuse and absence of intent to abandon;
4. one specimen showing current use in commerce;
5. statements made in affidavit or declaration form;[36]

---

34. *See* T.M.E.P. 1605.07.
35. Conwood Corp. v. Loew's Theatres, Inc., 173 U.S.P.Q. 829 (T.T.A.B. 1972).
36. A sample renewal form is contained in Appendix 5 (Trademark Renewal Form).

6. filing fee for renewal plus grace period fee where applicable.[37]

Updating a Registration

Chances are that a mark will undergo some change through the years. Type style may vary, design elements or some word portions may be added or deleted.

The goods identified by the mark may also change. Deletions and additions are common occurrences. What can the trademark owner do to be sure his registration protects his mark as currently used?

Changes in the Mark

A registration can be amended to reflect changes that do not materially alter the character of the mark.[38] An amendment will not be permitted if the mark presents a different commercial impression from the mark as originally registered. A new application is required to give interested parties a chance to oppose.

The application for amendment requires new drawings, new specimens, a declaration, and filing fee.[39]

Changes in the Goods

If the mark is no longer in use on certain goods listed in the registration, these goods should be deleted at the time the Section 15 or any renewal is filed. It is not necessary to take such action in advance of these filings.

If the mark is used on additional goods, the registration cannot be amended to add the new goods. But a new application can be filed. It is a good idea to review a company's registrations from

37. *See* Appendix 2 for Trademark Fees.
38. *Ex parte* Black & Decker Mfg. Co., 136 U.S.P.Q. 379 (Comm'r Pat. 1963).
39. 15 U.S.C. § 1057(d); T.M.R.P. 2.173.

time to time to see if additional applications are required to cover the current product line.

Correcting Mistakes

Mistakes contained in registrations may be corrected by filing an application for correction in the Patent and Trademark Office. If the mistake was the fault of the Office, a certificate of correction will be issued free of charge.[40] If the mistake was the fault of applicant, it may be corrected so long as the change involved does not require republication.[41] The application for correction should recite the facts, including applicant's good faith, and contain a declaration and a filing fee.[42]

40. 15 U.S.C. § 1057(b); T.M.R.P. 2.174.
41. 15 U.S.C. § 1057(g); *Ex parte* Black & Decker Mfg. Co., 136 U.S.P.Q. 379 (Comm'r Pat. 1963).
42. T.M.R.P. 2.175.

7

Protecting a Trademark from Infringement

It is not enough to:

- carefully select a mark;
- search it for possible conflicts;
- use it properly, publicly, and continuously in connection with the goods or services;
- register it with the U.S. Patent and Trademark Office and file the necessary maintenance documents.

So long as a trademark remains in use, the owner's job is never done. Constant vigilance against infringements by third parties is required to preserve the trademark owner's rights.

This chapter focuses on the factors considered in evaluating infringement under three major theories:

1. likelihood of confusion;
2. counterfeit; and
3. dilution.

Likelihood of Confusion

Likelihood of confusion is the central inquiry in a trademark infringement case under the Lanham Act or common law. The question is: "whether there is a 'likelihood of confusion' on the part of consumers between the names and symbols used by the two parties."[1]

> Section 32(1) of the Lanham Act, 15 U.S.C.A. § 1114(1), governs lawsuits for the infringement of a federally registered trademark. A defendant is liable for infringement if, without the consent of the registrant, he uses "in commerce any reproduction, counterfeit, copy, or colorable imitation of a registered mark" which "is likely to cause confusion, or to cause mistake, or to deceive."[2]

The Burden of Proof

The burden of proof is on plaintiff. Plaintiff must show by a preponderance of evidence that an appreciable number of ordinarily prudent purchasers are likely to be confused between the marks.[3]

Likelihood Means Probable, Not Possible

"Likelihood" does not mean a mere possibility of confusion, but rather a probability that confusion will occur:

> It should be noted that the Lanham Act . . . requires that confusion, mistake, or deception be "likely," not merely "possible."[4]

Factors to Consider in Determining Likely Confusion

To determine likely confusion, the courts consider:

a. the strength of plaintiff's mark;
b. the degree of similarity between plaintiff's and defendant's marks;
c. the proximity of the products or services;

---

1. Freedom S. & L. Ass'n v. Way, 757 F.2d 1176, 1179 (11th Cir. 1985), *cert. denied*, 106 S. Ct. 134 (1985).
2. John H. Harland Co. v. Clarke Checks, Inc., 711 F.2d 966, 972 (11th Cir. 1983).
3. Mushroom Makers, Inc. v. R.G. Barry Corp., 580 F.2d 44, 47 (2d Cir. 1978).
4. Sears, Roebuck & Co. v. All States Life Ins. Co., 246 F.2d 161, 168 (5th Cir. 1957).

d. the likelihood that plaintiff will bridge the gap;
e. defendant's good faith in adopting his mark;
f. evidence of actual confusion;
g. the sophistication of the buyers; and
h. the quality of defendant's products or services.

These factors were articulated in the Second Circuit *Polaroid* case and are sometimes known as the Polaroid factors.[5] Essentially the same factors are considered by other circuits although they may be expressed in slightly different terms. A discussion of each factor and its application in specific cases follows.

The Strength of Plaintiff's Mark

Trademark strength "refers to the distinctiveness of the mark, or more precisely, its tendency to identify the goods sold under the mark as emanating from a particular, although possibly anonymous, source."[6]

> The more distinctive a plaintiff's servicemark, the greater the likelihood that consumers will associate the registered mark and all similar marks with the registered owner. The law therefore provides the greatest protection to strong and distinctive servicemarks.[7]

Just how is distinctiveness measured? Courts look primarily to:

1. The type of mark, *e.g.*, arbitrary, suggestive, descriptive, or generic.[8] The more remote the relationship between the mark and the goods, the stronger the mark.
2. The extent of third party use. The more infrequent the use by others, the stronger the mark.

---

5. Polaroid Corp. v. Polarad Elecs. Corp., 287 F.2d 492, 495 (2d Cir.), *cert. denied*, 368 U.S. 820 (1961).
6. McGregor-Doniger, Inc. v. Drizzle, Inc., 599 F.2d 1126, 1131 (2d Cir. 1979).
7. Freedom S. & L. Ass'n v. Way, 757 F.2d 1176, 1182 (11th Cir. 1985), *cert. denied*, 106 S. Ct. 134 (1985).
8. For discussion of these trademark categories see chapter 2, pp. 17-23, *supra*.

3. Advertising and sales. The more extensive the use, the stronger the mark.

Trademark Strength Based on Type of Mark: Where there is no logical correlation between the meaning of the mark and the product, the mark is "strong" and will receive broad protection.[9]

Where the descriptive nature of the mark makes it a natural choice for a particular product or service, it is "weak" and will not receive broad protection.[10]

Generally, there are four categories of strength for trademark purposes. In descending order these categories are:

1. arbitrary and fanciful—coined words such as KODAK, or words having no connection with the product or service, such as CAMEL for cigarettes;
2. suggestive—terms that subtly connote something about the product or service, *e.g.*, CITIBANK for banking;[11]
3. descriptive—terms that immediately describe something about the product or service, *e.g.*, SECURITY CENTER for a secure storage facility;[12]
4. generic—terms that serve as the common name for the kind of product or service, *e.g.*, VIDEO BUYER'S GUIDE.[13]

A descriptive mark is protected only when secondary meaning (association with a single source) is shown. A generic term is free for all to use to describe their products and can never become a trademark.[14]

---

9. Jellibeans, Inc. v. Skating Clubs of Ga., Inc., 716 F.2d 833, 841 n.19 (11th Cir. 1983).
10. Freedom S. & L. Ass'n v. Way, 757 F.2d 1176, 1182 (11th Cir. 1985), *cert. denied*, 106 S. Ct. 134 (1985).
11. Citibank, N.A. v. Citibanc Group, Inc., 724 F.2d 1540, 1545 (11th Cir. 1984).
12. Security Center, Ltd. v. First Nat'l Sec. Centers, 750 F.2d 1295, 1299 (5th Cir. 1985).
13. Reese Publishing Co. v. Hampton Int'l Communications, Inc., 620 F.2d 7, 10-11 (2d Cir. 1980).
14. See chapter 2, pp. 18-19, *supra*, for discussion of generic terms.

Trademark Strength Based on Third Party Use: A mark commonly used by third parties receives less protection than a mark not in common use.[15] This is especially true where third party use is for similar goods. A profusion of third party uses in the game field supported the finding that KIK-IT was not infringed by KICK'ER:

> Affiliated cannot claim exclusive rights over every variation of the word "kick." In the game field alone there is a profusion of games whose names, designed to catch the fancy of either children or parents, are derived from the word kick and which involve typically a football or soccer format.[16]

Third party use outside plaintiff's field is also evidence of the weakness of plaintiff's mark. The use of TRIUMPH for many types of products supported the finding that TRIUMPH on hosiery was not infringed by DISTINCTION BY TRIUMPH OF EUROPE on brassieres, corsets, and panty girdles:

> The mark "Triumph" is a so-called weak mark, *i.e.*, has been used many times to identify many types of products and services.[17]

To the same effect is the *Exquisite* case:

> A further index of its weakness is the extent to which it is employed by other concerns, to identify other types of goods and services. [Citations omitted]. It is undisputed here, for example, that the Manhattan, Bronx and Brooklyn telephone directories contain at least a dozen listings of concerns whose names begin with "Exquisite" aside from the plaintiff and the defendant. Such widespread usage further undermines any pretense of distinctiveness which plaintiff might claim for it.[18]

---

15. Sun Banks v. Sun Federal S. & L. Ass'n, 651 F.2d 311, 316 (5th Cir. 1981); Amstar Corp. v. Domino's Pizza, Inc., 615 F.2d 252, 259 (5th Cir.), *cert. denied*, 449 U.S. 899 (1980).
16. Affiliated Hosps. Prods., Inc. v. Merdel Game Mfg. Co., 513 F.2d 1183, 1188 (2d Cir. 1975).
17. Triumph Hosiery Mills, Inc. v. Triumph Int'l Corp., 308 F.2d 196, 199 n.2 (2d Cir. 1962).
18. Exquisite Form Indus., Inc. v. Exquisite Fabrics of London, 378 F. Supp. 403, 410 (S.D.N.Y. 1974).

Trademark Strength Based on Advertising and Sales: Plaintiff's advertising and sales also build up trademark strength:

> Strength or weakness is primarily a question of assessment of a mark's distinctiveness or popularity. Where the public has been educated to recognize and accept a particular mark as the hallmark for a particular source of that product, or the mark itself is inherently unique or has been the subject of wide advertisement, it is a strong trademark.[19]

If the mark in issue rises to the status of "well known," it wears a "larger cloak of protection":

> The law today, however, rewards a famous or well-known mark with a larger cloak of protection than in the case of a lesser known mark because of the propensity of the consuming public to associate a relatively unknown mark with one to which they have long been exposed if the mark bears any resemblance thereto. Efforts that have resulted in making a designation a well-known mark should be encouraged and not be used as a basis to whittle away at the goodwill created thereby.[20]

Even a mark initially weak, because of its logical relationship to the product or because of third party use, may subsequently acquire strength from plaintiff's promotional efforts.[21]

The finding that a mark is "weak" does not end the inquiry. It just narrows the scope of protection to closely related products.

The Similarities in the Marks

Traditionally, similarity is judged by comparing the marks in terms of appearance, sound, and meaning. When the judge sees no

---

19. E.I. Du Pont de Nemours & Co. v. Yoshida Int'l, Inc., 393 F. Supp. 502, 512 (E.D.N.Y. 1975).
20. Volkswagenwerk Ag. v. D & R Sales, Inc., 189 U.S.P.Q. 549, 554 (T.T.A.B. 1975).
21. John H. Harland Co. v. Clarke Checks, Inc., 711 F.2d 966, 974, n.13 (11th Cir. 1983.)

similarity, hears no similarity, and understands no similarity, confusion is not likely.[22]

Judging Similarities: While comparison of similarities is inevitable in assessing likely confusion, there are strict rules as to how the comparison should be made.

1. No Side-by-side Comparison: Because consumers do not usually view the products side-by-side in the marketplace, side-by-side comparison is not the proper test:

> However, as the district court noted at an earlier point in its opinion, a side-by-side comparison of the marks is not the proper test. The test is the consumers' state of mind when faced with the marks individually.[23]

2. No Dissection: Along with the prohibition against side-by-side comparison is the prohibition against trademark dissection. It is the overall commercial impression conveyed by the marks as a whole that determines the issue of likely confusion:

> It is axiomatic that a mark should not be dissected and considered piecemeal; rather, it must be considered as a whole in determining likelihood of confusion.[24]

While the marks must be considered as a whole, certain features may be given more or less weight.[25]

3. No Perfect Recall: Judges, who have the products in issue sitting before them day after day of trial, have no problem spotting specific differences in trademarks and labels.

---

22. Haagen-Dazs, Inc. v. Frusen Gladje Ltd., 493 F. Supp. 73, 75 (S.D.N.Y. 1980) (Haagen-Dazs and Frusen Gladje clearly distinguishable—not even the remote possibility of confusion).
23. Union Carbide Corp. v. Ever-Ready Inc., 531 F.2d 366, 382 (7th Cir. 1976); G.D. Searle & Co. v. Chas. Pfizer & Co., 265 F.2d 385, 388 (7th Cir. 1959).
24. Franklin Mint Corp. v. Master Mfg. Co., 667 F.2d 1005, 1007 (C.C.P.A. 1981). Sun-Fun Prods., Inc. v. Suntan Research & Dev., Inc., 656 F.2d 186, 189 (5th Cir. 1981).
25. SMS, Inc. v. Byn-Mar, Inc., 228 U.S.P.Q. 219, 220 (T.T.A.B. 1985).

Purchasers, however, do not shop with a handy sample of plaintiff's product in their pocket:

> The law does not require that the reasonably prudent purchaser keep a handy file of photographs and labels which he or she must pull out to compare with the label of every product purchased.[26]

Purchasers must rely on their memories, and most purchasers do not have perfect recall:

> Consumers often do not retain a clear impression of the precise form in which a mark appears. This is not from carelessness but rather is due to the fallibility of the human memory.[27]

4. Distinctive Labels May Not Be Visible: Judges should be reminded that trademarks are often heard but not seen. Where advertising, *e.g.*, word of mouth, radio, etc. is removed from the physical product, label comparisons cannot be relied on to prevent likely confusion:

> Moreover, it is not only on the shelves the two products are advertised; radio and newspaper ads, as well as word of mouth, may carry an advertising message. In those media, distinctive labels will be absent.[28]

Acceptable Similarities: Some similarities are more acceptable than others. Where both marks include a generic portion, the focus must be on the nongeneric portion.

> [A]lthough the marks ultimately must be considered as a whole, the focus of the inquiry regarding appearance and sound is on the non-generic portion.[29]

---

26. 2 McCarthy, Trademarks and Unfair Competition § 23:17, at 99 (2d ed. 1984).
27. Union Carbide Corp. v. Ever-Ready, Inc., 531 F.2d 366, 382 (7th Cir. 1976).
28. Hills Bros. Coffee, Inc. v. Hills Supermarkets, Inc., 428 F.2d 379, 381 (2d Cir. 1970).
29. John H. Harland Co. v. Clarke Checks, Inc., 711 F.2d 966, 976 (11th Cir. 1983) (Memory Stub found confusing with Entry Stub for checkbook stubs).

By the same token, where both marks include a "weak" (descriptive) portion, the focus must be on the nondescriptive portion. In the *Nina Ricci* case, L'AIR D'OR for perfume flecked with gold was held not confusing with L'AIR DU TEMPS for perfume.[30] The court considered L'Air (translated as air or essence) "weak."

Another general rule is that where a mark is "weak," minor additions may negate any confusing similarity.[31]

Distinctions That May or May Not Make a Difference: Sometimes, distinctions in packaging, style of print, or the presence of defendant's company name make a difference.[32] But sometimes such distinctions will not "save the day."[33] The weight accorded these distinctions will vary in each case depending on all the other factors.

Proximity of the Goods

Common Sense and Common Experience: Steam Shovels Versus Butter: Generally speaking, goods are sufficiently related for purposes of likely confusion if the average purchaser believes they might come from the same source.[34]

Onc court summarized it this way: "the inquiry into similarity of products is ultimately one of common sense and common experience."[35] An early decision gave the graphic example of steam shovels and butter:

---

30. Nina Ricci, S.A.R.L. v. Gemcraft Ltd., 612 F. Supp. 1520 (S.D.N.Y. 1985).
31. Sun Banks of Fla., Inc. v. Sun Fed. S. & L. Ass'n, 651 F.2d 311, 316 (5th Cir. 1981) (holding SUN BANK and logo design not confusing to SUN FEDERAL SAVINGS and logo design).
32. Nina Ricci, S.A.R.L. v. Gemcraft Ltd., 612 F. Supp. 1520 (S.D.N.Y. 1985).
33. A.T. Cross Co. v. Jonathan Bradley Pens, Inc., 470 F.2d 689, 692 (2d Cir. 1972); (LA CROSSE by Bradley found confusing with CROSS for mechanical pens and pencils).
34. Communications Satellite Corp. v. Comcet, Inc., 429 F.2d 1245, 1252 (4th Cir.), *cert. denied*, 400 U.S. 942 (1970).
35. ITT Corp. v. XTRA Corp., 225 U.S.P.Q. 723, 732 (D. Mass. 1985).

> It is safe to say that no reasonable person would suppose that articles as dissimilar as steam-shovels and butter would come from the same source even though the trademarks thereon were practically identical, but, on the other hand, most purchasers would be inclined to believe that butter and cream, if marketed under trademarks bearing even slight similarity, were produced by the same manufacturer.[36]

The common experience test suggests that proximity of goods is more easily found in today's business climate than in the past. As licensing and corporate acquisitions become more prevalent, the public is educated to expect a variety of products to originate with one company.[37]

Pertinent Factors: In assessing proximity of the goods, relevant factors include similarities in retail outlets, purchasers, and advertising media as well as similarities in products,[38] *e.g.*, price and complementary nature of use.[39]

Examples of Closely Related Products: Certain product categories are traditionally treated as closely related. For example, similar marks on articles of wearing apparel are frequently found to cause likely confusion.[40] The same is true for similar marks on

---

36. Dwinell-Wright Co. v. National Fruit Prod. Co., 140 F.2d 618, 622 (1st Cir. 1944).
37. Tuxedo Monopoly, Inc. v. General Mills Fun Group, Inc., 648 F.2d 1335, 1336 (C.C.P.A. 1981).
38. Some circuits treat similarities in the goods, channels of distribution, and advertising as separate factors, but the analysis is pretty much the same. John H. Harland Co. v. Clarke Checks, Inc., 711 F.2d 966 (11th Cir. 1983).
39. Aunt Jemima Mills Co. v. Rigney & Co., 247 F. 407 (2d Cir. 1917) (AUNT JEMIMA pancake batter confusing with AUNT JEMIMA pancake syrup).
40. *In re* Pix of Am., Inc., 225 U.S.P.Q. 691 (T.T.A.B. 1985) and cases cited therein (NEWPORTS shoes confusing with NEWPORT outer shirts).

alcoholic beverages[41] and similar marks on food products.[42]

Exceptions That Prove There Is No Rule: The close proximity of goods is, of course, only one factor.[43] There is no hard and fast rule, even where identical marks are used on goods normally considered closely related. Startling examples of "exceptions that prove there is no rule" are found in both the apparel and food categories.

The owner of MUSHROOMS for ladies' shoes could reasonably be optimistic about prevailing against the use of MUSHROOM for ladies' sportswear. And, indeed, the Court of Appeals did find likelihood of confusion.[44] Nevertheless, the court refused to enjoin the second user of MUSHROOM because of his substantial good faith investment.

A similar scenario occurred in the BRAVOS case.[45] There, the identical marks were applied to crackers and tortilla chips. And again, the second user's substantial good faith investment militated against injunctive relief.

These exceptional decisions stand as potent reminders that each case is decided on its own facts.

---

41. E. Remy Martin & Co. v. Shaw-Ross Int'l Imports, Inc., 756 F.2d 1525 (11th Cir. 1985); (REMY MARTIN and REMY cognac and brandy confusing with F. REMY wine and liquors).
42. American Foods, Inc. v. Golden Flake, Inc., 312 F.2d 619 (5th Cir. 1963); (GOLDEN FLAKE potato chips and other foods confusing with RAINBO GOLDEN FLAKE dinner rolls).
43. Freedom S. & L. Ass'n v. Way, 757 F.2d 1176 (11th Cir. 1985) (no likely confusion between FREEDOM realty services and FREEDOM savings and loan services despite close proximity in services).
44. Mushroom Makers, Inc. v. R.G. Barry Corp., 580 F.2d 44, 47 (2d Cir. 1978).
45. Vitarroz v. Borden, Inc., 644 F.2d 960 (2d Cir. 1981).

Stricter Standard for Medicinal Products: One category of products is singled out for special treatment by the law: products that affect the purchaser's health.

Where confusion or mistake could have harmful health consequences, the courts have imposed a stricter standard of likely confusion. In other words, relief will be granted upon less proof of likely confusion where medicinal products are involved:

> Confusion between plaintiff's and defendant's marks here could result in physical harm to the consuming public, whether through failure to receive effective medication or through adverse reaction to inadvertently prescribed or dispensed drugs. Hence a stricter standard in order to prevent likelihood of confusion seems desirable.[46]

Bridging the Gap

Bridging the gap has been defined as "the senior user's interest in preserving avenues of expansion and entering into related fields."[47]

There appear to be two ways of crossing the bridge. One is by actual plans for expansion. Such plans must be more than "sheer possibility." They must be "sufficiently real or imminent" to justify the granting of equitable relief.[48]

Another route for crossing the bridge is marked not so much by plans for expansion as by the consumer's assumption that expansion is likely:

---

46. Syntex Laboratories, Inc. v. Norwich Pharmacal Co., 437 F.2d 566, 569 (2d Cir. 1971) (VAGESTROL for vaginal suppository found confusing with VAGITROL for vaginal cream); Morgenstern Chem. Co. v. G.D. Searle & Co., 253 F.2d 390 (3d Cir.), *cert. denied*, 358 U.S. 816 (1958) (MICTINE for diuretic tablets found confusing with MICTURIN for tablets to treat urinary tract infections).
47. Mushroom Makers, Inc. v. R.G. Barry Corp., 580 F.2d 44, 49 (2d Cir. 1978).
48. Schoenfeld Indus., Inc. v. Britannia Sales, Ltd., 512 F. Supp. 979, 983 (S.D.N.Y. 1981).

> [T]he law is well established that in order to prevail the owner need not show that he has in fact or is about to bridge the gap between his and the newcomer's presently noncompeting products. The ultimate test remains one of likelihood of confusion among prospective purchasers as to source of origin; the expansion of business factor turns not so much on objective evidence of actual expansion or potential therefor as it does on whether it is reasonable for the ordinary purchaser to assume such expansion.[49]

In judging the consumer's reasonable assumption of expansion, courts look to:

plaintiff's history of expansion;[50] and

the existence of other companies that have taken similar expansion steps.[51]

Defendant's Intent

Bad faith is not required to find trademark infringement.[52] But it sure does help! In fact, bad faith may alone be sufficient to justify the inference of likely confusion.

> If . . . a plaintiff can show that a defendant adopted a mark with the intent of deriving benefit from the reputation of the plaintiff, that fact alone "may be sufficient to justify the inference that there is confusing similarity."[53]

The theory here is that where defendant intends to trade on plaintiff's mark, the law presumes that defendant succeeded.

> In assessing the likelihood of confusion to the public, an important factor is whether or not the second comer created the similar

---

49. E.I. Du Pont de Nemours & Co. v. Yoshida Int'l, Inc., 393 F. Supp. 502, 517-18 (E.D.N.Y. 1975) (quoting 3 R. CALLMANN, UNFAIR COMPETITION, TRADEMARKS, AND MONOPOLIES § 82.2(c), at 808-09 (2d ed. 1969).
50. E.I. Du Pont de Nemours & Co. v. Yoshida Int'l, Inc., 393 F. Supp. 502 (E.D.N.Y. 1975).
51. Scarves by Vera, Inc. v. Todo Imports, Ltd., 544 F.2d 1167, 1174 (2d Cir. 1976).
52. HMH Publishing Co., Inc. v. Brincat, 504 F.2d 713, 720 (9th Cir. 1974).
53. Exxon Corp. v. Texas Motor Exch., 628 F.2d 500, 506 (5th Cir. 1980).

trade dress intentionally. If there was intentional copying the second comer will be presumed to have intended to create a confusing similarity of appearance and will be presumed to have succeeded.[54]

On the other hand, the mere copying of plaintiff's mark will not be held against defendant if the court finds that plaintiff's mark is generic.[55]

What Constitutes Bad Faith: Bad faith may be established by defendant's copying of type style, background designs, color schemes, and/or overall trade dress.[56] Bad faith may be found where defendant has no credible explanation for the adoption of his mark.[57] Failure to search a mark may also put defendant behind the bad faith eight ball.[58]

On the other hand, bad faith is usually not found simply because plaintiff's mark was turned up in the search conducted by defendant. Defendant may still have adopted his mark in good faith on the grounds that the search revealed other marks similar to plaintiff's.[59] Good faith may also be found because of defendant's belief that the different nature of the products presented no conflict.[60]

---

54. Perfect Fit Indus., Inc. v. Acme Quilting Co., 618 F.2d 950, 954 (2d Cir. 1980); Sun Banks v. Sun Fed. S. & L. Ass'n, 651 F.2d 311, 318-19 (5th Cir. 1981).
55. Liquid Controls, Corp. v. Liquid Control Corp., 802 F.2d 934, 940 (7th Cir. 1986).
56. Spring Mills, Inc. v. Ultracashmere House Ltd., 689 F.2d 1127, 1134-35 (2d Cir. 1982).
57. Kiki Undies Corp. v. Promenade Hosiery Mills, Inc., 411 F.2d 1097, 1101 (2d Cir. 1969).
58. ITT Corp. v. XTRA Corp., 225 U.S.P.Q. 723, 729-30 (D. Mass. 1985).
59. Lever Brothers Co. v. American Bakeries Co., 693 F.2d 251, 258 (2d Cir. 1982).
60. Mushroom Makers, Inc. v. R.G. Barry Corp., 441 F. Supp. 1220, 1230 (S.D.N.Y. 1977), *aff'd*, 580 F.2d 44 (2d Cir. 1978)

Advice of Counsel—A Questionable Antidote: Reliance on advice of counsel may or may not absolve defendant from a finding of bad faith. Such action, as pointed out in the *Harland* MEMORY STUB case, can be interpreted two ways:

> Clarke argues that any possible inference of intent to trade on the reputation of Harland's mark by adopting a confusingly similar mark is necessarily negated by evidence that Clarke officials consulted trademark counsel before adopting the Entry Stub mark. We disagree. Although the evidence of Clarke's consultations with counsel can be read to suggest that Clarke had no intent to adopt a mark which was confusingly similar to Harland's mark, the jury also might have inferred that Clarke merely was attempting to come as close to Harland's mark as the law would allow. Cf. *Chevron Chemical Co. v. Voluntary Purchasing Groups, Inc.*, 659 F.2d 695, 704, 212 USPQ 904, 912-13 (5th Cir. 1981) (Unit A) (district court found that defendant "meant to copy [plaintiff's] trade dress, 'at least as much as the law would allow' "; former Fifth Circuit stated that the only plausible explanation for such behavior was that defendant had intent to "cash in" on plaintiff's good will), cert. denied, 457 U.S. 1126 (1982). Thus, the fact that Clarke officials sought legal advice before adopting the Entry Stub mark does not preclude a finding that Clarke intended to trade on the good will associated with Harland's mark by adopting a mark which "approach[ed] so near to [the Memory Stub Mark] that the public may fail to distinguish between them." *Florence Manufacturing Co. v. J.C. Dowd & Co.*, 178 F. 73, 75 (2d Cir. 1910). Cf. *Wolf v. National Lead Co.*, 272 F.2d 867, 971, 123 USPQ 574, 576-77 (9th Cir. 1959) (fact that appellant acted on advice of counsel did not preclude an accounting of profits because "[w]hether he believed himself to be within the law or not, he was knowingly and deliberately cashing in upon the good will of appellee"), cert. denied, 362 U.S. 950, 80 S.Ct. 860, 4 L.Ed.2d 868 (1960).[61]

61. John H. Harland Co. v. Clarke Checks, Inc., 711 F.2d 966, 977-78 (11th Cir. 1983).

If the advice of counsel theory is pleaded, defendant should be ready to produce all attorney-client correspondence on the subject.[62]

Actual Confusion

Two Sides to Every Story: Trademark plaintiffs who have little or no proof of actual confusion are fond of pointing out:

1. Likely confusion, not actual confusion, is the test.[63] Evidence of actual confusion is not necessary to a finding of likely confusion.[64]
2. Evidence of actual confusion is almost impossible to come by.[65] This is because many purchasers do not realize confusion has occurred—or if they do, do not bother to notify the trademark owner.[66]
3. Very little proof of actual confusion will weigh strongly in favor of likely confusion.[67]
4. When the products have been on the market a relatively short time, the absence of actual confusion is of little weight.[68]

Defendants, on the other hand, are just as fond of pointing to the other side of the story:

---

62. Fonar Corp. v. Johnson & Johnson, Inc., 227 U.S.P.Q. 886, 887-88 (D. Mass. 1986).
63. Hills Bros. Coffee, Inc. v. Hills Supermarkets, Inc., 428 F.2d 379, 380 (2d Cir. 1970).
64. Amstar Corp. v. Domino's Pizza, Inc., 615 F.2d 252, 263 (5th Cir.), *cert. denied*, 449 U.S. 899 (1980).
65. Harold F. Ritchie, Inc. v. Chesebrough-Ponds, Inc., 281 F.2d 755, 761 (2d Cir. 1960).
66. Union Carbide Corp. v. Ever-Ready, Inc., 531 F.2d 366, 383 (7th Cir. 1976).
67. World Carpets, Inc. v. Dick Littrell's New World Carpets, 438 F.2d 482, 489 (5th Cir. 1971).
68. Nordica di Franco e Giovanni Vaccari v. Nordic Sport Ltd., 202 U.S.P.Q. 860, 863 (T.T.A.B. 1979).

1. Isolated instances of actual confusion are not persuasive.[69]
2. Plaintiffs who have selected a weak mark can expect a certain amount of confusion.[70]
3. Confusion must be judged in the context of the overall sales or transactions involved [less than fifteen instances of confusion in three years is negligible when compared with total number of transactions].[71]
4. Coexistence for a significant period of time without evidence of confusion weighs strongly against a finding of likely confusion.[72]

Quality and Quantity Count: Not all confusion is created equal. Evidence showing that an actual purchase was affected by confusion is highly probative.[73] Inquiries as to possible connection between the parties are regarded as persuasive by some courts,[74] and not so persuasive by others.[75]

Quantity is also important. As noted above, some courts will find the number of instances of confusion negligible when compared with total sales. There is no such thing as too much evidence of actual confusion.

---

69. Amstar Corp. v. Domino's Pizza, Inc., 615 F.2d 252, 263 (5th Cir.), *cert. denied*, 449 U.S. 899 (1980).
70. Scott Paper Co. v. Scott's Liquid Gold, Inc., 589 F.2d 1225, 1231 (3d Cir. 1978).
71. Sun Banks v. Sun Fed. S. & L. Ass'n, 651 F.2d 311, 319 (5th Cir. 1981).
72. Pignons S.A. de Mechanique de Precision v. Polaroid Corp., 657 F.2d 482, 490 (1st Cir. 1981) (coexistence for four years).
73. Astra Pharmaceutical Prods., Inc. v. Beckman Instruments, Inc., 718 F.2d 1201, 1207 (1st Cir. 1983).
74. ITT Corp. v. XTRA Corp., 225 U.S.P.Q. 723, 728-29 (D. Mass. 1985).
75. Trade Publications, Inc. v. Big Bear of N. C., Inc., 191 U.S.P.Q. 477, 478-79 (M.D. N.C. 1976); Pennzoil Co. v. Crown Cent. Petroleum Corp., 50 F. Supp. 891, 899 (D. Md. 1943), *aff'd*, 140 F.2d 387 (4th Cir. 1944).

Purchaser Sophistication

Simply put: "Sophisticated consumers may be expected to exercise greater care."[76] Some guidelines for determining purchaser sophistication follow.

The Credulous General Public Versus the Discriminating Professional: One way of analyzing buyer sophistication is to separate purchasers into two classes: The general public versus the professional. The general public encompasses:

> [T]hat vast multitude which includes the ignorant, the unthinking and the credulous, who, in making purchases, do not stop to analyze, but are governed by appearance and general impressions.[77]

The professional, on the other hand, who is buying for specific work related purposes is armed with greater knowledge and greater powers of discrimination.

The Ordinarily Prudent Purchaser: Whether the purchaser is a discriminating professional or a gullible member of the general public, he is presumed to exercise the care normally exercised by the "ordinarily prudent" purchaser of the goods in issue.[78] Of course, ordinary prudence varies with the type of product, the expense, the method of sales, and the channels of distribution.

Supermarket Hypnosis Versus Protracted Focus: The degree of care ranges from the low attention paid by harried supermarket shoppers to the careful selection made by technically trained purchasers of laboratory instruments costing thousands of dollars.

The supermarket shopper has been described as undergoing a "state of hypnosis" as he travels the aisles confronted by a myriad of products:

---

76. Pignons S.A. de Mechanique de Precision v. Polaroid Corp., 657 F.2d 482, 489-90 (1st Cir. 1981).
77. Florence Mfg. Co. v. J.C. Dowd & Co., 178 F. 73, 75 (2d Cir. 1910).
78. Dawn Donut Co. v. Day, 450 F.2d 332, 333 (10th Cir. 1971).

> [W]e are dealing neither with an unusual product which requires discriminating purchase nor with a purchasing public which is discriminating. To the contrary, it has been asserted that the average purchaser undergoes while in the supermarket, an experience not unlike that of hypnosis.[79]

In contrast, the decision to buy blood analyzers costing $35,000 to $60,000 and taking three months to a year to consummate:

> is obviously not done on an impulse, and involves a careful consideration of the reliability and dependability of the manufacturer and seller of the product.[80]

While likely confusion diminishes if expensive goods are purchased after careful consideration, even sophisticated purchasers are subject to confusion between very similar marks.[81]

Quality of Defendant's Goods

The quality of defendant's goods is sometimes included in the list of standard factors to consider in judging likely confusion.[82] But, defendant cannot avoid infringement just because his goods are currently of high quality since plaintiff has no control over defendant's future actions.

> Even if the infringer's goods are of high quality, the victim has the right to insist that its reputation not be imperiled by another's actions. *Processed Plastics Co. v. Warner Communications, Inc.*, 675 F.2d 852, 858 (7th Cir. 1982); see also 4 R. Callmann, *Unfair Competition, Trademarks and Monopolies*, § 88.3(b) at 205-06 (3rd ed. 1970). Bausch & Lomb's loss of control over its reputation

---

79. Pikle-Rite Co. v. Chicago Pickle Co., 171 F. Supp. 671, 676 (N.D. Ill. 1959); *see also* Lever Bros. Co. v. American Bakeries Co., 693 F.2d 251 (2d Cir. 1982).
80. Astra Pharmaceutical Prods., Inc. v. Beckman Instruments, Inc., 718 F.2d 1201, 1206 (1st Cir. 1983).
81. Omega Importing Corp. v. Petri-Kine Camera Co., 451 F.2d 1190, 1195 (2d Cir. 1971).
82. Polaroid Corp. v. Polarad Elecs. Corp., 287 F.2d 492, 495 (2d Cir.), *cert. denied*, 368 U.S. 820 (1961).

> justifies a finding of irreparable harm even if it could demonstrate no loss of sales or market share.[83]

Of course, there may be more immediate harm done where defendant's product is shoddy. With this in mind, plaintiff would do well to stress defendant's inferior quality if such be the case. But a claim should not be denied just because defendant's products are currently of high quality.

Balance of Harm

Injunctive relief, being an equitable remedy, reflects a balancing of the harms to each party. It logically follows from a finding of likely confusion that the harm to plaintiff and the interest of the public require the issuance of an injunction.

Nevertheless, there have been cases where confusion is found as a matter of law—but defendant's use is allowed. The Second Circuit reached this result in the *Mushrooms* case where the second user had made a substantial good faith investment in his mark. The second user's projected annual sales for MUSHROOM clothing at the time of trial approached the $20 million level. Sales of MUSHROOMS shoes by the first user amounted to $6 million from 1974 through the first half of 1977. The court concluded that:

> We therefore find, based upon the trial court record, that Mushroom Makers' [second user] interest in retaining the goodwill developed through concurrent use of an identical trademark far outweighs any conceivable injury to Barry [first user]; consequently we hold that the district court acted properly in denying the requested injunction.[84]

Balancing the harm may also tip a finding against likely confusion. In the BRAVOS case, defendant Borden had invested $1.3

83. Wesley-Jessen Div. of Schering Corp. v. Bausch & Lomb, Inc., 698 F.2d 862, 867 (7th Cir. 1983).

84. Mushroom Makers, Inc. v. R.G. Barry Corp., 580 F.2d 44, 49 (2d Cir. 1978).

million without knowledge of plaintiff's mark (which did not show up in Borden's search).[85] By trial, an additional $5 million was expended and sales were approximately $9 million. Plaintiff had total sales of $136,000 and advertising of $13,000. On these facts, the Court found no likely confusion between the identical marks used on crackers and tortilla chips.

While defendant's good faith investment can't be counted on to swing the balance, it is certainly a factor to be reckoned with.

Counterfeits

What Is a Counterfeit

All counterfeits are infringements but not all infringements are counterfeits. A counterfeit mark is identical to or substantially indistinguishable from plaintiff's mark. The Lanham Act defines counterfeit as:

> a spurious mark which is identical with, or substantially indistinguishable from, a registered mark.[86]

While the Lanham Act was born with a special definition of counterfeit, the remedies provided under that statute were the same for counterfeits as for ordinary infringements.

As counterfeiting activities escalated, trademark owners cried out for stricter penalties to deter what had become a billion dollar business. These cries were finally heeded and the Trademark Counterfeiting Act of 1984 was enacted.

---

85. Vitarroz v. Borden, Inc., 644 F.2d 960 (2d Cir. 1981).
86. 15 U.S.C. § 1127.

The Trademark Counterfeiting Act of 1984

Penalties

The Counterfeiting Act provides for criminal penalties as well as stricter civil remedies.[87] Individuals are subject to criminal penalties of up to $250,000 and/or five years of imprisonment. Corporations can be fined up to $1 million. The civil remedies mandate the award of treble damages or profits (whichever is greater) and attorneys' fees, absent a finding of "extenuating circumstances."

Definitions

The Counterfeit Act adopts the original Lanham Act definition of counterfeit, namely:

> A "counterfeit" is a spurious mark which is identical with, or substantially indistinguishable from, a registered mark.

However, the "counterfeit" mark must be used on the same goods or services covered by plaintiff's registration.[88]

Intent Required

In addition to likely confusion, the Act requires intentional trafficking or attempted trafficking and knowing use of a counterfeit mark.

Ex Parte Seizure

To prevent counterfeiters from dumping their records and counterfeit merchandise at the first hint of suit, the Act authorizes ex parte seizure of counterfeit goods and pertinent documents.

While district courts had already been granting ex parte seizure orders before the Act was passed, the Act confirms the availability

---

87. 15 U.S.C. §§ 1116(d), 1117(b); 18 U.S.C. § 2320.
88. 15 U.S.C. §§ 1127, 1116(d)(1)(B)(i); 18 U.S.C. § 2320(d)(1)(A)(i), (ii).

of this relief and details the specific findings that the court must make, namely that:

(1) No other adequate remedy exists;
(2) The applicant has not publicized the requested seizure;
(3) The applicant is likely to succeed in showing that the person against whom seizure would be ordered used a counterfeit mark;
(4) An immediate and irreparable injury will occur if seizure is not ordered;
(5) The harm to applicant outweighs the harm to the person against whom seizure is ordered;
(6) The matter to be seized is located at the place identified in the application; and
(7) The person against whom seizure would be ordered would destroy the allegedly counterfeit goods if notice was provided.[89]

Wrongful Seizure

The Act requires security for damages suffered as a result of wrongful seizure. In addition, punitive damages may be recovered where the seizure was sought in bad faith.

What Is Not a Counterfeit

Specifically excluded from the Act are "overruns" and parallel imports (grey market goods).[90] Overruns are unauthorized goods produced by a licensed manufacturer. The sponsors of the Act indicated that the trademark owner has effective contractual and civil remedies against such unauthorized use.[91]

As to parallel imports, these goods are legitimately manufactured and sold overseas, but may be excluded from the U.S. market when the U.S. owner has deposited his registration with Customs.[92] There is considerable debate as to whether such goods

89. 15 U.S.C. § 1116(d)(4)(B)(i)-(vii).
90. See chapter 13, pp. 271-76, *infra*, for methods of barring parallel imports.
91. *See* El Greco Leather Prods. Co. v. Shoe World, Inc., 599 F. Supp. 1380, 1396 (E.D.N.Y. 1984); *rev'd on other grounds*, 806 F.2d 392 (2d Cir. 1986).
92. 19 U.S.C. § 1526(a).

are infringements[93] and so it is not surprising that they are excluded from the harsher penalties provided by the Counterfeit Act.

The Average Purchaser Is Alive and Well

There is little case law as to what meets the definition of counterfeit mark, *i.e.*, when is a mark "substantially indistinguishable" from a registered mark. It is clear, however, that the determination will be made from the point of view of the average purchaser. In the *Rolex* case, decided before the passage of the Act, the court rejected Customs' argument that the question of counterfeit should be judged from the perspective of an expert who can spot distinctions with a jeweler's loupe.[94]

Dilution: "Yes, Virginia, There Really Is a Dilution Cause of Action"

The Spirit and Letter of the Law

To trademark owners having trouble proving likely confusion, state anti-dilution statutes promised welcome relief.[95] These statutes provide protection against the "dilution" of distinctive marks, notwithstanding the absence of confusion or competition between the parties.[96]

Dilution is characterized as a "whittling down" of the identity or reputation of a tradename or mark.[97] Dilution is also defined as:

93. *See* chapter 13, pp. 271-76, *infra*.
94. Montres Rolex, S.A. v. Snyder, 718 F.2d 524 (2d Cir. 1983).
95. As of 1986, twenty-three states have passed anti-dilution statutes.
96. Query if dilution may also be recognized under the common law in the absence of a statute. A case that appeared to apply a dilution theory without reference to the word dilution is Chemical Corp. of Am. v. Anheuser-Busch, Inc., 306 F.2d 433 (5th Cir. 1962) (Floorwax-insecticide slogan WHERE THERE'S LIFE THERE'S BUGS found likely to be confused with beer slogan WHERE THERE'S LIFE THERE'S BUD).
97. Mortellito v. Nina of Cal., Inc., 335 F. Supp. 1288, 1296 (S.D.N.Y. 1972).

> [A]n act which threatens two separable but related components of advertising value. Junior uses may blur a mark's product identification or they may tarnish the affirmative associations a mark has come to convey.[98]

The "evil" that the anti-dilution statutes seek to remedy is:

> not public confusion caused by similar products or services sold by competitors, but a cancer-like growth of dissimilar products or services which feeds upon the business reputation of an established distinctive trade-mark or name.[99]

Despite the plain words and intent of the anti-dilution statutes, the courts took several decades to acknowledge that confusion is not required for relief. Today, the law has finally developed to the point where attorneys can confidently say to their clients, "Yes, there really is a dilution cause of action."

This section will review the attitude of the courts toward dilution in the past, the elements of a dilution cause of action in the present, and finally some questions about dilution in the future.

The Past: Ignoring the Plain Wording of the Statute

Anti-dilution statutes date back to the late 1940s. The first statute was enacted in Massachusetts in 1947. The New York statute, which uses language typical of the statutes in other states, was enacted in 1961. It reads:

> Likelihood of injury to business reputation or of dilution of the distinctive quality of a mark or trade name shall be a ground for injunctive relief in cases of infringement of a mark registered or not registered or in cases of unfair competition, notwithstanding the absence of competition between the parties or the absence of confusion as to the source of goods or services.[100]

---

98. 3 R. CALLMANN, THE LAW OF UNFAIR COMPETITION, TRADEMARKS, AND MONOPOLIES § 84.2, at 954-55.
99. Allied Maintenance Corp. v. Allied Mechanical Trades, Inc., 42 N.Y.2d 538, 543, 399 N.Y.S.2d 628, 369 N.E.2d 1162 (N.Y. Ct. App. 1977).
100. N.Y. GEN. BUS. LAWS § 368-d.

For many years the courts interpreted the dilution statutes as though competition and confusion were required—despite the explicit statutory language to the contrary.[101] Those cases that did find dilution did so only after a finding of confusion.[102] The reverse was also true; those cases that did not find confusion did not find dilution.[103] This "tying" phenomenon continued even after courts began to acknowledge that dilution did not require confusion.[104]

The Present: The Statute Means What It Says: Confusion and Competition Are Not Required

A breakthrough in the dilution arena occurred in 1977. And strangely enough it occurred in connection with one of the most diluted names imaginable: ALLIED.[105] While the New York Court of Appeals divided on the issue of whether ALLIED was distinctive enough to be diluted, the Court was unanimous in holding that the dilution statute did not require likelihood of confusion.

The strong signal broadcast by *Allied* was clearly received by the Second Circuit Court of Appeals. Following *Allied*, the Second Circuit has consistently affirmed that:

> injury to a recognized trade name, rather than damage arising from confusion among consumers, lies at the heart of the wrong.[106]

---

101. Berlitz Schools of Languages of Am. v. Everest House, 619 F.2d 211, 215 (2d Cir. 1980); HMH Publishing Co., Inc. v. Lambert, 482 F.2d 595, 599 (9th Cir. 1973); Carter-Wallace, Inc. v. Procter & Gamble Co., 434 F.2d 794, 803 (9th Cir. 1970).
102. Coca-Cola Co. v. Gemini Rising, Inc., 346 F. Supp. 1183 (S.D.N.Y. 1972).
103. Girl Scouts of United States v. Personality Posters Mfg. Co., 304 F. Supp. 1228 (S.D.N.Y. 1969).
104. Tetley, Inc. v. Topps Chewing Gum, Inc., 556 F. Supp. 785 (E.D.N.Y. 1983).
105. Allied Maintenance Corp. v. Allied Mechanical Trades, Inc., 42 N.Y.2d 538, 543, 399 N.Y.S.2d 628, 369 N.E.2d (N.Y. Ct. App. 1977).
106. Mushroom Makers, Inc. v. R.G. Barry Corp., 580 F.2d 44, 49 (2d Cir. 1978), *cert. denied*, 439 U.S. 1116 (1979); Dallas Cowboys Cheerleaders, Inc. v. Pussycat Cinema, Ltd., 604 F.2d 200, 205 n.8 (2d Cir. 1979).

There is no doubt now that the statute means what it says: "Neither competition between the parties nor confusion about the source of products . . . [is] necessary to state a cause of action for dilution."[107] The next question, of course, is what is necessary?

The Elements of a Dilution Cause of Action

Under current law, a cause of action for dilution arises where:

a. The mark or name is "truly of distinctive quality."[108]

b. There is likelihood of dilution.

The Requirement of Distinctiveness

It is still unsettled as to just how distinctive a mark must be to qualify for protection against dilution. Some commentators have suggested that only "famous" or "celebrated" marks should be protected by anti-dilution statutes.[109]

Fame, however, was not specifically mentioned by the *Allied* majority as the touchstone for distinctiveness. The court phrased the test this way: the mark must be "truly of distinctive quality or have a secondary meaning in the mind of the public."[110]

In cases decided after *Allied*, courts in New York as well as other states have protected less well known marks under the anti-dilution statutes; for example:

---

107. Sally Gee, Inc. v. Myra Hogan, Inc., 699 F.2d 621, 624 (2d Cir. 1983).

108. *Id.* at 625.

109. Note, *Dilution: Trademark Infringement or Will-o'-the-Wisp?*, 77 HARV. L. REV. 520, 530 (1964). Examples of famous diluting marks were given in the legislative history of the New York statute: Dupont shoes, Buick aspirin tablets, Schlitz varnish, Kodak pianos, and Bulova gowns. 1954 N.Y. Legis. Annual 49.

110. Allied Maintenance Corp. v. Allied Mechanical Trades, Inc., 42 N.Y.2d 538, 545-46, 399 N.Y.S.2d 628, 369 N.E.2d 1162 (N.Y. Ct. App. 1977) (over 300 uses of ALLIED for companies in the New York telephone directory precluded a finding of distinctiveness).

1. CINNABAR for beauty products versus CINNABAR for haircutting salon;[111]
2. COOKIE JAR and Design for banking services versus COOKIE JAR and Design for topless go-go bar;[112]
3. WEDGWOOD for residential real estate versus WEDGWOOD for retirement apartments.[113]

The Court in *Wedgwood* analyzed the distinctiveness requirement as follows:

> The words "distinctive quality" do not connote to us only the high degree of strength or renown that defendant contends a name must have to be protected by ORS 647.107. Moreover, if the statute does have such a limited application, we cannot understand why the legislature enacted it; the only persons who could avail themselves of it would be those who are peculiarly well protected by the common law remedy. For instance, defendant gives KODAK as an example of the very limited class of names to which the antidilution statute should apply. If someone unaffiliated with the owner of the KODAK name were to open a chain of restaurants called "Kodak's Burgers," the owner of the name would have an excellent chance of prevailing in an unfair competition action.[114]

In *Wedgwood*, the court granted protection to the WEDGWOOD mark on real estate because of its reputation in the local Portland metropolitan area, despite the argument that on a national scale the name WEDGWOOD was associated with the well known china.[115]

The *Wedgwood* approach is similar to the "big fish in a small pond" theory proposed in the McCarthy treatise. The idea is that a mark may not have to be well known on a national scale but would

---

111. Estee Lauder, Inc. v. Cinnabar 2000 Haircutters, Inc., 218 U.S.P.Q. 191 (S.D.N.Y. 1982).
112. Community Fed. S. & L. Ass'n v. Orondorff, 678 F.2d 1034 (11th Cir. 1982).
113. Wedgwood Homes, Inc. v. Lund, 221 U.S.P.Q. 174 (Or. Ct. App. 1982).
114. *Id.* at 178.
115. *Id.* at 179.

have to be sufficiently well known in its territory or product area to deserve protection under dilution.[116]

The Requirement of Likely Dilution

The Second Circuit has suggested two distinct forms of dilution:

1. the blurring of a mark's product identification; and
2. the tarnishment of the affirmative associations a mark has come to convey.[117]

Blurring the Identity of a Mark: The blurring theory requires proof that the product evoking quality of plaintiff's mark is likely to be weakened by defendant's mark.[118] In the *Sally Gee* case, the Second Circuit did not believe the name SALLY LEE would blur the identity of SALLY GEE—apparently because of the difference in marks.

> Sophisticated retailers and discerning consumers of women's apparel are unlikely to have blurred vision causing them to see "Sally Gee" upon viewing a Sally Lee label.[119]

Tarnishment: Tarnishment was not found in SALLY GEE because defendant's clothing was higher in price and higher in quality than plaintiff's clothing.

Tarnishment, however, has been successfully established in a number of other cases. In the *Steinway* case, the piano people enjoined use of the name STEINWAY for beer can holders. The Court stated:

> Defendants' use of the designation STEIN-WAY in connection with its business and its products, unless enjoined, will associate or tend to associate plaintiff's high quality pianos and plaintiff's business and cultural activities with defendants' inexpensive, mass-produced products and with the retail liquor stores, supermarkets

---

116. 2 MCCARTHY, TRADEMARKS & UNFAIR COMPETITION 24:14, 226 (1984).
117. Sally Gee, Inc. v. Myra Hogan, Inc., 699 F.2d 621, 624-25 (2d Cir. 1983).
118. *Id.*
119. *Id.* at 626.

> and similar merchandising concerns which sell defendants' products. Such association will inevitably tarnish plaintiff's reputation and image with the public of manufacturing and/or sponsoring only products and activities of taste, quality and distinction.[120]

In the *Pillsbury Doughboy* case, defendant's magazine was enjoined from using the PILLSBURY DOUGHBOY and DOUGHGIRL in lewd poses.[121] This was one of the first cases to make a clear distinction between the confusion and dilution causes of action. After a thorough review of the pertinent factors, the court rejected the argument that confusion was likely, but upheld plaintiff's dilution claim.

The Role of Defendant's Bad Faith

Bad faith is not a prerequisite for finding dilution, despite some case law to the contrary.[122] Bad faith is, however, a relevant factor, just as it is in any action seeking equitable relief.[123]

Dilution Inapplicable to Patent and Trademark Office Proceedings

If dilution is your strongest suit, you will do better leading with court action. The Lanham Act does not provide for a dilution cause of action. Hence, dilution is not available in Patent and Trademark Office proceedings.[124]

---

120. Steinway & Sons v. Robert Demars & Friends, 210 U.S.P.Q. 954, 961 (C.D. Cal. 1981).
121. Pillsbury Co. v. Milky Way Productions, Inc., 215 U.S.P.Q. 124 (N.D. Ga. 1981).
122. Estee Lauder, Inc. v. Cinnabar 2000 Haircutters, Inc., 218 U.S.P.Q. 191, 192 (S.D.N.Y. 1982).
123. Sally Gee, Inc. v. Myra Hogan, Inc., 699 F.2d 621, 626 (2d Cir. 1983).
124. Geo. A. Dickel Co. v. General Mills, Inc., 317 F.2d 954, 956 (C.C.P.A. 1963); Tiffany & Co. v. National Gypsum Co., 459 F.2d 527 (C.C.P.A. 1972).

The Future: Does Competition Preclude Dilution? The Pendulum Swings Back!

For decades, competition was treated as a necessary element of dilution—despite the clear statutory wording to the contrary. As late as 1982, district courts were requiring direct competition under a dilution theory.[125]

Now, some decisions have not only dispensed with the requirement of competition—they have suggested that competition precludes a finding of dilution.[126] Talk about a swinging pendulum!

On the other hand, a number of decisions have afforded relief for dilution where directly competitive products are involved.[127] As pointed out in the *Le Sportsac* case, nothing in the statutory language reflects an intent to treat competition as the death knell of dilution. The statute says dilution is a ground for relief "notwithstanding the absence of competition between the parties or the absence of confusion . . . ."

We can expect to hear much more about dilution in years to come. Some open questions are:

Should comparative advertising references be actionable under a dilution theory?[128]

Should the Lanham Act preempt application of a state dilution statute when a mark is used in commerce?[129]

---

125. *See* Sally Gee, Inc. v. Myra Hogan, Inc., 699 F.2d 621, 624 (2d Cir. 1983).

126. Olay Co. v. Cocacare Prods., Inc., 218 U.S.P.Q. 1028, 1038 (S.D.N.Y. 1983); EZ Loader Boat Trailers, Inc. v. Cox Trailers, Inc., 706 F.2d 1213, 1214-15 (Fed. Cir. 1983).

127. Le Sportsac, Inc. v. K Mart Corp., 227 U.S.P.Q. 151 (E.D.N.Y. 1985); W. Goebel Porzellanfabrik v. Action Indus., Inc., 589 F. Supp. 763 (S.D.N.Y. 1984).

128. Greiwe, *Antidilution Statutes: A New Attack on Comparative Advertising*, 72 TRADEMARK REP. 178, 186 (1982).

129. *Compare* Golden Door, Inc. v. Oshido, 646 F.2d 347 9th Cir. 1980 (state laws that grant greater protection to federal registrants than is granted by the Lanham Act do not conflict with Congressional intent of preventing deception or confusion) *with* United States Jaycees v. Commodities Magazine, Inc., No. C-85-2018, slip op. (N.D. Iowa Jan. 2, 1987) (state dilution statutes conflict with purpose of Lanham Act to provide uniform rights for marks used in interstate commerce).

8

Defenses to Infringement

There are basically two lines of defense to trademark infringement charges. The first line of defense focuses on the argument that there is no likelihood of confusion. This argument is supported by: a) all the differences in the parties' marks, goods, channels of trade, and purchasers; and b) all the similar marks in use by third parties.

The second line of defense does not hinge on absence of likely confusion. Rather, defendant argues that even if there is likelihood of confusion, plaintiff is not entitled to relief because of a defect in his mark or improper behavior pertaining to his mark.

The second line of defense includes a number of different claims known as "affirmative defenses." Generally, these affirmative defenses must be pleaded and proven by defendant. Both lines of defense are reviewed in this chapter.

Disputing Confusion

Vive la Différence!

Differences that individually may not be significant, when added together can tip the scales against likely confusion.

The previous chapter set forth some general rules applied in judging similar marks and similar goods. Here is a checklist of specific differences defendant should keep in mind:

1. differences in sound, appearance, and meaning of marks, including type style, design, number of words, syllables, and letters;

2. differences in appearance of packaging, *e.g.*, size, shape, color, composition;
3. differences in house marks or company names;
4. differences in nature of goods—running from the extreme of steam shovels versus butter to butter versus cream;
5. differences in retail outlets or sections of retail outlets;
6. differences in advertising media;
7. differences in quality and price;
8. differences in purchasers and their degree of care.

The effect of these differences, singly or in combination, will, of course, depend on the facts of each case.

Third Party Use—or—Everybody Else Is Using It

Third party use is treated under the section dealing with the strength of plaintiff's mark.[1] Where plaintiff's mark is commonly used by others, it is a "weak" mark with a narrow scope of protection.

Third party use also bears directly on the issue of likely confusion.[2] A public that has been exposed to extensive use of similar marks has presumably learned to distinguish among them. As the Court noted in the *Sun Banks* case:

> [W]e find the extensive third-party use of the word "Sun" impressive evidence that there would be no likelihood of confusion between Sun Banks and Sun Federal. See, e.g., *Amstar Corp. v. Domino's Pizza, Inc., supra* (72 third-party registrations of the mark "Domino"); *Armstrong Cork Co. v. World of Carpets, Inc., supra* (multiple uses of the mark "World"); *American Heritage Life Ins. Co. v. Heritage Life Ins. Co., supra* (multiple uses of the mark "Heritage"); *Holiday Inns, Inc. v. Holiday Out in America*, 481 F.2d 445, 178 USPQ 257 (5th Cir. 1973) (multiple uses of the mark "Holiday"); *El Chico, Inc. v. El Chico Cafe*, 214 F.2d 721,

1. *See* chapter 7, pp. 119-22, *supra*.
2. Armstrong Cork Co. v. World Carpets, Inc., 597 F.2d 496, 505 (5th Cir. 1979).

102 USPQ 657 (5th Cir. 1954) (27 third-party registrations of the mark "Chico," "El Chico" and other similar names).[3]

On the other hand, third party marks are not impressive evidence of no likely confusion where the public is unaware of them:

> We have frequently said that little weight is to be given such registrations in evaluating whether there is likelihood of confusion. The existence of these registrations is not evidence of what happens in the marketplace or that customers are familiar with them. . . .
>
> We think the listing of trademarks . . . in various trade magazines should be treated in a similar manner as are third-party registrations. They give no indication as to actual sales, when the mark was adopted, customer familiarity with the marks, etc.[4]

In broad outline, the arguments on third party use stack up like this:

For Plaintiff

1. The third party marks have limited, if any, public exposure.
2. Defendant, unlike the third parties, is guilty of bad faith.[5]
3. The third parties are not as close to plaintiff as defendant in terms of goods, geographical location, or similarity of marks.[6]

For Defendant

1. The third party marks even without evidence of use show the descriptive significance of plaintiff's mark.

---

3. Sun Banks v. Sun Fed. S.&L. Ass'n, 651 F.2d 311, 316 (5th Cir. 1981) (Over 4,000 uses of SUN by Florida businesses, including twenty-five in the financial field).
4. AMF Inc. v. American Leisure Prods., Inc., 474 F.2d 1403, 1406 (C.C.P.A. 1973).
5. Tisch Hotels, Inc. v. Americana Inn, Inc., 350 F.2d 609, 614 (7th Cir. 1965).
6. National Lead Co. v. Wolfe, 223 F.2d 195, 204 (9th Cir. 1955); University of Ga. Athletic Ass'n v. Bill Laite, 756 F.2d 1535, 1545 (11th Cir. 1985).

2. If plaintiff can live with similar third party marks for similar goods, defendant should not be singled out for complaint.
3. Widespread third party use makes it unlikely that purchasers will associate defendant's mark with plaintiff.

The bottom line on third party use is its effect on public perception.[7] In light of the third party use, does defendant's mark still suggest an immediate connection with plaintiff?

Affirmative Defenses

Affirmative defenses that must be pleaded and proven by defendant include:

1. laches;
2. abandonment;
3. genericness;[8]
4. fair use;
5. fraud;
6. unclean hands;
7. trademark misuse; and
8. violation of the antitrust laws.

Each of these defenses is discussed below.

---

7. University of Ga. Athletic Ass'n v. Bill Laite, 756 F2d 1535, 1545, n.27 (11th Cir. 1985); Sun Banks v Sun Fed. S.&L. Ass'n, 651 F.2d 311, 316 (5th Cir. 1981).
8. Plaintiff's federal registration creates a presumption that his mark is not generic, placing the burden on defendant to prove genericness. Plaintiff's unregistered mark, however, carries no presumptions, so that if defendant raises a generic claim the burden will be on the plaintiff to prove lack of genericness. National Conference of Bar Examiners v. Multistate Legal Studies, Inc., 692 F.2d 478, 488 (7th Cir. 1982).

Laches

Laches applies where plaintiff has unreasonably delayed in asserting his rights against defendant, and defendant has relied on this delay to his prejudice. Laches is based on the principle that equity aids the vigilant and not those who sleep on their rights. Plaintiff's cry of harm has a hollow ring when he has sat by for years without taking action.

The Policy Underlying Laches

The requirement that plaintiff act with reasonable diligence in pursuing his legal rights encourages:

1. the prompt resolution of disputes;
2. the conduct of litigation when evidence and witness recollection is fresh;
3. a climate of certainty for the defendant who is proceeding to invest capital and labor in his property.[9]

The Elements of the Laches Defense

To establish laches as a defense to permanent injunctive or monetary relief in a trademark action, defendant must prove that:

1. Plaintiff had knowledge of defendant's use.
2. Plaintiff inexcusably delayed in taking action.
3. Defendant will be prejudiced if plaintiff is now permitted to assert his rights.[10] In other words, defendant must prove that he reasonably relied on plaintiff's delay to his prejudice.

Plaintiff's delay may be excused by:

a) ongoing settlement negotiations;

---

9. NAACP v. N.A.A.C.P. Legal Defense & Educational Fund, Inc., 753 F.2d 131, 137 (D.C. Cir. 1985).
10. Saratoga Vichy Spring Co. v. Lehman, 625 F.2d 1037, 1040 (2d Cir. 1980) (quoting Cuban Cigar Brands, N.V. v. Upmann Int'l, Inc., 457 F. Supp. 1090, 1096 (S.D.N.Y. 1978), *aff'd*, 607 F.2d 995 (2d Cir. 1979).

b) conscious fraud or bad faith by defendant;[11]
c) pending litigation against other infringers.[12]

The elements of the laches defense and plaintiff's excusable delay are reviewed in more detail below.

Plaintiff's Knowledge of Defendant's Use: The clock starts ticking for the purpose of laches when plaintiff first learns of defendant's use. In some cases, there is no dispute as to when plaintiff acquired knowledge of defendant's infringement. For example, there may be correspondence between the parties' officers, or prior affiliation between the parties.[13]

Nor can plaintiff play the ostrich with his head in the sand. A claim to lack of knowledge will not pass muster when plaintiff should have known of defendant's infringement.[14]

1. Imputing Knowledge to a Corporation: Corporate plaintiffs may seek to deny knowledge of defendant's infringing use because the use was known only to low-level corporate employees. The general rule is that knowledge will be imputed to a corporation when it is held by those whose duties encompass the protection of the trademark's goodwill. One court cited bookkeepers and truck drivers as examples of personnel whose duties did not require trademark sensitivity; salespersons, on the other hand, had better watch out!

> Knowledge of mark usage gained by bookkeepers in receiving checks and dock workers in loading Great Plains' trucks should not normally be imputed to the corporation. Their duties are not of the type that would require sensitivity of the value of their employer's marks in the marketplace. However, salespeople produce the

11. NAACP v. N.A.A.C.P. Legal Defense & Educational Fund, Inc., 753 F.2d 131, 137 (D.C. Cir. 1985).
12. See this chapter, pp. 161, *infra*, for further discussion of excusable delay.
13. NAACP v. N.A.A.C.P. Legal Defense & Educational Fund, 753 F.2d 131 (D.C. Cir. 1985).
14. Armco, Inc. v. Armco Burglar Alarm Co., Inc., 693 F.2d 1155, 1161 (5th Cir. 1982); Chandon Champagne Corp. v. San Marino Wine Corp., 335 F.2d 531, 535 (2d Cir. 1964).

"stuff" of which a corporation's "goodwill" is made. Salespeople, if they are to be effective, must be present in the marketplace and cognizant of the various factors that effect present and future sales. Product "goodwill" is one such factor. A corporation which employs a professional salesperson who has knowledge of an offending trademark use will have imputed to it the knowledge of the employee.[15]

2. Progressive Encroachment: If defendant's encroachment is progressive, the laches clock may not be turned back to plaintiff's first knowledge of defendant. Rather, laches will only start to run at the point when plaintiff became aware of defendant's expanded activities. The Court in *Parrot Jungle* observed the "substantial difference" between plaintiff's early knowledge of defendant's local use and plaintiff's recent knowledge of defendant's national franchising efforts:

> [T]here is a substantial difference between plaintiff's awareness of a pet store or stores in New York and its awareness of a national franchising effort. It was the latter which triggered plaintiff's prompt assertion of its rights. A modest encroachment is one thing, a sudden proposed national exploitation of plaintiff's name is quite another, and plaintiff's failure to challenge the former will not entirely disable plaintiffs from preventing the latter.[16]

Plaintiff's Inexcusable Delay:

1. How Much Delay is Too Much?: The test for laches is a flexible one. The court will examine the amount of delay, the prejudice caused by that delay, and the confusion to the public resulting from defendant's continued use. Long periods of delay invite defendant's reasonable reliance by strengthening his belief that his rights will not be challenged.[17]

---

15. Georgia-Pacific Corp. v. Great Plains Bag Co., 614 F.2d 757, 763 (C.C.P.A. 1980); Dawn Donut Co. v. Hart's Food Stores, 267 F.2d 358, 363 (2d Cir. 1959).
16. Parrot Jungle, Inc. v. Parrot Jungle, Inc., 512 F. Supp. 266, 270 (S.D.N.Y. 1981).
17. NAACP v. N.A.A.C.P. Legal Defense & Educational Fund, 753 F.2d 131, 137-38 (D.C. Cir. 1985).

Delays of thirteen years[18], eleven years[19], and ten years[20] have amounted to laches. Delays of from two years up to twenty years have been found insufficient to establish laches.[21]

One court has suggested that a delay of two years is rarely enough to find laches.[22] In the *Simon Says* case, however, where defendant had gained a national reputation in its SIMON games over the critical two-year period of delay, suit by the owner of a SIMON SAYS nightclub act was barred by laches.[23]

Since multimedia advertising campaigns can now result in tremendous dollar expenditures and development of goodwill in short periods of time, plaintiffs would do well to make their position known promptly.

2. *Following the Analogous Statute of Limitations:* The Sixth Circuit has determined to follow the closest analogous statute of limitations in deciding what amounts to an unreasonable delay.[24] In the *Tandy* case, plaintiff, owner of the mark RADIO

---

18. Seven-Up Co. v. O-So-Grape Co., 283 F.2d 103, 105-06 (7th Cir. 1960), *cert. denied*, 365 U.S. 869 (1961).
19. Polaroid Corp. v. Polarad Elecs. Corp., 287 F.2d 492 (2d Cir.), *cert. denied*, 368 U.S. 820 (1961).
20. Congress of Racial Equality v. Pinn, (Slip Op. N.Y. Sup. Ct. 1985).
21. Piper Aircraft Corp. v. Wag-Aero, Inc., 741 F.2d 925, 933 (7th Cir. 1984) (two-year delay); San Francisco Ass'n for the Blind v. Industrial Aid for the Blind, 152 F.2d 532, 537 (8th Cir. 1946) (eight-year delay did not bar injunction but did bar monetary relief); University of Pittsburgh v. Champion Prods., Inc. 686 F.2d 1040, *cert. denied*, 459 U.S. 1087 (1982) (twenty-year delay).
22. Piper Aircraft Corp. v. Wag-Aero, Inc., 741 F.2d 925, 932-33 (7th Cir. 1984); *See also* Ambrit, Inc. v. Kraft, Inc., 805 F.2d 974, 989 (11th Cir. 1986) (defendant cited no case where delay of less than two years was found to constitute laches).
23. Simon Says Enters., Inc. v. Milton Bradley Co., 522 F. Supp. 986 (S.D.N.Y. 1981).
24. Tandy Corp. v. Malone & Hyde, Inc., 769 F.2d 362 (6th Cir. 1985), *cert. denied*, 106 S. Ct. 2277 (1986).

SHACK, delayed thirty-two months before filing suit to enjoin use of AUTO SHACK. The District Court granted summary judgment dismissing the complaint on the grounds of laches.

The Court of Appeals reversed, holding that the reasonableness of the delay for the purposes of an action for monetary relief should be measured by the closest analogous statute of limitations. This would provide the courts and the parties with the advantage of a measure of certainty.[25] The pertinent statute in *Tandy* was the Tennessee property tort three-year statute of limitations. On the basis of this statute, the Sixth Circuit found that a trademark action brought within three years of plaintiff's knowledge was clothed with a strong presumption of reasonableness. The presumption may be overcome only in extraordinary or unusual circumstances.[26]

Defendant's Prejudicial Reliance on Plaintiff's Delay: Unless plaintiff's delay is outrageously long, defendant must prove that he reasonably relied to his prejudice on plaintiff's delay.[27]

1. Plaintiff's Acquiescence as Supporting Defendant's Reliance: Defendant's reasonable reliance on plaintiff's delay can be proven by plaintiff's affirmative conduct. Plaintiff's affirmative conduct may have encouraged defendant's belief that his use would not be challenged. This express or implied consent by plaintiff to defendant's use is known as "acquiescence."

Affirmative acts of encouragement have been found where:

---

25. In *Tandy*, there is some question whether suggested that in the context of purely equitable relief, the correct standard may be the more general one of unreasonable delay and prejudice to defendant. *Id.* at 366, n.2.

26. *Id.* at 365-66.

27. NAACP v. N.A.A.C.P. Legal Defense & Educational Fund, 753 F.2d 131, 137-38 (D.C. Cir. 1985); University of Pittsburgh v. Champion Prods., Inc., 686 F.2d 1040, 1044 (3d Cir.), *cert. denied*, 459 U.S. 1087 (1982) (court gives example of a hundred-year delay as so outrageous and unreasonable that equity will not enjoin even a fraudulent infringer's use).

1. The parties were previously related and plaintiff agreed to defendant's independence;[28]
2. Plaintiff's sales people voiced approval of defendant's use;[29]
3. Plaintiff and defendant cooperated with each other in business, e.g., plaintiff continued as defendant's client;[30]
4. Plaintiff threatened to file suit but did not.[31]

2. To Protest or Not to Protest: Where plaintiff does not contemplate prompt legal action, is he better off protesting defendant's use, or not protesting until he is prepared to follow through? On the one hand, plaintiff's act in making his objection known to defendant bolsters defendant's reliance argument—plaintiff's protest clearly shows that defendant knew plaintiff knew about defendant's use. Hence, defendant had reason to rely on plaintiff's ensuing delay. On the other hand, plaintiff's protest undermines defendant's reliance argument because defendant is arguably proceeding at his risk.[32]

On balance, a protest letter is probably advisable. In the *Saratoga Vichy* case, where plaintiff acquiesced in New York State's infringing conduct for seven years, the Second Circuit stated:

> [a] simple warning letter would have sufficed.[33]

---

28. *Id.*
29. Georgia-Pacific Corp. v. Great Plains Bag Co., 614 F.2d 757, 762-63 (C.C.P.A. 1980).
30. NAACP v. N.A.A.C.P. Legal Defense & Educational Fund, 753 F.2d 131 (D.C. Cir. 1985); *See also* Seven-Up Co. v. O-So-Grape Co., 283 F.2d 103 (7th Cir. 1960), *cert. denied*, 365 U.S. 869 (1961).
31. NAACP v. N.A.A.C.P. Legal Defense & Educational Fund, 753 F.2d 131, 138 (D.C. Cir. 1985), (Plaintiff's threat to sue in the form of a Board of directors resolution was expressly withdrawn); Continental Coatings Corp. v. Metco, Inc., 464 F.2d 1375 (7th Cir. 1972); Anheuser-Busch, Inc. v. Du Bois Brewing Co., 175 F.2d 370 (3d Cir. 1949).
32. Citibank, N.A. v. Citibanc Group, Inc., 215 U.S.P.Q. 884, 906 (N.D. Ala. 1982); *aff'd*, 724 F.2d 1540 (11th Cir 1984).
33. Saratoga Vichy Spring Co. v. Lehman, 625 F.2d 1037, 1041 (2d Cir. 1980).

And in the *NAACP* case, the court repeated several times that plaintiff "did not give clear notice of his exclusive claim to the NAACP initials."[34]

3. ***Proof of Defendant's Prejudicial Reliance:*** Typically, defendant's prejudicial reliance is proven by sales and advertising dollars invested in reliance on plaintiff's failure to protest. In the *NAACP* case, the court stated:

> The prejudice resulting from the reliance interest building during the years of delay in this case was substantial. The LDF continued to develop "[t]he universal esteem in which the [NAACP] initials are held." The LDF invested substantial labor and millions of dollars in pressing important civil rights suits, soliciting gifts, and recruiting talent using the NAACP initials. Because many organizations have names virtually identical to the LDF's except for the NAACP initials, it is only these initials that distinguish the LDF from its emulators.[35]

Defendant must establish that his investment was incurred in reliance on the inaction of plaintiff. Laches will not be invoked where defendant's promotion and use was based upon his own opinion of no conflict, or the invalidity of plaintiff's registration, rather than defendant's misapprehension of plaintiff's intentions.[36]

The Effect of Laches Short of an Absolute Bar

Plaintiff's Delay as Bearing on Likely Confusion: Some decisions, while not finding laches an absolute bar, factor plaintiff's delay into the determination of likely confusion. The theory is that

34. NAACP v. N.A.A.C.P. Legal Defense & Educational Fund, 753 F.2d 131, 138 (D.C. Cir. 1985). *See also* Cuisinarts, Inc. v. John Boos & Co., 227 U.S.P.Q. 153, 156 (S.D.N.Y. 1985) (no laches where defendant failed to respond to plaintiff's protest letter or prove that plaintiff had knowledge of defendant's continued use).
35. NAACP v. N.A.A.C.P. Legal Defense & Educational Fund, 753 F.2d 131, 138-39 (D.C. Cir. 1985).
36. Citibank, N.A. v. Citibanc Group, Inc., 215 U.S.P.Q. 884, 906 (N.D. Ala. 1982), *aff'd*, 724 F.2d 1540, 1546 (11th Cir. 1984).

if confusion was really a problem, plaintiff wouldn't be sitting on his hands for any lengthy period.[37]

Plaintiff's Delay as a Bar to Monetary Relief: A number of older authorities speak in terms of laches as a bar to monetary relief, but not injunctive relief. This does not mean that laches cannot bar injunctive relief. Where defendant's detrimental reliance is substantial, laches may bar both injunctive and monetary relief.[38]

Plaintiff's Delay as Affecting Scope of Relief: Plaintiff's delay in filing suit may not be so excessive as to pose an absolute bar, but still be an equitable consideration limiting the scope of relief. For example, plaintiff's delay may suggest that limited relief such as a disclaimer of association will suffice.[39] In the *Grenadier* case, plaintiff first protested defendant's use by telephone in 1977 or 1978. Defendant disregarded plaintiff's protest and plaintiff's next protest was by letter in 1980. A two-year period of negotiation followed. The court held that plaintiff did not forego or intend to forego his claim. However, plaintiff was aware of defendant's substantial investment and expansion and failed to bring action until 1982. Thus, equity precluded an absolute injunction, but a disclaimer of association with plaintiff was required to minimize likely confusion.

37. Amstar Corp. v. Domino's Pizza, Inc., 615 F.2d 252, 265 (5th Cir.), *reh'g denied*, 617 F.2d 295, *cert. denied*, 449 U.S. 899 (1980).
38. NAACP v. N.A.A.C.P. Legal Defense & Educational Fund, 753 F.2d 131, 137-38 (D.C. Cir. 1985).
39. Grenadier Corp. v. Grenadier Realty Corp., 568 F. Supp. 502 (S.D.N.Y. 1983).

Excuses, Excuses

Laches by definition involves inexcusable delay. Plaintiff's delay may be excused when:

1. The delay was the result of ongoing settlement negotiations;
2. Defendant was guilty of deliberate infringement;
3. Plaintiff was involved in litigation against third parties.

Ongoing Settlement Negotiations: It makes sense that ongoing negotiations stop the laches clock. It is hard to argue that negotiations led defendant to believe his use would go unchallenged.[40] Moreover, the policy of fostering out-of-court settlements would be severely handicapped if the time required for negotiations counted as inexcusable delay.

Defendant's Deliberate Infringement: Laches is premised on the theory that a defendant who invested in his mark in reliance on plaintiff's inaction should not be deprived of his investment. But if defendant is a deliberate infringer, he should not be allowed to profit from his use of the mark in any event.

Another reason for disregarding laches in the case of deliberate infringement is the public interest in protection against confusion. Presumably, confusion is more certain to result from defendant's deliberate effort to trade on plaintiff's mark than from defendant's good faith use.

Where a court weighs plaintiff's laches on the one hand, against defendant's deliberate infringement and public confusion on the other, laches will not bar injunctive relief.[41]

Plaintiff's Pending Litigation: Plaintiff is not required to sue everyone at once. Accordingly, plaintiff's delay in bringing suit

40. Armco, Inc. v. Armco Burglar Alarm Co., Inc., 693 F.2d 1155 (5th Cir. 1982).
41. Quill Corp. v. Quill Printing Corp., 215 U.S.P.Q. 986 (N.D. Ill. 1982). *See also* Cuban Cigar Brands N.V. v. Upmann Int'l, Inc., 457 F. Supp. 1090 (S.D.N.Y. 1978), *aff'd*, 607 F.2d 995 (2d Cir. 1979).

may be excusable where he is occupied pursuing other infringers. In the *Oil of Olay* case, plaintiff Olay had delayed filing suit from 1977 to 1981.[42] Between 1977 and 1978, Olay was preoccupied with what it considered to be a more pressing problem, namely, the termination of private label brands imitating OIL OF OLAY. When that was accomplished, Olay turned its attention to defendant. According to the Court, "[i]t was not necessary for Olay to jump on its horse and ride off in all directions at the same time."

Plaintiff should, however, consider notifying defendant of his plan to ride against defendant as soon as the other rustlers have been corralled. In patent cases, pending litigation will not excuse plaintiff's delay unless plaintiff gives notice of his plan to act against defendant as soon as the pending infringements are resolved.[43]

In summary, the key point to remember about laches is the equitable nature of this defense. Even where defendant suffers some prejudice as a result of plaintiff's delay, the public interest in avoiding confusion might outweigh that prejudice.[44]

Estoppel

Estoppel Arising from Laches and Acquiescence

The terms laches and estoppel are often used together. Laches occurs where plaintiff has unreasonably delayed in the pursuit of his claim, and defendant has relied to his prejudice on plaintiff's delay. Estoppel is the result of plaintiff's laches. Where laches is found, plaintiff is estopped from asserting infringement.

Plaintiff may also be estopped as a result of his acquiescence. Acquiescence is proven where plaintiff's conduct amounts to an assurance to defendant that plaintiff would not assert his mark

42. Olay Co., Inc. v. Cococare Prods., Inc., 218 U.S.P.Q. 1028 (S.D.N.Y. 1983).
43. A.C. Aukerman Co. v. Miller Formless Co., Inc., 693 F.2d 697, 700 (7th Cir. 1982).
44. Conagra, Inc. v. Singleton, 743 F.2d 1508, 1517 (11th Cir. 1984).

against defendant.[45] Where defendant has relied to his prejudice on plaintiff's acquiescence, plaintiff is estopped from challenging defendant's use.

Equitable Estoppel

Equitable estoppel is applied in trademark actions to prevent a party from taking a position factually inconsistent with his prior position. The theory is that plaintiff should not be able to speak or act to obtain a benefit at one time, and then reverse himself, when it appears to his advantage to do so:

> There is a kind of evidential estoppel which, though it may not amount to a complete estoppel in pais, is raised when persons who have spoken or acted one way under one set of circumstances, and with one objective in mind, undertake under other circumstances and when their objective has changed, to testimonially give a different color to what they formerly said and did. We think that principle applies here.[46]

This theory of estoppel was applied in the *Hiland* KITTY CLOVER potato chip case.[47] Plaintiff, who had announced the elimination of his KITTY CLOVER brand, was estopped from denying that the announcement constituted abandonment. The court defined the elements of equitable estoppel as follows:

> (1) defendant's lack of knowledge and of the means of knowledge of the truth as to the facts in question;
>
> (2) defendant's reliance, in good faith, upon plaintiff's misleading conduct or false representations; and
>
> (3) defendant's change in position based thereon to his injury, detriment or prejudice.

---

45. Carl Zeiss Stiftung v. V.E.B. Carl Zeiss, Jena, 293 F. Supp. 892, 917 (S.D.N.Y. 1968); *aff'd*, 433 F.2d 686 (2d Cir. 1970); *cert. denied*, 403 U.S. 905 (1971).
46. Holly Hill Citrus Growers' Ass'n v. Holly Hill Fruit Prods., Inc., 75 F.2d 13, 17 (5th Cir. 1935).
47. Hiland Potato Chip Co. v. Culbro Snack Foods, Inc., 585 F. Supp. 17, 22-23 (S.D. Iowa 1982), *aff'd*, 720 F.2d 981 (8th Cir. 1983).

Abandonment

The function of a trademark is to identify the origin and quality of goods. When a mark no longer serves to identify origin and quality, the mark is considered "abandoned."[48] Abandonment means that the owner has forfeited his trademark rights and the mark is free for use by the next person.[49]

The Heavy Burden of Proof

The burden of proof is on the party claiming abandonment. Because abandonment is in the nature of a forfeiture, the burden of proof is a heavy one.[50]

One decision characterized the burden as requiring evidence that "leaves no room for doubt or speculation" and leads to "but one inescapable conclusion, namely, that the use of the mark was discontinued with intent to abandon it to the world."[51]

Types of Abandonment

Under the Lanham Act, a mark is deemed abandoned when:

1. the trademark owner discontinues use with intent not to resume;
2. the trademark owner causes the mark to lose its significance as an indication of origin.[52]

---

48. 1 McCarthy, Trademarks and Unfair Competition § 17:2, at 769 (2d ed. 1984).
49. Sutton Cosmetics (P.R.), Inc. v. Lander Co., 455 F.2d 285, 288 (2d Cir. 1972); P. Daussa Corp. v. Sutton Cosmetics (P.R.), Inc., 462 F.2d 134, 136 (2d Cir. 1972).
50. Saratoga Vichy Spring Co., Inc. v. Lehman, 625 F.2d 1037, 1044 (2d Cir. 1980).
51. Miller Brewing Co. v. Oland's Breweries, Ltd., 189 U.S.P.Q. 481, 488 (T.T.A.B. 1975), *aff'd*, 548 F.2d 349 (C.C.P.A. 1976).
52. 15 U.S.C. § 1127.

Abandonment Through Discontinued Use with Intent Not to Resume: The Lanham Act states:

> A mark shall be deemed to be abandoned—
>
> (a) When its use has been discontinued with intent not to resume use. Intent not to resume may be inferred from circumstances. Nonuse for two consecutive years shall be prima facie abandonment.[53]

Nonuse of the mark for two consecutive years creates a prima facie case of abandonment. Where defendant proves that plaintiff has not used his mark for two years, the burden shifts to plaintiff to demonstrate his intent to resume use:

> Acts which unexplained would be sufficient to establish an abandonment may be answered by showing that there was never an intention to give up and relinquish the right claimed.[54]

1. Intent to Resume "Commercial" Use: While many cases speak in terms of intent to abandon, the specific statutory language requires "intent to resume use." In the *Exxon* case, the court noted that this distinction becomes important where a plaintiff wants to retain a mark only to prevent its use by others (warehousing cases).[55]

An owner may not wish to abandon his mark, but may not intend to resume its use. It is the intent to resume "commercial" use that is critical to rebut a prima facie case of abandonment.[56]

In *Exxon*, defendant claimed that plaintiff's HUMBLE mark was abondoned when plaintiff changed the name of all its HUMBLE gas stations to EXXON. The court found that defendant's prima facie case of abandonment was rebutted by plaintiff's resumed use after three years of nonuse, marketing department proposals, and

53. 15 U.S.C. § 1127(a).
54. Saxlehner v. Eisner & Mendelson Co., 179 U.S. 19, 31 (1900).
55. Exxon Corp. v. Humble Exploration Co., Inc., 695 F.2d 96, 103 (5th Cir. 1983).
56. *Id.*

periodic shipments to targeted customers. This evidence established plaintiff's intent to resume commercial use.[57]

2. The Continued Existence of Goodwill: The continued existence of goodwill may help to rebut a prima facie case of abandonment. The fact that goodwill does not ordinarily disappear overnight was a cause for rejecting the abandonment claim in the *Defiance* case.[58]

Other cases have also emphasized the continued existence of goodwill. In finding that the mark RAMBLER for automobiles had not been abandoned, the Trademark Trial and Appeal Board stated:

> While opposer has discontinued the use of "RAMBLER" as a trademark for vehicles produced by opposer over the past few years, the record falls short of establishing any abandonment thereof. In fact, there is a considerable reservoir of goodwill in the mark "RAMBLER" in this country that inures to opposer as a consequence of the large number of "RAMBLER" vehicles still on the road; opposer's activities in supplying "RAMBLER" parts and accessories to owners of these vehicles; and the use by dealers of the term "RAMBLER" as a portion of their corporate or business names and their maintenance of "RAMBLER" signs on their premises.[59]

Indeed, goodwill can survive even without any ongoing marketplace activities. Thus, there was no abandonment when the goodwill of a trademark for beer had not dissipated after the brewery had been closed for eight years.[60] The efforts to maintain the brewery during the eight-year period of nonuse and the refusal to sell rights to the mark separate from the business demonstrated

---

57. Exxon Corp. v. Humble Exploration Co., Inc., 592 F. Supp. 1226 (N.D. Tex. 1984).
58. Defiance Button Mach. Co. v. C & C Metal Prods. Corp., 759 F.2d 1053 (2d Cir. 1985).
59. American Motors Corp. v. Action-Age, Inc., 178 U.S.P.Q. 377, 378 (T.T.A.B. 1973).
60. Sterling Brewers, Inc. v. Schenley Indus., Inc., 441 F.2d 675, 679 (C.C.P.A. 1971).

"an intent to maintain conditions conducive to resumption of production under the mark on relatively short notice."[61]

On the other hand, the claim to residual goodwill did not stave off a finding of abandonment where the owner unequivocally declared his intention to discontinue use.[62] In the *Hiland* KITTY CLOVER case, plaintiff's predecessor sent a letter to the trade announcing the elimination of KITTY CLOVER brand potato chips and their replacement by HILAND brand products. KITTY CLOVER was discontinued as announced, and defendant, in reliance on the announcement, immediately expanded his own use of KITTY CLOVER into the territory occupied by plaintiff's predecessor. The court held that the unequivocal public declaration of intent to discontinue sales was a circumstance from which intent not to resume use could be inferred. The court also noted that testimony by plaintiff's predecessor that he did not intend to abandon his mark was outweighed by the objective evidence of his actions.

3. The Nature of the Product as a Factor in Evaluating Intent to Resume Use: The nature of the product and other related factors, *e.g.*, feasibility of production, potential market, and efforts to market, are taken into account in determining the intent to resume use.[63]

In *Televator*, the Board noted the "expensive," "complex" nature of the cargo and passenger traffic system that "would take a great deal of time to develop and modify to a particular airport's needs."[64] The Board also noted the limited potential market for the system, as well as respondent's efforts to obtain financial backing, find customers, and develop a prototype. While not even one Televator System had been installed over a seven-year period,

61. *Id.* at 680.
62. Hiland Potato Chip Co. v. Culbro Snack Foods, Inc., 720 F.2d 981 (8th Cir. 1983).
63. Reynolds Televator Corp. v. Pfeffer, 173 U.S.P.Q. 437, 439-40 (T.T.A.B. 1972).
64. *Id.*

respondent's continued efforts to market the product precluded a finding of abandonment.

4. Suspension of Use Beyond Owner's Control: Where use of a mark is suspended because of events beyond the owner's control, courts are reluctant to find abandonment. Such events include war, fires, and strikes. It is important, however, to resume use as soon as the catastrophe has passed.[65]

It is also important to distinguish between lack of sales success and events preventing sales. Where use was discontinued for more than two years after negative test market results, vague testimony about efforts to reposition the product did not rebut the prima facie case of abandonment.[66]

Abandonment Through Loss of Significance as an Indication of Origin: The second prong of the Lanham Act definition of abandonment provides:

> A mark shall be deemed to be "abandoned"—
>
> (b) When any course of conduct of the registrant, including acts of omission as well as commission, causes the mark to lose its significance as an indication of origin.[67]

A mark may lose its significance as an indication of origin where:

1. Uncontrolled licensing results in the loss of consistent quality;
2. Failure to protest use by others results in the mark becoming generic;

---

65. Chandon Champagne Corp. v. San Marino Wine Corp., 335 F.2d 531, 535 (2d Cir. 1964).
66. *See* Colgate-Palmolive Co. v. Sanford Chem. Co., 162 U.S.P.Q. 424, 426 (T.T.A.B. 1969). *But see* STAR-KIST Foods, Inc. v. P.J. Rhodes & Co., 769 F.2d 1393, 1396 (9th Cir. 1985) (discontinued use because of unprofitability of importation did not constitute abandonment).
67. 15 U.S.C. § 1127(b).

3. Assignment without goodwill results in the assignee being unable to produce products of the same quality as the assignor's;
4. Substantial changes in product result in a highly inferior or wholly different product; or substantial changes in the mark create a different commercial impression.

1. Uncontrolled Licensing: The trademark owner has a duty to control the nature and quality of the goods sold under his mark. If quality control is not maintained, the consumer will not be getting what he expected. The consumer will be, in a word, deceived. This would be directly at odds with the purpose of trademark law: to prevent consumer deception.

Where a trademark is licensed for use by another, the licensor must exercise control over the quality of the goods produced by the licensee.[68]

> The purpose of the control requirement is the protection of the public. If a licensor does not maintain control of his licensees in their use of the license, the public may be damaged by products that, despite their trademark, do not have the normal quality of such goods. "The amount of control required varies with the circumstances."[69]

If the licensor fails to control the quality of the licensee's merchandise, the licensor may cause the mark "to lose its significance as an indication of origin."[70] Because the mark no longer stands for the quality previously associated with the licensor's mark, the licensor abandons (loses his rights in) the mark:

> If a trademark owner allows licensees to depart from its quality standards, the public will be misled, and the trademark will cease

68. For further discussion of trademark licensing, see chapter 15, pp. 319-28, *infra*.
69. United States Jaycees v. Philadelphia Jaycees, 639 F.2d 134, 140 (3d Cir. 1981).
70. See Lanham Act definition of abandonment, 15 U.S.C. § 1127(b).

to have utility as an informational device. A trademark owner who allows this to occur loses its right to use the mark.[71]

In *Sheila Shine*, the court found abandonment through uncontrolled licensing where the trademark owner made no effort to control his licensee for eleven years. The *Sheila Shine* court also found that three to six years' lapse in exercise of control was not enough to work an abandonment.[72]

2. Failure To Police: Failure to take action against third party infringers is sometimes referred to as abandonment. As the Fourth Circuit points out, however, it is a rare situation where third party use causes the mark to lose all significance as an indication of origin. The more usual effect of failure to police is the diminished strength of plaintiff's mark:

> In the typical trademark litigation, the relevance of failure to prosecute others is not to abandonment, but to strength. The issue is hardly ever abandonment, because that requires proof that the mark has lost all significance as an indication of origin. That is, the mark is completely without signs of life.[73]

3. Assignment Without Goodwill:

a) Goodwill Must Be Transferred: A trademark does not exist in a vacuum. A trademark is attached to a business—it symbolizes the goodwill of the business.[74] When the trademark is assigned without the goodwill of the business, the assignment is invalid.[75] Some courts characterize the effect of such an invalid assignment (a/k/a a "naked" assignment or assignment in gross) as abandonment.

---

71. Kentucky Fried Chicken Corp. v. Diversified Packaging Corp., 549 F.2d 368, 387 (5th Cir. 1977).
72. Sheila's Shine Prods., Inc. v. Sheila Shine, Inc., 486 F.2d 114, 124-25 (5th Cir. 1973).
73. Sweetheart Plastics, Inc. v. Detroit Forming, Inc., 743 F.2d 1039, 1046 (4th Cir. 1984).
74. Kidd v. Johnson, 100 U.S. 617 (1879).
75. For further discussion of trademark assignments see chapter 16, pp. 329-38, *infra*.

Where goodwill is not transferred, there may be some question as to whose rights are abandoned. Usually it is the assignor's rights that are abandoned so the assignee cannot rely on the assignor's date of first use.[76] As a result of the abandonment, the assignee must establish his own goodwill and is limited to his own date of first use. In addition, the assignee will abandon all his rights to the mark if he changes the assignor's product so as to defraud the public.[77]

b) Evidence of the Transfer of Goodwill: The Lanham Act provides for transfer of ownership by an assignment that includes "that part of the goodwill of the business connected with the use of and symbolized by the mark."[78] But the mere use of the statutory language may not be enough to prove the transfer of goodwill. In some cases, it is also necessary to transfer tangible assets to prove that goodwill has in fact been transferred.

In deciding if the transfer of tangible assets is required, the general rule is: the assignment should include sufficient tangible assets to enable the assignee to carry on the business of the assignor. In some cases, this means that secret formula, customer lists, patterns, or other business tangibles must be assigned.[79]

In other cases, the assignee will be able to carry on the assignor's business even though tangible assets were not transferred. For example, the assignee of the HY-CROSS trademark was able to carry on the assignor's chicken breeding business even though no chickens were transferred:

> Unlike the cases relied on, Osborne, so far as the record shows, was using the mark at the time he executed the assignment of it. He had a valid registration which he also assigned. With these two legal properties he also assigned, in the very words of the statute,

76. 1 McCARTHY, TRADEMARKS AND UNFAIR COMPETITION § 18:5, at 806 (2d ed. 1984).
77. Mulhens & Kropff, Inc. v. Ferd. Muelhens, Inc., 43 F.2d 937 (2d Cir.), *cert. denied*, 282 U.S. 881 (1930).
78. 15 U.S.C. § 1060.
79. Merry Hull & Co. v. Hi-Line Co., 243 F. Supp. 45 (S.D.N.Y. 1965).

> "that part of the goodwill of the business connected with the use of and symbolized by the mark." . . . Thus, what had once been Osborne's business in "HY-CROSS" chicks became Welp's business. We do not see what legal difference it would have made if a crate of eggs had been included in the assignment, or a flock of chickens destined to be eaten.[80]

In determining whether goodwill has in fact been transferred, the guiding principle is consumer protection.[81] The assignee should be looking to acquire any tangible assets necessary to insure that the consumer is getting trademarked goods equal in quality to the assignor's original goods.

4. Material Changes in the Product or Mark: Product changes, *e.g.*, "new and improved," are a way of American commercial life. Such changes are to be expected and normally do not result in consumer deception. However, if the assignee makes a material alteration that results in a wholly inferior or substantially different product, he will find himself on the short end of the abandonment stick.[82]

A similar principle applies to changes in the trademark itself. If the assignee makes a material alteration in the mark that creates a substantially different commercial impression, a new mark is created and the old mark is abandoned.[83]

Fair Use

The doctrine of fair use provides a defense to the infringing use of plaintiff's mark where defendant's use is solely to describe

---

80. Hy-Cross Hatchery, Inc. v. Osborne, 303 F.2d 947, 950 (C.C.P.A. 1962).
81. Visa, U.S.A., Inc. v. Birmingham Trust Nat'l Bank, 696 F.2d 1371, 1377 (Fed. Cir. 1982); Syntex Laboratories, Inc. v. Norwich Pharmacal Co., 315 F. Supp. 45, 55 (S.D.N.Y. 1970), *aff'd*, 437 F.2d 566 (2d Cir. 1971); *In re* Roman Cleanser Co. v. Patterson Laboratories, Inc., 802 F.2d 207 (6th Cir. 1986).
82. Independent Baking Powder Co. v. Boorman, 175 F. 448 (C.C.D.N.J. 1910) (Trademark owner's change from alum baking powder to phosphate baking powder results in forfeiture of owner's rights).
83. Polo Fashions, Inc. v. Extra Special Prods., Inc., 451 F. Supp. 555, 563 (S.D.N.Y. 1978) (change from MARCO POLO to POLO creates different commercial impression).

defendant's goods. Fair use is backed by the public interest in allowing competitors to make free use of the English language to describe their goods. So long as defendant's use is descriptive, in good faith, and not as a trademark, it will be permitted—even if it causes likely confusion.[84]

The common law fair use defense is embodied in the Lanham Act.[85] Section 1115(b)(4) provides a specific defense to registrant's exclusive right to use the mark where:

> [U]se of the name, term or device charged to be an infringement is a use, otherwise than as a trade or service mark, *** of a term or device which is descriptive of and used fairly and in good faith only to describe to users the goods or services of such party, or their geographic origin.

The key to the fair use defense is the concept of "use otherwise than as a trademark."

> The use of a word such as "joy" which is in the public domain is only unfair when a competitor uses it in its trade-mark or secondary sense. The competitor is free to use the word in its common or primary sense.[86]

In deciding whether defendant's use is in a trademark sense, many decisions focus on the prominence of the use. Where defendant uses the term "as a symbol to attract public attention," fair use has been rejected:

> Here "mobile," [used in type style copied from plaintiff] while it may serve some descriptive function, is indisputably the attention-getting symbol on the defendants' signs, letterhead, and advertisements.[87]

---

84. Q-Tips, Inc. v. Johnson & Johnson, Inc., 206 F.2d 144, 148 (3d Cir. 1953); Soweco, Inc. v. Shell Oil Co., 617 F.2d 1178, 1189 n.30 (5th Cir. 1980); John O. Butler Co. v. Oral B Co., 185 U.S.P.Q. 594, 576 (N.D. Ill. 1975).
85. Venetianaire Corp. of Am. v. A & P Import Co., 429 F.2d 1079, 1081 (2d Cir. 1970).
86. Jean Patou, Inc. v. Jacqueline Cochran, Inc., 201 F. Supp. 861, 865 (S.D.N.Y. 1962), *aff'd*, 312 F.2d 125 (2d Cir. 1963).
87. Mobil Oil Corp. v. Mobile Mechanics, Inc., 192 U.S.P.Q. 744, 749 (D. Conn. 1976).

> But here the defendant obviously used the term ["hygienic"] "as a symbol to attract public attention". . . .[88]

> But the [term "featherlight"] did take on trademark characteristics because of Solo's clear attempts to give it a conspicuous position in its marketing and display techniques, without giving prominence to the mark "Solo."[89]

Of course, if defendant's use does not really describe defendant's goods, it will not qualify as a fair use:

> "Frosty" does not describe to prospective users the goods sold by Dr. Pepper Company. It is a description of something else, as all parties agree. It is used in such a manner as to attract prospective customers to the product of the Dr. Pepper Company.[90]

Fair Use Distinguished from Comparative Advertising

Use of a competitor's mark in comparative advertising is sometimes called a fair use. This is a misnomer. The fair use doctrine excuses defendant's infringing use of plaintiff's mark where defendant's use is solely to describe defendant's goods. Defendant's fair use may cause likely confusion but is allowed because of the public interest in the free use of descriptive words. In comparative advertising, however, defendant uses plaintiff's mark to identify plaintiff's product—not to describe defendant's goods. Comparative advertising uses, unlike fair descriptive uses, are governed by the likelihood of confusion standard.[91]

A leading case on comparative advertising is *Smith v. Chanel.*[92] Defendant promoted its SECOND CHANCE perfume as equivalent to plaintiff's CHANEL NO. 5 perfume. The parties stipulated that

---

88. Venetianaire Corp. of Am. v. A & P Import Co., 429 F.2d 1079, 1082 (2d Cir. 1970).
89. Feathercombs, Inc. v. Solo Prods. Corp., 306 F.2d 251, 256 (2d Cir. 1962).
90. Frostie Co. v. Dr. Pepper Co., 341 F.2d 363, 366-67 (5th Cir. 1965).
91. Smith v. Chanel, Inc., 402 F.2d 562, 563 (9th Cir. 1968); See this chapter pp. 172-73, *supra*, for case law on fair use.
92. *Id.*

the products were in fact equivalent. The Court held that defendant's use of CHANEL NO. 5 was justified because of the public interest in being informed of an equivalent product at a lesser price:

> It is the unimpeded availability of substantially equivalent units that permits the normal operation of supply and demand to yield the fair price society must pay for a given commodity. *American Safety Table Co. v. Schreiber*, 269 F.2d 255, 272 (2d Cir. 1959). But this public benefit might be lost if appellants could not tell potential purchasers that appellants' product was the equivalent and cheaper**." Alexander, *Honesty and Competition*, 39 So. Cal. L. Rev. 1, 4 (1966). The most effective way (and, where complex chemical compositions sold under trade names are involved, often the only practical way) in which this can be done is to identify the copied article by its trademark or trade name. To prohibit use of a competitor's trademark for the sole purpose of identifying the competitor's product would bar effective communication of claims of equivalence. Assuming the equivalence of "Second Chance" and "Chanel No. 5," the public interest would not be served by a rule of law which would preclude sellers of "Second Chance" from advising consumers of the equivalence and thus effectively deprive consumers of knowledge that an identical product was being offered at one third the price.[93]

Some forty years before *Smith v. Chanel*, the Supreme Court dealt with reference to a competitor's mark for informational purposes. In *Prestonettes, Inc. v. Coty*, the COTY mark was used on the Prestonettes compact label to inform purchasers that the compact contained COTY powder. The Court observed that use of a competitor's mark is not "taboo"—it can be used "to tell the truth". But the use of COTY approved by the Court was strictly limited as to size and plainly set forth that Prestonettes was not connected with Coty. The approved use read:

> "Prestonettes, Inc., not connected with Coty, states that the compact of face powder herein was independently compounded by it from Coty's - (giving the name) loose powder and its own

93. Smith v. Chanel, Inc., 402 F.2d 562, 568 (9th Cir. 1968).

> binder. Loose powder - percent. Binder - percent," every word to be in letters of the same size, color, type, and general distinctiveness.[94]

The Court recognized that use of the competitor's mark should not be so prominent that purchasers might look no further, *i.e.*, that purchasers would notice only the competitor's mark and think the product was made by or associated with the competitor.

The type of restriction sanctioned in *Coty* was adopted sixty years later in the *Searle* case.[95] Defendant Hudson copied elements of Searle's METAMUCIL trade dress and used the statement "equivalent to METAMUCIL" on the Hudson product. In order to avoid confusion, Hudson was required to:

1. use the word "equivalent" in type at least as large as Searle's mark METAMUCIL;
2. use an ® next to METAMUCIL; and
3. state that METAMUCIL was made by G.D. Searle and that Searle did not make or license REGACILIUM (Hudson's product).

Thus we see the teachings of *Coty* are still followed. Plaintiff's mark may be used to inform the public about defendant's equivalent product if:

1. defendant's use is truthful; and
2. defendant's use does not cause likely confusion.

Fair Use Distinguished from Parody

Owners of well-known marks may find themselves subjected to "parody" uses. The defendant is clearly imitating plaintiff's mark, and justifies the imitation on the grounds of humorous social comment. But a parody trademark, no matter how funny, will not be permitted if it is likely to cause confusion with plaintiff's mark.

94. Prestonettes, Inc. v. Coty, 264 U.S. 359, 368 (1924).
95. G.D. Searle & Co. v. Hudson Pharmaceutical Corp., 715 F.2d 837, 839 (3d Cir. 1983).

Parody is sometimes likened to the defense of fair use. But parody, unlike the fair use of plaintiff's mark to describe defendant's goods, is not an absolute defense. Parody is just a way of arguing that consumers are not likely to be confused because the parody mark creates a distinction between plaintiff's mark and defendant's mark. Thus, the very nature of parody tends to diminish confusion.

Parodies that are used to sell a competitive product, as opposed to parodies used solely for entertainment or social criticism, may have a harder time surviving court scrutiny. There may also be a greater likelihood of confusion when the trademark owner's mark (albeit in parodied form) is used in conjunction with a directly competitive product. This was the case where the mascot of Wendy's hamburger chain, LITTLE WENDY, was used to advertise the competitive BIG BITE sandwich outlet.[96]

A parody may also be enjoinable under a dilution cause of action.[97] Indeed, many parodies are objectionable as tarnishing the image of the famous mark and appear particularly vulnerable to a dilution argument. Parody uses enjoined because of their unwholesome association with plaintiff's mark include:

> ENJOY COCAINE on a poster using the famous ENJOY COCA-COLA format, colors, and logo.[98]
>
> Lewd poses by The PILLSBURY DOUGHBOY and DOUGHGIRL depicted in defendant's *Screw* magazine.[99]
>
> WHERE THERE'S LIFE THERE'S BUGS as a slogan for floor wax insecticide reminiscent of the famous beer slogan WHERE THERE'S LIFE THERE'S BUD.[100]

---

96. Wendy's Int'l, Inc. v. Big Bite, Inc., 576 F. Supp. 816 (S.D. Ohio 1983).
97. See chapter 7, pp. 140-47, *supra*, on dilution.
98. Coca-Cola Co. v. Gemini Rising, Inc., 346 F. Supp. 1183 (E.D.N.Y. 1972).
99. Pillsbury Co. v. Milky Way Prods., 215 U.S.P.Q. 124 (N.D. Ga. 1981).
100. Chemical Corp. of Am. v. Anheuser-Busch, Inc., 306 F.2d 433 (5th Cir. 1962).

DEBBIE DOES DALLAS pornographic movie featuring performers wearing uniforms simulating Dallas Cowboys Cheerleader uniforms.[101]

MUTANT OF OMAHA (play on MUTUAL OF OMAHA) for T-shirts protesting nuclear arms.[102]

The LL BEAM sex catalog parody of the LL BEAN catalog.[103]

Parodies that have survived court action because of no likely confusion or dilution include:

The Pregnant Girl Scout poster headlined BE PREPARED.[104]

The unflattering portrayal of the cartoon figure REDDY KILOWATT in a publication critical of public utilities.[105]

PETLEY FLEA BAGS sticker parodies of TETLEY TEA BAGS.[106]

MIAMI MICE T-shirt cartoon figures imitating the MIAMI VICE television series.[107]

LARDASHE large size designer jeans play on JORDACHE designer jeans.[108]

---

101. Dallas Cowboys Cheerleaders, Inc. v. Pussycat Cinema, Ltd., 604 F.2d 200 (2d Cir. 1979).
102. Mutual of Omaha Ins. Co. v. Novak, 775 F.2d 247 (8th Cir. 1985).
103. L.L. Bean, Inc. v. Drake Publishers, Inc., 228 U.S.P.Q. 733 (D. Me. 1986).
104. Girl Scouts of United States v. Personality Posters Mfg. Co., 304 F. Supp. 1228 (S.D.N.Y. 1969).
105. Reddy Communications v. E.A.F., 199 U.S.P.Q. 630 (D.C. Cir. 1977). While the court found no likely confusion or dilution, it rejected defendant's First Amendment (freedom of speech) defense on the grounds that defendant could get his message across without using plaintiff's trademark.
106. Tetley, Inc. v. Topps Chewing Gum, Inc., 556 F. Supp. 785 (E.D.N.Y. 1983).
107. Universal City Studios, Inc. v. Casey & Casey, Inc., 622 F. Supp. 201 (S.D. Fla. 1985).
108. Jordache Enters., Inc. v. Hogg Wyld, Ltd., 625 F. Supp. 48 (D.N.M. 1985).

Some of these decisions appear downright inconsistent. This may be explained by the different interpretation of dilution under recent law, the different facts, or simply the different judicial senses of humor. Permissible parody, like beauty, may very well lie in the eye of the beholder.

Genericness

The generic defense is available throughout the life of the trademark. A defendant may assert that plaintiff's mark is generic ab initio, or that it has become the generic name of the goods. The fact that the trademark has been registered and has even achieved incontestable status will not preclude the generic defense. Since plaintiff's registration is presumed valid, defendant will have the burden of proving that the registered mark is generic.[109]

To prove a mark generic, defendant must show that the public does not understand the term as a trademark, *i.e.*, as identifying the goods as coming from a single source.[110]

Genericness is not proven just because consumers ask for the particular product by the trademark.[111] For example, consumers may ask for TIDE. This does not mean that TIDE is a generic term. Consumers still understand that TIDE identifies a detergent made only by one company.

The generic issue does not turn on the term used by consumers when asking for the product. Rather, the issue turns on what consumers understand the term to mean. Does the public understand the term to identify goods made only by a single source?[112]

Evidence relevant to the generic issue includes:

---

109. 15 U.S.C. §§ 1057(b), 1064(c), 1065(4); See this chapter pp. 152, n.8, *supra*.
110. A.J. Greenbaum, *A Proposal For Evaluation Of Genericness After "Anti-Monopoly"*, 73 TRADEMARK REP. 101 (1983).
111. *In re* DC Comics, Inc., 689 F.2d 1042, 1051 (C.C.P.A. 1982).
112. 15 U.S.C. § 1064(c); Bayer Co., Inc. v. United Drug Co., 272 F. 505, 509 (S.D.N.Y 1921).

1. the absence or presence of the term in dictionaries and its definition in relationship to the goods;
2. the manner of use by the trademark owner—as a trademark or as a common name for the goods;
3. the manner of use by competitors and the trade;
4. consumer surveys.[113]

Fraud in the Procurement and Maintenance of Trademark Registrations

Heavy Burden of Proof

A party alleging fraud has a heavy burden of proof.[114] "Clear and convincing evidence" is required.[115]

Pleading the Elements of Fraud

Fraud must be pleaded with particularity.[116] Legal conclusions will not do. The pleader must state the time, place, and content of the false representation; the fact misrepresented; and what was obtained by the misrepresentation.[117]

The following elements must be proven to sustain the claim that plaintiff's registration was obtained by fraud:

1. Plaintiff made a false representation to the Patent and Trademark Office regarding a material fact, or willfully withheld material information;
2. Plaintiff knew that the representation was false;

---

113. E.I. Du Pont de Nemours & Co. v. Yoshida Int'l, Inc., 393 F. Supp. 502, 527 (E.D.N.Y. 1975). See chapter 2, pp. 18-19, 24-25, *supra*, for a more detailed discussion of evidence and case law pertinent to the generic issue.
114. King-Size, Inc. v. Frank's King Size Clothes, Inc., 547 F. Supp. 1138, 1166 (S.D. Tex. 1982).
115. Smith Int'l, Inc. v. Olin Corp., 209 U.S.P.Q. 1033, 1044 (T.T.A.B. 1981).
116. FED. R. CIV. P. 9(b).
117. W.R. Grace & Co. v. Arizona Feeds, 195 U.S.P.Q. 670, 672 (Comm'r Pats. 1977).

3. The Patent and Trademark Office would not have issued the registration but for its reliance on plaintiff's false representation.

False Versus Fraudulent: Honest misunderstanding does not amount to fraud.[118] The party must know the statement is false.[119]

Materiality: The false representation must be material to the issuance of plaintiff's registration. Materiality is sometimes referred to as the "but for" test—but for the misrepresentation the registration would not have been granted.[120]

Fraudulent and Nonfraudulent Conduct

Fraud has been found as a result of the following actions:

- claiming belief as to trademark ownership when U.S. distributor knew his company did not own the mark;[121]
- filing renewal affidavit when mark not used for many years;[122]
- claiming use on all goods of registration when mark used only on some goods;[123]
- failing to disclose the fact that a term is generic.[124]

Conduct held not to constitute fraud includes:

---

118. King-Size, Inc. v. Frank's King Size Clothes, Inc., 547 F. Supp. 1138, 1167 (S.D. Tex. 1982).
119. Abercrombie & Fitch Co. v. Hunting World, Inc., 537 F.2d 4, 14 (2d Cir. 1976).
120. National Trailways Bus Sys. v. Trailway Van Lines, Inc., 269 F. Supp. 352, 356 (E.D.N.Y. 1965).
121. Global Maschinen GmbH v. Global Banking Sys., Inc., 227 U.S.P.Q. 862, 867 (T.T.A.B. 1985).
122. Polo Fashions, Inc. v. Extra Special Prods., Inc., 208 U.S.P.Q. 421, 427 (S.D.N.Y. 1980).
123. Western Farmers Ass'n v. Loblaw, Inc., 180 U.S.P.Q. 345, 347 (T.T.A.B. 1973).
124. Deflecta-Shield Corp. v. Kar-rite Corp., 229 U.S.P.Q. 743, 747 (N.D. Ill. 1986).

- misstatements as to dates of first use so long as there was use before the filing date;[125]
- failure to disclose descriptive or functional nature of mark;[126]
- good faith allegations of belief regarding ownership of the mark;[127] and
- failure to disclose use by others.[128]

With respect to the failure to disclose, the "duty" imposed on trademark owners is much less strict than the duty imposed on patentees.[129] This is because a trademark registration is not dispositive of the trademark owner's rights. Even if the registration is found invalid, the trademark owner can still rely on his common law rights. In the case of a patent, however, the failure to disclose provides the patentee with a monopoly he would not have but for his failure to disclose. Also, the trademark registration proceedings provide for opposition and cancellation actions. Thus the burden is on the third party claiming rights rather than the registrant to investigate and report on possible users.[130]

The Consequences of Fraud

What happens when the heavy burden is carried as to the essential elements of fraud? Not as much as a defendant would like. Plaintiff's registration may be cancelled, or plaintiff may be

---

125. CarX Serv. Sys., Inc. v. Exxon Corp., 215 U.S.P.Q. 345, 351 (T.T.A.B. 1982).
126. Schwinn Bicycle Co. v. Murray Ohio Mfg. Co., 339 F. Supp. 973, 984 (M.D. Tenn. 1971).
127. Kemin Indus., Inc. v. Watkins Prods., Inc., 192 U.S.P.Q. 327, 330 (T.T.A.B. 1976).
128. *Id.* Good faith subjective belief that no other firm has legal right to use precludes finding of fraud.
129. Yocum v. Covington, 216 U.S.P.Q. 210, 216 (T.T.A.B. 1982).
130. Money Store v. Harriscorp Fin. Inc., 689 F.2d 666, 670-71 (7th Cir. 1982).

precluded from relying on his registration and its attendant presumptions.[131] If plaintiff's business is geographically limited, losing the benefits of federal registration could have significant consequences in the allocation of territorial rights. Also, if the fraudulent registration was incontestable, the defenses precluded by incontestability, such as descriptiveness, will become available.

Whatever happens to plaintiff's registration, however, will not prevent plaintiff from enforcing his common law rights.[132]

Fraud in the procurement of a registration also subjects plaintiff to an action for damages under Section 38[133] of the Lanham Act:

> Any person who shall procure registration in the Patent and Trademark Office of a mark by a false or fraudulent declaration or representation, oral or in writing, or by any false means, shall be liable in a civil action by any person injured thereby for any damages sustained in consequence thereof.[134]

The courts have followed a restrictive approach in granting damages under Section 38. Damages have generally been denied unless the fraudulently obtained registration is used offensively. For example, attorneys' fees incurred in defending an infringement suit based on a fraudulent registration were allowed as damages under Section 38, while fees incurred in bringing an action to cancel a fraudulent registration were not allowed.[135]

---

131. Duffy-Mott Co. v. Cumberland Packing Co., 424 F.2d 1095, 1098-99 (C.C.P.A. 1970).

132. *Id.* at 1100.

133. 15 U.S.C. § 1120. While this section refers to false statements used to "procure registration," it also applies to false statements used in "maintaining" a registration. Polo Fashions, Inc. v. Extra Special Prods., 208 U.S.P.Q. 421, 427 (S.D.N.Y. 1980).

134. 15 U.S.C. § 1120.

135. L.E. Graybeal, *Section 38—A Remedy for Fraud in the Procurement of a Trademark Registration*, 75 TRADEMARK REP. 27, 33-34 (1985); DeMert & Dougherty, Inc. v. Chesebrough-Pond's, Inc., 348 F. Supp. 1194, 1198 (N.D. Ill. 1972); Academy Award Prods., Inc. v. Bulova Watch Co., Inc., 129 F. Supp. 780, 784 (S.D.N.Y. 1955), *aff'd*, 233 F.2d 449 (2d Cir. 1956).

Unclean Hands

The doctrine that plaintiff must come into a court of equity with "clean hands" is yet another reflection of the equitable nature of trademark law. A plaintiff who requests the assistance of a court of equity must not himself be guilty of inequitable conduct.

However, the doctrine has significant limitations. Plaintiff's dirty hands will only be disabling if related directly to the subject matter of the action:

> The principle that "he who comes into equity must do so with clean hands" . . . does not repel all sinners from courts of equity. . . . The inequity which will repel him must have an immediate and necessary relation to the equity for which he sues.[136]

Moreover, where plaintiff has washed his hands (discontinued the inequitable conduct), the defense may not apply.[137]

Conduct held not to constitute unclean hands because it was too remote from plaintiff's claim of trademark infringement includes:

> violation of state license laws (*e.g.*, failure to take out license or pay taxes);[138]
>
> violation of Security and Exchange Commission regulations;[139] and
>
> plaintiff's infringement of third party rights.[140]

Conduct held to constitute unclean hands includes:

---

136. Shaver v. Heller & Merz Co., 108 F. 821, 834 (8th Cir. 1901).
137. Funds of Funds, Ltd. v. First American Fund of Funds, Inc., 274 F. Supp. 517, 519-20 n.1 (S.D.N.Y. 1967).
138. United States Light & Heating Co. v. United States Light & Heating Co., 181 F. 182, 187 (S.D.N.Y. 1910).
139. Funds of Funds, Ltd. v. First American Fund of Funds, Inc., 274 F. Supp. 517, 520 n.1 (S.D.N.Y. 1967).
140. Potter-Wrightington, Inc. v. Ward Baking Co., 288 F. 597, 602-03 (D. Mass. 1923), *aff'd*, 298 F. 398 (1st Cir. 1924).

intentional material misrepresentation as to product ingredients;[141]

use of a deceptive mark;[142] and

deliberate misuse of trademark registration symbol.[143]

The public interest factor also comes into play in ruling on an unclean hands defense. Courts are reluctant to find unclean hands where the result will be public confusion generated by both parties' continued use.[144]

Trademark Misuse

Again, keeping in mind the equitable nature of trademark rights, "misuse" of these rights is a recognized defense. Misuse includes activities that may themselves be the basis of a counterclaim, *e.g.*, enforcement of a fraudulently obtained registration,[145] violation of the antitrust laws,[146] as well as use in violation of other laws.

Trademark misuse has been found where a trademark license was terminated as a result of illegal discrimination.[147] The licensor of the JAYCEES mark terminated a licensee who refused to observe the license requirement of excluding women from membership. When the licensor sued to enjoin the licensee's continued use of JAYCEES, the District Court denied injunctive relief. The Eighth Circuit affirmed the District Court finding that:

---

141. Mulhens & Kropff v. Ferd. Muelhens, Inc., 43 F.2d 937, 939 (2d Cir. 1929), *cert. denied*, 282 U.S. 881 (1930).
142. Clinton E. Worden & Co. v. California Fig Syrup Co., 187 U.S. 516, 521 (1903).
143. Urecal Corp. v. Masters, 413 F. Supp. 873, 875-76 (N.D. Ill. 1976).
144. *See* Bell v. Streetwise Records, Ltd., 761 F.2d 67, 76 (1st Cir. 1985) (reversing District Court and refusing to apply unclean hands defense).
145. See pp. 180-83, *supra*, on fraud.
146. See pp. 186-91, infra, on antitrust violations.
147. United States Jaycees v. Cedar Rapids Jaycees, 614 F. Supp. 515, 518 (N.D. Iowa 1985), *aff'd*, 794 F.2d 379 (8th Cir. 1986).

When a terminated licensee shows that illegal discrimination was underlying the termination of the trademark license, it would be inequitable to grant injunctive relief.[148]

Violation of Antitrust Laws

Trademark use in violation of the antitrust laws is a specific defense to an incontestable registration under the Lanham Act.[149] Although strictly speaking, proof of the defense simply means plaintiff's registration is deprived of incontestable status, courts have interpreted the defense as barring enforcement of the registration on grounds of misuse or unclean hands.[150]

Trademark use to violate the antitrust laws may also be the basis for a counterclaim seeking treble damages resulting from illegal monopolization, conspiracy in restraint of trade, etc.

Direct Relation Between Antitrust Violation and Trademark Required

Like other unclean hands defenses, the antitrust violation must relate directly to plaintiff's trademark.[151] The trademark must be the "fundamental vehicle" required and used to accomplish the antitrust violation.[152]

The trademark was used as the fundamental vehicle for accomplishing the antitrust violation in the *Phi Delta* case.[153] There, the maker of jewelry for fraternal organizations conspired with the

148. *Id.*
149. 15 U.S.C. § 1115(b)(7).
150. Carl Zeiss Stiftung v. V.E.B. Carl Zeiss, Jena, 298 F. Supp. 1309, 1314 (S.D.N.Y. 1969), *modified*, 433 F.2d 686 (2d Cir. 1970), *cert. denied*, 403 U.S. 905 (1971).
151. *Id.*
152. *Id.*
153. Phi Delta Theta Fraternity v. J. A. Buchroeder & Co., 251 F. Supp. 968 (W.D. Mo. 1966).

leading college fraternities and sororities to use trademark registrations for the fraternal insignia for the purpose of excluding competition in the sale of fraternal jewelry.

The antitrust violation must also relate directly to plaintiff's claim of infringement against defendant. In *Coca-Cola v. Howard Johnson*, Coca-Cola sued Howard Johnson for passing off its cola beverage in response to order for COKE or COCA-COLA. Howard Johnson counterclaimed alleging trademark misuse in violation of the antitrust laws because Coca-Cola had allegedly imposed illegal territorial resale restrictions and tie-ins on its licensees (not parties to the suit). The court dismissed Howard Johnson's counterclaim because Coca-Cola's antitrust violations were too remote from Coca-Cola's infringement claim against Howard Johnson.[154]

Patents and Trademarks Distinguished

There are important differences between patents and trademarks vis-à-vis antitrust violations. The exclusionary power of a patent is greater because it bestows a monopoly on the product. The trademark only bestows a monopoly on the name or symbol identifying the product.

This basic difference between trademarks and patents was commented on in the *Car-Freshner* case. Plaintiff claimed infringement of its pine tree design trademark for car air freshener products. Defendant counterclaimed alleging that plaintiff's trademark enforcement action was an attempt to monopolize competition in violation of the antitrust laws. The court dismissed defendant's counterclaim, holding that plaintiff's trademark enforcement could not as a matter of law monopolize the relevant market in all car air freshener products. The court stated:

---

154. Coca-Cola Co. v. Howard Johnson Co., 386 F. Supp. 330, 336-37 (N.D. Ga. 1974).

> Unlike a patent or copyright, a trademark does not in any way represent a monopoly conferred upon a particular product. [155]

Courts are also more reluctant to bar enforcement of a trademark, as opposed to a patent, because of the public interest in protection from confusion.

Bad Faith Trademark Enforcement: The *Noerr-Pennington* Doctrine and the "Sham" Exception

An increasingly common antitrust misuse defense alleges that the suit brought by plaintiff was brought in bad faith as part of an attempt to monopolize or restrain trade.

Plaintiff may try to combat this defense by claiming immunity under the *Noerr-Pennington* doctrine.[156] Under this doctrine, plaintiff has a constitutional right of access to the courts, which immunizes him from antitrust liability based on his filing suit against defendant.

The immunity conferred by the *Noerr-Pennington* doctrine, however, is not absolute. There is an exception to the doctrine known as the "sham exception": If the law suit is a mere sham brought to harass a competitor and damage competition, it will not qualify for immunity under *Noerr-Pennington*.[157]

The "sham" exception should be defeated where plaintiff can show his suit was a genuine attempt to secure a decision on the merits and that he had a reasonable basis for his claim.[158]

In some cases, courts have made a determination as to plaintiff's good faith in bringing suit prior to a decision on the merits.[159] In

---

155. Car-Freshner Corp. v. Auto Aid Mfg. Corp., 438 F. Supp. 82, 86 (N.D.N.Y. 1977).
156. The *Noerr-Pennington* doctrine has its roots in two Supreme Court cases: Eastern R.R. Presidents Conference v. Noerr Motor Freight, Inc., 365 U.S. 127 (1961) and United Mine Workers v. Pennington, 381 U.S. 657 (1965).
157. California Motor Transp. Co. v. Trucking Unlimited, 404 U.S. 508 (1972).
158. Adolph Coors Co. v. A & S Wholesalers, Inc., 185 U.S.P.Q. 515, *aff'd on point, modified on other grounds*, 561 F.2d 807 (10th Cir. 1977).
159. Coca-Cola Co. v. Overland, Inc., 692 F.2d 1250, 1257 (9th Cir. 1982).

other cases, plaintiffs have succeeded in staying the antitrust claim until after a decision is reached on the trademark claim. The theory is that the antitrust claim will automatically fail if plaintiff succeeds on the merits of his trademark claim.[160]

One decision in Connecticut has suggested that a single suit, absent some other conduct involving abuse or corruption of judicial process, cannot be the basis of a sham exception.[161] Otherwise, a defendant's threats to invoke the antitrust laws would have a chilling effect on plaintiff's right to obtain court determination of his claim. Other courts maintain that a single suit may be the basis for a sham exception.[162]

The Elements of Monopolization and Attempted Monopolization

Section 2 of the Sherman Act provides:

> Every person who shall monopolize, or attempt to monopolize, or combine or conspire with any other person or persons, to monopolize any part of the trade or commerce among the several States, or with foreign nations, shall be deemed guilty of a felony.[163]

Monopolization under Section 2 requires: (1) the willful acquisition or maintenance of monopoly power in the relevant market; and (2) the existence of actual injury to competition in that market.[164]

Attempted monopoly requires:

> (1) specific intent to control prices or destroy competition in some part of commerce; (2) predatory or anticompetitive conduct

160. Helene Curtis Indus., Inc. v. Church & Dwight Co., 560 F.2d 1325, 1336, *cert. denied*, 434 U.S. 1070 (7th Cir. 1978).
161. Mountain Grove Cemetary v. Norwalk Vault Co., 428 F. Supp. 951, 955-56 (D. Conn. 1977).
162. Clipper Exxpress v. Rocky Mountain Motor Tariff Bureau, 690 F.2d 1240, 1254 (9th Cir. 1982).
163. 15 U.S.C. § 2.
164. General Business Sys. v. North Am. Philips Corp., 699 F.2d 965 (9th Cir. 1983).

directed to accomplishing the unlawful purpose; and (3) a dangerous probability of success.[165]

The Relevant Market

The relevant market is composed of products that are reasonably interchangeable for the purpose for which they were made. Interchangeability is determined by reference to price, use, and quality.[166]

A number of cases have held that a relevant market cannot be limited to those products identified by a particular owner's trademark.[167]

A definition of the relevant market as consisting of products similar in appearance to plaintiff's product design trademark has also been rejected as a matter of law.[168]

Conspiracy in Restraint of Trade

Section 1 of the Sherman Act prohibits "Every contract, combination . . . or conspiracy, in restraint of trade or commerce among the several states".[169] The courts have construed this provision as applying only to those contracts or combinations that "unreasonably" restrain competition.[170]

Practices condemned under Section 1 include arrangements controlling price, divisions of territories or customers, refusals to deal, and certain tying and exclusive dealing arrangements.

The use of trademarks in connection with all these restraints is beyond the scope of this text. However, as to trademark licensing arrangements that are frequently pleaded as defenses to these restraints, a general statement can be made: Anti-competitive

165. *Id.* at 975.
166. United States v. E. I. Du Pont De Nemours & Co., 351 U.S. 377, 395 (1956).
167. Domed Stadium Hotel, Inc. v. Holiday Inns, Inc., 732 F.2d 480, 488 (5th Cir. 1984).
168. Car-Freshner Corp. v. Auto Aid Mfg. Corp., 438 F. Supp. 82, 87 (N.D.N.Y. 1977).
169. 15 U.S.C. § 1.
170. Northern Pac. Ry. Co. v. United States, 356 U.S. 1, 4-5 (1958).

conduct is not justified because it is incident or ancillary to a valid trademark licensing system.[171]

171. Specific application of the principle is found in the following cases: General Leaseways, Inc. v. National Truck Leasing Ass'n, 744 F.2d 588 (7th Cir. 1984); Evans v. S.S. Kresge Co., 544 F.2d 1184 (3d Cir. 1976), *cert. denied*, 433 U.S. 908 (1977) (trademark license may not be used to avoid Sherman Act liability); Fontana Aviation, Inc. v. Beech Aircraft Corp., 432 F.2d 1080 (7th Cir. 1970), *cert. denied*, 401 U.S. 923 (1971) (restraints of trade cannot be justified as reasonable steps taken to implement a valid trademark licensing system); Switzer Bros., Inc. v. Locklin, 297 F.2d 39 (7th Cir. 1961), *cert. denied*, 369 U.S. 851 (1962) (quality control provisions of the Lanham Act relating to trademark licenses cannot condone a violation of the antitrust laws); Jack Winter, Inc. v. Koratron Co., Inc., 375 F. Supp. 1 (N.D. Cal. 1974) (use of trademark license to effect a horizontal territorial division of a market is a per se violation of Section 1 of the Sherman Act).

9

Negotiating a Settlement

"I'd Rather Switch Than Fight"

Litigation has many drawbacks—it is expensive, takes up valuable executive time, and the outcome is uncertain. In many cases, the sensible conclusion for defendant is: "I'd rather switch than fight."

How does defendant go about deciding if switching is preferable to fighting? Here are some preliminary steps that will help defendant assess his position.

Making Sure Who's First

Before throwing in the towel, defendant should confirm that he is in fact the second user. It is surprising how often a hasty notice of infringement is sent by a company who turns out not to have prior rights.

Getting the Facts

In addition to verifying that plaintiff is really the first user, defendant should get some basic facts on plaintiff's mark, *e.g.*, length of use, channels of distribution, sample products, and literature. Defendant should also order a search on plaintiff's mark to assess the chances of establishing an "everybody is using it" defense.[1]

---

1. See chapter 7, p. 121, *supra*, on third party use.

Methods of getting the facts include: direct inquiry to plaintiff; investigation by outside agencies and review of Patent and Trademark Office records. The file on plaintiff's registration or application may contain statements of no confusion with third party marks similar to defendant's, or assertions that portions of plaintiff's mark are descriptive. These statements could substantially weaken plaintiff's case.[2]

Defendant should also take a look at his own use. What is the commercial importance of the mark? Will a significant advertising investment be lost by a change? Can a slight change be made that would:

1. satisfy plaintiff; and
2. carry over the good will already developed by defendant.

Creating the Right Atmosphere

The Honey Versus Vinegar Principle

Letters are written and received by people, not faceless companies. Unless plaintiff is dead set on litigation, he would do well to write a courteous letter. A courteous reply can also go a long way toward creating an atmosphere conducive to settlement.

Telephone Versus Correspondence

Sometimes a letter does not give an accurate signal of the writer's intentions. It usually helps to establish telephone communications. The parties can sound each other out before committing themselves to a firm position in writing. Plaintiff may be able to get a feel for defendant's willingness to change. Defendant, in turn, can better assess plaintiff's insistence on achieving each and every element of relief demanded.

2. See chapter 5, pp. 95-96, *supra,* for case law on effect of statements made in prosecuting trademark applications.

Common Settlement Arrangements

Gradual Name Change

Alternatives to all-out litigation include various phase-out periods for changing over to a new name, such as:

a change of name to be accomplished over a set period of time, *e.g.*, six months or a year;

a change of name to be accomplished as soon as existing stock is used up;

a change of name to be accompanied by the use of "Formerly Brand X" for a period of time.

Limitations on Use

Another option is permitting defendant's use under certain conditions, for example:

limitation to specific goods;

limitation to specific channels of commerce;

limitation to specific geographical areas;

requirement that defendant's use be accompanied by prominent reference to his house mark or company name;

requirement that defendant's use be accompanied by a disclaimer of association with plaintiff.

In deciding whether to permit defendant's use under any of these conditions, plaintiff should consider the effect of the settlement on future cases. If this particular use is allowed, plaintiff may have to live with other similar uses.

Monetary Settlements

Sometimes it is worth plaintiff's while to pay the expenses incurred by defendant's change to a different mark. In deciding if and how much to pay, consider:

defendant's good faith;

possible advantages to acquiring defendant's rights, *e.g.*, broadened product line or geographical rights;

the effect such payment may have on other infringements—will others demand similar payments?

the strength of plaintiff's case; and

the effect of an adverse court decision on plaintiff's business.

If a payment seems appropriate, how can a reasonable figure be negotiated? Some attorneys will always start negotiations off by asking for twice what their client is willing to take. If the client will accept $10,000, they ask for $20,000. Other attorneys will make an offer fairly close to what their client is ready to accept, on the theory that too high a demand will cause settlement discussions to break down before they start. As a general rule, you should be prepared to make some movement from the first offer—otherwise your adversary will not be satisfied that a compromise has been reached.

The negotiation process also involves many "body" or "voice" signals. Your adversary may hint that a certain range would be acceptable—while appearing to ask for more.

License Agreements

Permitting defendant to continue his use under license is another settlement alternative. The license may require a royalty on percentage of sales or may be royalty free.

The critical element of any license agreement is the licensor's control over the quality of the licensee's goods or services. For a license agreement to stand up under court scrutiny, the license should not only provide the means of exercising control, the licensor should be sure that quality is in fact maintained. This can be done by periodic examination of the product, the setting of standard specifications, *e.g.*, the use of certain materials, inspection of the licensee's premises, etc.[3]

Getting the Client into the Act

Sometimes it helps to let the two clients thrash out settlement terms. Especially when the lawyers are at an impasse, direct contact between the parties may produce a breakthrough. The danger to guard against here is any discussion by the client on the merits that could be used against him if the case is not settled.

Leading from Strength

Creating the right atmosphere for settlement does not necessarily mean plaintiff should abandon a firm approach. Especially where plaintiff is prepared to sue, it is important to show defendant that plaintiff means business. One way to do this is to set deadlines for reply. Setting deadlines makes it harder for defendant to stall and drag out settlement discussions.

Another way to emphasize the importance of the matter is to bring outside counsel in at an early stage.

Delivering a copy of a "draft" complaint before filing can also move settlement quickly to a head. Defendant knows you are ready to proceed, as, of course, you will be. The danger here, as with any threat to file suit, is that defendant may beat you to the punch by filing a declaratory judgment action.[4] You could end up

---

3. See chapter 15, pp. 319-26, *infra*, on trademark license agreements.
4. See chapter 13, pp. 279-81, *infra*, on declaratory judgment actions.

in court before there has been a thorough exploration of settlement.

10

Litigating in Court

Preparing the Complaint: Common Causes of Action

In drafting a complaint for trademark infringement, the following causes of action should be considered:

1. infringement of plaintiff's federally registered mark;
2. violation of Section 43(a) of the Lanham Act;
3. common law trademark infringement and unfair competition;
4. violation of state deceptive trade practices acts;
5. dilution; and
6. misappropriation.

Infringement of Plaintiff's Federally Registered Mark

Section 32 of the Lanham Act provides a cause of action for use of a mark likely to cause confusion, mistake, or deception with a registered mark.[1] The federal registration supplies a basis for federal court jurisdiction.[2]

A complaint asserting infringement of a federal registration generally alleges: the nature of plaintiff's business; the adoption and use of plaintiff's mark; the status of plaintiff's federal registration; the promotion and advertising of plaintiff's mark; the valuable goodwill associated with plaintiff's mark; the association of

1. 15 U.S.C. § 1114(1).
2. 15 U.S.C. § 1121.

plaintiff's mark with a single source; plus facts pertaining to defendant's mark and his use.

Typical exhibits to the complaint are: plaintiff's federal registration; photographs showing both parties' marks applied to their products (especially where defendant has also simulated plaintiff's trade dress); and any other material that demonstrates the similarity in the marks.

In answering the complaint, defendant will have to admit, deny, or state he is without knowledge sufficient to form a belief as to the truth of each allegation.[3] Thus, it is a good idea to limit each complaint paragraph to a single allegation and avoid conclusory hyperbole. By this tactic, you may draw some useful admissions in the answer.

Violation of Section 43(a)

Section 43(a) of the Lanham Act imposes civil liability upon "(a)ny person who shall . . . use in connection with any goods . . . a false designation of origin, or any false description or representation, including words or other symbols tending falsely to describe or represent the same."[4]

Section 43(a) provides a cause of action in federal court for infringement of an unregistered mark where defendant's use has an effect on commerce.[5] The likely confusion standard for judging infringement of registered marks also applies to unregistered marks under Section 43(a).[6]

Unregistered marks protected by Section 43(a) include packaging and product design marks (trade dress).[7] Plaintiffs who assert

---

3. FED. R. CIV. P. 8(b).
4. 15 U.S.C. § 1125(a).
5. Shatel Corp. v. Mao Ta Lumber & Yacht Corp., 697 F.2d 1352 (11th Cir. 1983).
6. Amstar Corp. v. Domino's Pizza, Inc., 615 F.2d 252, 258-59 (5th Cir. 1980).
7. Warner Bros., Inc. v. Gay Toys, Inc., 658 F.2d 76 (2d Cir. 1981).

trade dress rights should be sure to allege nonfunctionality and secondary meaning (association with a single source).

Even if an unregistered mark is clearly not descriptive and does not require proof of secondary meaning, it is a good idea to allege secondary meaning. It is easier to plead secondary meaning than fight an ill-founded motion to dismiss.

In addition to protecting unregistered marks, Section 43(a) provides an action for false advertising by defendant as to his own goods.[8] Section 43(a) does not provide relief, however, for disparagement of plaintiff's goods in defendant's advertising.[9]

To make out a false advertising claim under 43(a), plaintiff must establish three elements: 1) involvement of goods or services, 2) effect on interstate commerce, and 3) a false designation of origin or false description of defendants' goods or services.[10]

Most courts do not require likelihood of confusion between plaintiff's and defendant's products to succeed in a false advertising claim under 43(a). It is enough if the advertising statement is literally false or tends to create a misleading impression as to defendant's goods.[11]

Not only does Section 43(a) extend the relief provided by the Lanham Act to unregistered marks and false advertising, but it extends the class of plaintiffs who have standing to bring suit. Under Section 32(a), the infringer is "liable in a civil action by the registrant."[12] Under Section 43(a), the civil action may be brought

8. Section 43(a) prohibits any "false description or representation" as to defendant's goods or services. 15 U.S.C. § 1125(a). *See* Vidal Sassoon, Inc. v. Bristol-Myers Co., 661 F.2d 272, 278 (2d Cir. 1981).

9. Vidal Sassoon, Inc. v. Bristol-Myers Co., 661 F.2d 272, 277-78 (2d Cir. 1981).

10. CBS Inc. v. Springboard Int'l Records, 429 F. Supp. 563, 566 (S.D.N.Y. 1976).

11. American Home Prods. Corp. v. Johnson & Johnson, 577 F.2d 160 (2d Cir. 1978). *But see* Coca-Cola Co. v. Procter & Gamble Co., 642 F. Supp. 936 (W.D. Ohio 1986) (false advertising claim under Section 43(a) dismissed because plaintiff failed to plead likelihood of confusion between plaintiff's and defendant's products).

12. 15 U.S.C. § 1114(a).

"by any person who believes that he is or is likely to be damaged by the use of any such false description or representation."[13]

Thus, a 43(a) plaintiff need not own a federal registration or even common law rights in the mark. Exclusive and nonexclusive distributors, recipients of royalty interests—any commercial party with a "reasonable interest to be protected"—have standing under 43(a).[14]

Common Law Trademark Infringement and Unfair Competition

Unfair competition includes common law trademark infringement, trade dress infringement (copying of packaging or product appearance), false advertising, trade name infringement, and any "unfair" business practice. While unfair competition covers a broader spectrum of activities than trademark infringement, plaintiff must still prove likely confusion.[15]

The same facts as to plaintiff's and defendant's use pleaded under the federal counts may be pleaded under the common law unfair competition count. Frequently, plaintiff will incorporate by reference the paragraphs previously pleaded.

Plaintiff should also plead individual acts that separately may not amount to unfair competition, but that taken together: 1) create a cumulative effect that adds up to unfair competition; and 2) show defendant's bad intent.[16]

Deceptive Trade Practices

A number of states have adopted deceptive trade practices acts. Plaintiff should check for such statutes in the suit forum.

---

13. 15 U.S.C. § 1125(a).
14. PPX Enters. v. Audiofidelity, 746 F.2d 120, 125 (2d Cir. 1984).
15. Universal City Studios, Inc. v. Nintendo Co., Ltd., 746 F.2d 112, 115 (2d Cir. 1984).
16. See Kentucky Fried Chicken v. Diversified Packaging, 549 F.2d 368, 385 (5th Cir. 1977).

A typical deceptive trade practices act is the one in Minnesota that provides:

> Subdivision 1. A person engages in a deceptive trade practice when, in the course of his business, vocation, or occupation, he:
>
> * * *
>
> (2) causes likelihood of confusion or of misunderstanding as to the source, sponsorship, approval or certification of goods or services,
>
> (3) causes likelihood of confusion or of misunderstanding as to affiliation, connection, or association with, or certification by, another;
>
> * * *
>
> (8) disparages the goods, services, or business of another by false or misleading representation of fact;
>
> * * *
>
> (12) engages in any other conduct which similarly creates a likelihood of confusion or of misunderstanding.
>
> In order to prevail in an action under Sections 325D.43 to 325D.48 a complaint need not prove competition between the parties or actual confusion or misunderstanding.[17]

For the most part, plaintiff must show some likelihood of confusion or misunderstanding to make out a claim under a deceptive practices act.[18] This is the same element required for statutory and common law trademark infringement. There are some differences in the various state acts, *e.g.*, mandatory recovery of attorney's fees under certain circumstances.[19] Plaintiff should look to see if he might end up paying defendant's fees before leaping in to plead a violation of a particular state's act.

---

17. MINN. STAT. § 325D.43 *et seq.*; Scott v. Mego Int'l, Inc., 519 F. Supp. 1118, 1137 (D. Minn. 1981).
18. Scott v. Mego Int'l, Inc., 519 F. Supp. 1118, 1137 (D. Minn. 1981).
19. Evans & Assocs. v. Continental Homes, Inc., 785 F.2d 897, 917 (11th Cir. 1986).

Dilution

State anti-dilution statutes prohibit a use likely to injure plaintiff's business reputation or dilute the distinctiveness of plaintiff's mark.

Unlike the causes of action discussed above, likely confusion is not necessary to succeed on a dilution cause of action. The necessary elements are: 1) distinctiveness of the mark (because of its uniqueness and/or plaintiff's advertising); and 2) dilution by defendant's use through a) the blurring of the mark's product identification; or b) the tarnishing of the affirmative associations conveyed by the mark.[20]

Misappropriation

The elements of a misappropriation action are:

1. plaintiff's investment of substantial time, effort, and money in the subject;
2. defendant's appropriation of the fruits of plaintiff's labor at little or no cost; and
3. injury to plaintiff as a result of defendant's misappropriation.[21]

Confusion is not a necessary element of misappropriation. Hence, it is tempting to use misappropriation as an alternative theory to trademark infringement. The Eighth Circuit gave some credence to this approach in the *Truck Equipment* case. The Court of Appeals relied on *International News Service* (the source of the misappropriation doctrine) in upholding an injunction against defendant's use of the exterior design of plaintiff's trailer:

> Fruehauf argues, however, that consumers could not have associated the exterior design of the Cornhusker 800 as the product of TESCO because, after it entered the market, a similar trailer was

---

20. See chapter 7, pp. 140-47, *supra*, for wording of typical anti-dilution statute and discussion of case law.
21. International News Serv. v. Associated Press, 248 U.S. 215 (1918).

> made that was clearly labeled as the product of Fruehauf. This argument is a reformulation of the proposition that the law of unfair competition protects only against palming off or misrepresentation. The law of unfair competition, however, protects also against misappropriation. See *International News Service* v. *Associated Press*, 248 U.S. 215, 242, 39 S. Ct. 68, 63 L. Ed. 211 (1918); note 5 *supra*. As the Supreme Court has said: "The fault in the reasoning lies in applying as a test the right of the complainant as against the public, instead of considering the rights of complainant and defendant, competitors in business, as between themselves."[22]

The *Truck Equipment* language suggests that misappropriation affords relief against copying regardless of whether plaintiff has established the standard elements of trademark infringement.

Other decisions, however, have specifically refused to provide relief under a misappropriation theory where plaintiff failed to prove trademark validity and likely confusion.[23]

It would seem that a misappropriation action is most apt to succeed where the subject appropriated is not claimed as a trademark. See, for example, the *Standard & Poors* case where defendant misappropriated plaintiff's *Standard & Poor's* index.[24]

Choosing the Forum: Plaintiff's Choice and Defendant's Convenience

The venue statute limits plaintiff's choice of forum in an action under the Lanham Act to where defendant "resides" or "where the claim arose."[25] A corporate defendant "resides" in any district where it is doing business.[26]

22. Truck Equip. Serv. Co. v. Fruehauf Corp., 536 F.2d 1210, 1220 (8th Cir. 1976).
23. Toho Co., Ltd. v. Sears, Roebuck & Co., 645 F.2d 788, 794 (9th Cir. 1981).
24. Standard & Poor's Corp. v. Commodity Exch., Inc., 683 F.2d 704 (2d Cir. 1982).
25. 28 U.S.C. § 1391(b).
26. 28 U.S.C. § 1391(c).

On its face, the venue provision permitting plaintiff to sue where "the claim arose" gives the trademark owner a wide choice of forums. Because trademark infringement arises where the infringement occurs,[27] plaintiff theoretically may bring suit in any forum where defendant is selling the infringing product. The courts, however, have been gradually limiting plaintiff's choice.

In the *Honda Associates* case, the Court rejected the idea that suit could be brought where any part of the claim arose, no matter how small.[28] The Court required that the largest part of the claim, or at least a substantial part of the claim, arise in the district.

The *Honda* test was recast by the Supreme Court decision in the *Leroy* case. The Supreme Court restricted plaintiff's choice to those districts of equal plausibility in terms of availability of witnesses, evidence and the convenience of defendant—but not plaintiff:

> [I]t is absolutely clear that Congress did not intend to provide for venue at the residence of the plaintiff or to give that party an unfettered choice among a host of different districts. . . . In our view . . . the broadest interpretation of the ["claim arose"] language of § 1391(b) that is even arguably acceptable is that in the unusual case in which it is not clear that the claim arose in only one specific district, a plaintiff may choose between those two (or conceivably even more) districts that with approximately equal plausibility—in terms of the availability of witnesses, the accessibility of other relevant evidence, and the convenience of the defendant (but not of the plaintiff)—may be assigned as the locus of the claim.[29]

Any doubt that *Leroy* governs trademark cases was quashed by the Court of Appeals for the District of Columbia in the *Firehouse* case.[30] There the defendants sold 200 cases (1.5 percent of their

27. Vanity Fair Mills, Inc. v. T. Eaton Co., 234 F.2d 633 (2d Cir.), *cert. denied*, 352 U.S. 871, *reh'g denied*, 352 U.S. 913 (1956).
28. Honda Assocs., Inc. v. Nozawa Trading, Inc., 374 F. Supp. 886, 891-92 (S.D.N.Y. 1974).
29. Leroy v. Great W. United Corp., 443 U.S. 173, 185 (1979).
30. Noxell Corp. v. Firehouse No. 1 Bar-B-Que Restaurant, 760 F.2d 312 (D.C. Cir. 1985).

total sales of FIREHOUSE barbecue sauce) in the Washington, D.C. forum where plaintiff brought suit. Forty percent of defendants' product was sold in California. Defendants' employees, records, and key witnesses were California based.

Rather than transfer plaintiff's suit to California, the Court dismissed the suit and awarded attorneys' fees to defendants.[31] The Court chastised plaintiff for flouting Supreme Court precedent and haling defendants, a small company and its firefighter owner, into a forum 3,000 miles away from home. The Court branded this conduct as "exceptional" for fee award purposes under Section 35 of the Lanham Act.

Under *Leroy* and its progeny, the convenience of defendant has emerged as a paramount consideration in deciding where "the claim arose." If the availability of witnesses and accessibility of evidence are equally balanced between plaintiff's chosen forum and defendant's place of business, defendant's convenience will rule.[32]

Researching Your Judge

Once the complaint is filed, it is usually assigned to a particular judge. It is extremely useful to get a line on your judge—as to his procedures, his schedule, and his substantive decisions. This can be done by:

Checking the Local Law Journal

The daily or weekly newspaper of court activity sets out facts as to each judge's days for hearing motions, requirements for conferences prior to motions, chambers telephone hours, etc.

---

31. Noxell Corp. v. Firehouse No. 1 Bar-B-Que Restaurant, 771 F.2d 521, 526-27 (D.C. Cir. 1985).
32. Manufacturer's Hanover Corp. v. Maine Sav. Bank, 225 U.S.P.Q. 525, 528-29 (S.D.N.Y. 1985).

Checking for Biographical Data

Who's Who, Bar association publications and trade journal summaries are usual sources for biographical information.

Checking with Local Counsel

If you are litigating out of town, experienced local counsel can provide valuable data on the judge's procedures, timetable for discovery, participation in settlement efforts, etc.

Checking the Judge's Decisions

Computer research gives quick access to all your judge's decisions. You should review at least his trademark decisions, plus any decisions pertinent to motions you are contemplating, *e.g.*, summary judgment.

If your judge has decided a number of trademark cases, you may get a feel for his overall attitude towards trademarks: Is he a protector of property? Will he come down hard on any hint of bad faith? If you know what your judge will focus on, you can do a better job presenting your side of the case. Or you might decide that your case is better suited for presentation to a jury.

To Jury or Not to Jury

There are usually two jury questions that confront the parties:

1. Should a jury be requested?
2. If a jury demand is made, is the other side stuck with it?

Should a Jury Be Requested?

It is useful to list the pros and cons of a jury trial as it applies to your case. Factors to be balanced include the following:

Strong Versus Weak Case

If you have a strong case you will generally do better with a judge. Juries are less predictable and may misunderstand some of the intricacies of trademark law.

Big Guy Versus Little Guy

You have probably heard that juries favor the little guy. This is not always the case, especially if you are a large company with a good reputation. Nevertheless, the small company or individual whose rights have been trampled upon by the big commercial bully would do well to opt for a jury.[33]

The Home Field Advantage

Juries supposedly favor the home-town boy. In today's more cosmopolitan world, however, this is less of a factor. The home field advantage can also be reduced by giving local counsel a prominent role.

The Registration Advantage

Juries are impressed with registrations. A judge is less reluctant to say the Patent and Trademark Office made a mistake in granting a registration. If there is a descriptiveness issue and your registration is not yet incontestable (*i.e.*, can still be challenged on the basis of descriptiveness), a jury may be a good bet.

Time, Money, and Appealability

Juries will decide the case immediately after trial. The judge's decision could take months.

A jury trial requires jury instructions and more strict attention to admissible and inadmissible evidence. Judges are prone to say "I'll take it for what it's worth." Arguments over admissibility of

33. Big O Tire Dealers, Inc. v. Goodyear Tire & Rubber, 408 F. Supp. 1219, 1232 (D. Col. 1976), *aff'd with modification as to amount*, 561 F.2d 1365 (10th Cir. 1977).

evidence and propriety of jury instructions may increase the time and expense of trial.

A jury decision is also usually harder to overturn on appeal.[34]

Demanding A Jury Trial

If you opt for a jury trial, you must make a jury demand. The demand must be served no later than ten days after the last pleading directed to the issue to be tried has been served.[35] Failure to timely demand a jury constitutes a waiver.[36]

Avoiding a Jury Trial

The right to a jury trial as to legal issues is preserved by the Seventh Amendment to the Constitution.[37] There is no right to a jury trial as to equitable issues.

Legal versus equitable are defined by the relief requested. Money damages are traditionally a legal remedy. Injunctive relief is traditionally an equitable remedy.

When a request for injunctive relief is combined with a request for money damages, with common questions of fact, a right to jury trial exists. So says the Supreme Court in the leading *Dairy Queen* case.[38]

There is an argument, however, that a claim for profits is only incidental to the claim for injunctive relief and does not require trial by jury. At least one court has adopted this argument without mentioning *Dairy Queen*.[39]

There is also an argument that a claim to profits and damages under the Lanham Act is equitable and is to be awarded by "the

34. A jury verdict will not be overturned where it is supported by substantial evidence. Transgo, Inc. v. Ajac Transmission Parts Corp., 768 F.2d 1001, 1013-14 (9th Cir. 1985), *cert. denied*, 106 S. Ct. 802 (1986).
35. FED. R. CIV. P. 38(b).
36. FED. R. CIV. P. 38(d).
37. U.S. CONST. amend. 7 (1791). Implemented in FED. R. CIV. P. 38(a).
38. Dairy Queen, Inc. v. Wood, 369 U.S. 469 (1962).
39. Coca-Cola Co. v. Wright, 55 F.R.D. 11 (W.D. Tenn. 1971).

court" because the statute says so. Section 35 provides for an award of defendant's profits and plaintiff's damages "subject to the principles of equity."[40] Further, "the Court shall assess such profits and damages" or "cause the same to be assessed under its direction"; and if "the Court" finds that "recovery based on profits is inadequate or excessive the Court may . . . enter judgment for such sum as the Court shall find to be just." This statutory language was the basis for the court's reduction of a jury award in *Stuart v. Collins.*[41] Query whether the same reasoning could be used to avoid a jury trial altogether on the Lanham Act claims.

One way of skirting the jury is to move for preliminary injunctive relief. The motion will be decided by the court and frequently brings the litigation to an end without a full trial.[42]

Another way around a jury is summary judgment—if you can establish that there are no genuine issues of material fact.[43] Partial summary judgment on the monetary issue, if granted, would also eliminate the jury trial on the remaining equitable issues.

Preparing the Answer

Defendant's answer to a complaint is due twenty days after service.[44] Usually, plaintiff or the court will grant a thirty-day extension. Some courts have strict rules limiting the number of extensions and the parties should check the local rules on this point.

---

40. 15 U.S.C. § 1117.
41. Stuart v. Collins, 489 F. Supp. 827, 832-33 (S.D.N.Y. 1980) (jury award of $500,000 reduced by trial judge to $250,000).
42. See chapter 11, pp. 219-24, *infra*, on requirements for preliminary injunction.
43. FED. R. CIV. P. 56; see chapter 11, pp. 224-32, *infra*, for discussion of trademark summary judgment cases.
44. FED. R. CIV. P. 12(a).

Before answering the complaint, defendant should review possible grounds for a motion to strike or dismiss.[45]

In answering plaintiff's allegations, defendant has three options:

- admit;
- deny; or
- allege without knowledge or information sufficient to form a belief as to the truth of plaintiff's allegation and therefore deny.[46]

Defendant should not be too ready to admit allegations, even if he expects plaintiff will be able to prove them. For example, where plaintiff pleads ownership of a federal registration, defendant should limit his admission to the issuance of the registration (assuming Patent and Trademark Office records reflect the issuance) and plead "without knowledge" as to other claims, *e.g.*, ownership, validity, incontestability.

Affirmative Defenses

Affirmative defenses must be pleaded or they are waived.[47]

Of course, pleadings can be amended to add defenses, *e.g.*, if the facts supporting the defense are revealed by discovery.[48] Defenses may also be tried by implied consent of the parties.[49] It is advisable, however, to think out your case in advance and to plead known defenses at the outset.

Affirmative defenses to consider in responding to a trademark action include:

- laches;
- estoppel;
- acquiescence;

45. FED. R. CIV. P. 12(b), (e), (f).
46. FED. R. CIV. P. 8(b).
47. FED. R. CIV. P. 12.
48. FED. R. CIV. P. 15(a).
49. FED. R. CIV. P. 15(b).

- abandonment;
- fair use;
- fraud;
- misuse; and
- unclean hands.[50]

Procedural Defenses

There is also a group of procedural defenses that are waived unless pleaded at the outset. These include lack of personal jurisdiction, insufficient process, insufficient service of process, and improper venue.[51]

Counterclaims

The answer may include one or more counterclaims. There are permissive and compulsory counterclaims. Compulsory counterclaims are those that arise out of the same transaction or occurrence that is the subject matter of the original claim.[52] They are "compulsory" in the sense that if not raised, they cannot be raised in a later proceeding.

The time to reply to a counterclaim is twenty days after service of the answer.[53]

Beware the Sanctions of Rule 11

Rule 11 requires all pleadings and motions filed in court to be "well grounded in fact" and "warranted by existing law or a good faith argument for the extension, modification or reversal of existing law." The attorney's or party's signature on the pleadings certifies that:

50. See chapter 8, *supra*, for detailed discussion of these affirmative defenses.
51. *See* FED. R. CIV. P. 12(h).
52. FED. R. CIV. P. 13(a).
53. FED. R. CIV. P. 12(a).

> he has read the pleading, motion, or other paper; that to the best of his knowledge, information, and belief formed after reasonable inquiry it is well grounded in fact and is warranted by existing law or a good faith argument for the extension, modification, or reversal of existing law, and that it is not interposed for any improper purpose, such as to harass or to cause unnecessary delay or needless increase in the cost of litigation.

Sanctions for violation of Rule 11 include the award of attorneys' fees, (either jointly or severally against an attorney and the client) and dismissal of the case. Bad faith is no longer a requirement for Rule 11 sanctions. More and more, courts are applying Rule 11 sanctions for the filing of baseless pleadings and motions.[54]

The Discovery Process

Discovery is just what the word suggests. One party is discovering the basis for the other side's case. Discovery is designed to prevent surprise at trial.

The test as to what constitutes proper discovery is information "reasonably calculated to lead to the discovery of admissible evidence."[55] The methods of discovery include:

1. **Interrogatories**—written questions required to be answered under oath in writing in thirty days;[56]
2. **Depositions**—oral questions and answers under oath recorded by a court reporter;[57]
3. **Document Requests**—written requests to produce documents in possession or control of the adverse party—

---

54. For recent decisions applying Rule 11, see Eastway Constr. Corp. v. City of New York, 762 F.2d 243, 253-54 (2d Cir. 1985); Giant Food v. Standard Terry Mills, Inc., 229 U.S.P.Q. 955 (T.T.A.B. 1986), *reconsideration denied*, 231 U.S.P.Q. 626 (T.T.A.B. 1986).
55. FED. R. CIV. P. 26(b)(1).
56. FED. R. CIV. P. 33.
57. FED. R. CIV. P. 31.

written responses and production required in thirty days;[58]

4. **Requests for Admissions**—written requests that the adverse party admit or deny statements or opinions of fact or the application of law to fact—written responses required in thirty days.[59]

A few words about the strategic use of these discovery tools follow.

Interrogatories Versus Depositions

Many clients expect their attorneys to serve a comprehensive set of interrogatories as the first step in the discovery process. This approach has several pitfalls.

A "boilerplate" set of interrogatories rarely advances a case. For one thing, it is fairly easy to evade the written question. There is no one around to immediately follow up with another question.

Secondly, boilerplate questions tend to distract the interrogator from the specific facts of his case. By trying to cover the waterfront, it is easy to miss the boat.[60]

Thirdly, the boilerplate has a habit of landing back on your doorstep with a big clunk. In other words, the same questions will be directed to your client. Remember the Golden Rule of Discovery: Do not do unto others what you would not do unto yourself.

Finally, by serving interrogatories as the first step, you might start your opponent thinking about his case in depth. He is forced to check out the facts and will be much better prepared with a coherent story.

---

58. FED. R. CIV. P. 34.
59. FED. R. CIV. P. 36.
60. Some courts have recognized the limited value and unwarranted burden of comprehensive interrogatories and restricted the number allowed absent a showing of good cause. In the same vein, some local rules limit the interrogatory by subject matter such as identification of witnesses. Be sure to check the local court rules on this point.

For all of these reasons, the early deposition is often the most useful discovery tool. After the deposition, then interrogatories can be served to develop specific points, *e.g.*, dates of use, dollar sales, etc.

Document Requests—Before or after Depositions

The timing of document requests will depend in part on the timetable for the case. If a preliminary injunction is being sought, you may have little choice but to demand that production take place at or before the first scheduled deposition.

Where time is less critical, consider waiting until during or after the depositions to frame your requests. Document requests, like interrogatories, start your opponent thinking about his case. He may even color his testimony to jibe with the documents. The early deposition, taken before your opponent has considered how to present the facts his way, can draw admissions that you are unlikely to get at some later stage in the proceeding. Also, the deposition may reveal the existence of records and will enable the proponent to tailor the document requests accordingly.

Don't overlook third party sources for documents and depositions. One fertile area for document requests is advertising agency files. Ad men tend to be rather explicit in their memos and may even put in writing the intent to benefit from a competitor's good will. Also, former employees and licensees may provide useful information.

Requests for Admission

The purpose of requests for admission is to avoid the burden and delay of proving the admitted statement and to narrow the issues for trial. Requests for admission cover facts and opinion as well as the genuineness of documents. Admissions are a much under-utilized discovery tool—their value in pinning down your opponent to a definite position early in the case should not be overlooked.

Requests for admission can also be helpful in establishing critical facts, such as the trademark owner's toleration of third party uses. This kind of admission can sometimes be dodged at a deposition because the witness is not aware of corporate policy or does not have knowledge of the third party uses. Admissions cannot be avoided on the basis of lack of knowledge if such knowledge is available upon reasonable inquiry to the responding party.

11

Terminating the Litigation Before Trial

Either one or both parties may be interested in the quick knock out blow or the fast settlement that could terminate the case before trial. Procedures to be considered for this purpose include:

1. Preliminary Injunction Motion;
2. Summary Judgment Motion; and
3. Offer of Judgment.

Preliminary Injunctive Relief

Preliminary injunctions are designed to afford temporary relief to trademark owners pending a full trial.[1] But since the preliminary injunction decision frequently forecasts the ultimate outcome, as a practical matter, it often ends the litigation. This is especially true if defendant is forced to select another mark while the court battle continues. Even if defendant ultimately prevails after a full trial and appeal (perhaps a year or two later), he may have little interest in changing back to his original mark.

Preliminary Injunction Standards

Preliminary injunctions are granted where:

1. Plaintiff will suffer irreparable harm (harm not compensable by money damages) during the period before trial;
2. Plaintiff has some probability of success on the merits;

1. See chapter 13, pp. 251-57, *infra*, on types of injunctive relief, *e.g.*, injunctions against use of defendant's mark, product recall, etc.

3. The harm to plaintiff resulting from denying the injunction outweighs the harm to defendant from granting the injunction; and
4. Plaintiff has moved quickly to halt the infringement.

The standard for preliminary injunctive relief is similar throughout the United States, although there are slight variations among the circuits.

A typical preliminary injunction standard is the one employed by the Second Circuit, requiring proof of:

1. irreparable harm, and either
2. likelihood of success on the merits, or sufficiently serious questions going to the merits to make them a fair ground for litigation, and a balance of hardships tipping decidedly in favor of the moving party.[2]

A number of circuits also consider the public interest, *i.e.*, any harm that the injunction might cause the public. The trademark owner should be sure his proof meets the specific test for the circuit where he has filed suit.

Irreparable Harm to Plaintiff

In trademark cases, irreparable harm is often considered the inevitable result of likely confusion.

> Where there is, then, such high probability of confusion, injury irreparable in the sense that it may not be fully compensable in damages almost inevitably follows. While an injured plaintiff would be entitled to recover the profits on the infringing items, this is often difficult to determine; moreover, a defendant may have failed to earn profits because of the poor quality of its product or its own inefficiency. Indeed, confusion may cause purchasers to refrain from buying either product and to turn to those of other competitors. Yet to prove the loss of sales due to infringement is also notoriously difficult. . . . Furthermore, if an infringer's product is

---

2. Dallas Cowboys Cheerleaders, Inc. v. Pussycat Cinema, Ltd., 604 F.2d 200, 206-07 (2d Cir. 1979).

of poor quality, or simply not worth the price, a more lasting but not readily measurable injury may be inflicted on the plaintiff's reputation in the market.[3]

Injury to plaintiff occurs even if defendant's goods are of high quality, because plaintiff has no control over the future quality of defendant's goods.

Courts readily find irreparable harm in trademark infringement cases because of the victim's inability to control the nature and quality of the infringer's goods, *Ideal Industries v. Gardner Bender, Inc., supra*, 612 F.2d at 1026, not because the infringer's goods are necessarily inferior. Even if the infringer's goods are of high quality, the victim has the right to insist that its reputation not be imperiled by another's actions. *Processed Plastics Co. v. Warner Communications, Inc.*, 675 F.2d 852, 858 (7th Cir. 1982); see also 4 R. Callman, *Unfair Competition, Trademarks and Monopolies*, § 88.3(b) at 205-06 (3rd ed. 1970). Bausch & Lomb's loss of control over its reputation justifies a finding of irreparable harm even if it could demonstrate no loss of sales or market share.[4]

While good quality will not excuse defendant's infringement, bad quality will be held against defendant. A court is naturally sympathetic to a plaintiff whose reputation stands to be harmed by the sale of shoddy merchandise under a similar mark.

There has been some waffling in the Second Circuit as to whether likely confusion is enough by itself to establish irreparable harm.[5] While some decisions have suggested that proof of actual harm beyond likelihood of confusion is required, the Second Circuit has recently reiterated: "our traditional rule that a

3. Omega Importing Corp. v. Petri-Kine Camera Co., 451 F.2d 1190, 1195 (2d Cir. 1971).

4. Wesley-Jessen Div. of Schering Corp. v. Bausch & Lomb, Inc., 698 F.2d 862, 867 (7th Cir. 1983).

5. *Compare* Citibank, N.A. v. Citytrust, 756 F.2d 273, 275-76 (2d Cir. 1985) *with* Joseph Scott Co. v. Scott Swimming Pools, Inc., 764 F.2d 62, 66 (2d Cir. 1985).

finding of irreparable harm follows from a trademark plaintiff's showing of infringing use and likelihood of confusion."[6]

Likely Success on the Merits

In assessing likely success on the merits, the court examines the same issues that determine the outcome of a full trial. These normally include trademark ownership, validity, and likelihood of confusion, as well as any affirmative defenses.

As will be seen below, the degree of likely success required for preliminary relief varies depending on how strongly the balance of harm tips in plaintiff's favor.

Balancing the Harms

Many courts employ a sliding scale in the balancing process. Only some likelihood of success is required for preliminary relief where the harm to plaintiff significantly outweighs the harm to defendant. Conversely, the more likely plaintiff is to win, the less heavily the balance of harms need weigh in his favor.[7]

The harms weighed on defendant's side include his lost investment in the mark, the effect of an injunction on defendant's overall business (is the product in issue a small or large part of his business), and damage to customer relations. For plaintiff, the countervailing harms include damage to reputation by defendant's inferior quality goods, damage to prospective business and licensing negotiations, and damage from the inability to control defendant.

Naturally, where defendant chose his mark with knowledge of plaintiff's mark, a court puts much less weight on the loss of defendant's investment.

> We also observe that "[o]ne entering a field already occupied by another has a duty to select a trademark that will avoid confusion."

---

6. Church of Scientology Int'l v. Elmira Mission of the Church of Scientology, 794 F.2d 38, 42 (2d Cir. 1986).
7. Hyatt Corp. v. Hyatt Legal Servs., 736 F.2d 1153, 1159 (7th Cir. 1984).

> Having failed in this duty, Wesley-Jessen "cannot now complain that having to mend its ways will be too expensive." *Processed Plastic v. Warner Communications, Inc., supra*, 675 F.2d at 859.[8]

Plaintiff's Speed in Seeking Preliminary Relief

A party seeking preliminary relief should move quickly. A claim of immediate and irreparable harm sounds hollow where plaintiff has sat idly by suffering this harm for months or even years before action.

> Although a particular period of delay may not rise to the level of laches and thereby bar a permanent injunction, it may still indicate an absence of the kind of irreparable harm required to support a preliminary injunction.[9]

Preliminary Injunction Procedure

Preliminary injunction motions can be filed with the complaint, shortly following the complaint or after an initial round of discovery. The motion is accompanied by affidavits, depositions, exhibits, and briefs. Most courts also hold a preliminary injunction hearing where witnesses can testify and be cross-examined.

If the injunction is granted, plaintiff will usually be required to post a bond.[10] The figure ordered by the court is designed to cover the costs and damages to defendant should it turn out the injunction was wrongfully issued.

It is also possible to combine the hearing on a motion for preliminary relief with a trial on the merits.[11] Some advantages of this procedure are speed of final disposition and saving of expense;

---

8. Wesley-Jessen Div. of Schering Corp. v. Bausch & Lomb Inc., 698 F.2d 862, 867 (7th Cir. 1983).
9. Citibank, N.A. v. Citytrust, 756 F.2d 273, 276 (2d Cir. 1985) (more than ten-week delay). *See also* Programmed Tax Sys., Inc. v. Raytheon Co., 419 F. Supp. 1251, 1255 (S.D.N.Y. 1976) (four months delay) and Le Cordon Bleu S.a.r.l. v. BPC Publishing Ltd., 327 F. Supp. 267 (S.D.N.Y. 1971) (thirteen-week delay).
10. Fed. R. Civ. P. 65(c).
11. Fed. R. Civ. P. 65(a)(2).

some disadvantages are loss of the second bite of the apple and insufficient preparation time, especially as to proof of damages and surveys.

Appeal of Preliminary Injunction

The party seeking to reverse the grant or denial of a preliminary injunction faces a heavy burden.[12] Reversal requires a showing that the lower court's findings were clearly erroneous or represented a mistake of law,[13] or that there has been a clear abuse of the lower court's discretion.[14] If the district court makes no detailed findings in support of its decision, the appeal court "must engage in a somewhat more searching review."[15]

Summary Judgment

Purpose of Summary Judgment

The purpose of summary judgment is to avoid the time and expense involved in a full proceeding by early disposal of cases "where there is no genuine issue of material fact."[16]

An issue of fact is "material" if it "affects the outcome of the litigation," and "genuine" if it is supported by "substantial" evidence "going beyond the allegations of the complaint."[17]

In deciding if genuine issues exist, the party opposing summary judgment is given the benefit of all reasonable doubt:

---

12. SK&F, Co. v. Premo Pharmaceutical Laboratories, Inc., 625 F.2d 1055, 1066 (3d Cir. 1980).
13. Atari, Inc. v. North Am. Philips Consumer Elecs. Corp., 672 F.2d 607, 613 (7th Cir. 1982).
14. California Cedar Prods. Co. v. Pine Mountain Corp., 724 F.2d 827, 828 (9th Cir. 1984).
15. Kampmeier v. Nyquist, 553 F.2d 296, 299 (2d Cir. 1977).
16. FED. R. CIV. P. 56.
17. Hahn v. Sargent, 523 F.2d 461, 464 (1st Cir. 1975), *cert. denied*, 425 U.S. 904 (1976).

> The party opposing the motion should be given the benefit of all reasonable doubt in determining whether genuine issues of material fact exist.[18]

Summary judgment is not intended as a device to weigh the evidence or decide the issues in avoidance of a full trial. On the other hand, summary judgment will not be defeated by mere conclusory allegations or denials or the presence of complex legal issues:

> —an adverse party may not rest upon mere conclusory allegations or denials. The party opposing the motion must set forth "concrete particulars," [citation omitted] and cannot make a secret of his evidence, holding it close to his chest until the trial. It is not sufficient merely to assert a conclusion without supplying supporting arguments or facts in opposition to the motion.
>
> * * *
>
> Summary judgment, however, is not necessarily precluded merely because the legal issue is complex. Indeed, the policy favoring efficient resolution of disputes, which is the cornerstone of the summary judgment procedure, would be completely undermined if unsubstantiated assertions were sufficient to compel a trial. [Citations omitted.][19]

The Modern Trend

Traditionally, likelihood of confusion, the crucial issue in trademark infringement actions, has been considered a question of fact and inappropriate for summary judgment.[20]

The modern view, however, is that summary judgment is appropriate in trademark cases where the material facts pertaining to likely confusion are not in dispute. This is true whether the jurisdiction treats the issue of likely confusion as one of law or as

---

18. Litton Indus., Inc. v. Litronix, Inc., 577 F.2d 709, 712 (C.C.P.A. 1978).
19. SEC v. Research Automation Corp., 585 F.2d 31, 32 (2d Cir. 1978).
20. Albert Dickinson Co. v. Mellos Peanut Co., 179 F.2d 265, 270 (7th Cir. 1950); American Hosp. Supply Corp. v. Advanced Health Sys., Inc., 212 U.S.P.Q. 181, 184 (N.D. Ill. 1980).

one of fact. In those jurisdictions where likely confusion is an issue of law, summary judgment will be granted if there is no dispute as to the underlying factors used to determine likely confusion.[21] Even a dispute as to one or two minor factors may not defeat summary judgment.[22]

In those jurisdictions where likelihood of confusion is purely an issue of fact, summary judgment will be granted if the undisputed evidence as to the material factors persuades the court that reasonable men could not differ on the issue of likely confusion.[23]

A number of recent cases have been decided on summary judgment and the use of this device is increasing. For example, the Court of Appeals for the Federal Circuit in the *Pure Gold* case specifically encouraged the use of summary judgment by the Trademark Trial and Appeal Board:

> The practice of the U.S. Claims Court and of the former U.S. Court of Claims in routinely disposing of numerous cases on the basis of cross-motions for summary judgment has much to commend it. The adoption of similar practice is to be encouraged in inter partes cases before the Trademark Trial and Appeal Board, which seem particularly suitable to this type of disposition.[24]

---

21. Lois Sportswear U.S.A., Inc. v. Levi Strauss & Co., 799 F.2d 867 (2d Cir. 1986); WSM, Inc. v. Tennessee Sales Co., 709 F.2d 1084 (6th Cir. 1983). See chapter 7, pp. 118-36, *supra*, for discussion of Polaroid factors used to determine likelihood of confusion issue. See chapter 13, pp. 280-81, *infra*, for identification of those jurisdictions where likely confusion is issue of fact and those jurisdictions where it is issue of law.
22. Programmed Tax Sys., Inc. v. Raytheon Co., 439 F. Supp. 1128, 1132 (S.D.N.Y. 1977).
23. Pignons S.A. de Mecanique de Precision v. Polaroid Corp., 498 F. Supp. 805 (D. Mass. 1980), *aff'd*, 657 F.2d 482 (1st Cir. 1981).
24. Pure Gold, Inc. v. Syntex (U.S.A.), Inc., 739 F.2d 624, 627 n.2 (Fed. Cir. 1984).

Cases Where Summary Judgment Granted and Denied

Completeness of Record

Summary judgment has been granted where there has been extensive discovery, the basic facts are not contested, and the record requires no enlargement by trial. The completeness of the record was noted in the *ITT* XTRA case:

> The parties have compiled an extensive record of pleadings, depositions, affidavits, exhibits, and memoranda. On this record, a record which is not likely to be helpfully enlarged by a trial, I find that there is no genuine dispute of material fact.[25]

On the other hand, if a jury trial is in the offing, a court may be reluctant to decide the issue of likely confusion without a trial.[26] Or a court may feel that the record will benefit from additional evidence introduced at trial.[27]

Relationship Between Goods

Summary judgment has been granted where there is no close relationship between plaintiff's and defendant's goods. The theory is that no matter how the other factors are weighed, the remoteness between the goods prevents likely confusion.

Cases receiving summary disposition primarily because of unrelated goods are:

> PURE GOLD shampoo versus FERMODYL PURE GOLD citrus fruits;[28]

---

25. ITT Corp. v. XTRA Corp., 225 U.S.P.Q. 723, 727 (D.Mass. 1985).
26. *See* Sun-Fun Prods. v. Suntan Research & Dev., 656 F.2d 186 (5th Cir. 1981). The District Court's grant of a directed verdict for defendant was reversed on the grounds that the jury should be permitted to weigh the similarities in appearance of the products.
27. Lord Jeff Knitting Co. v. Warnaco, Inc., 594 F. Supp. 579, 581 (S.D.N.Y. 1984).
28. Pure Gold, Inc. v. Syntex (U.S.A.), Inc., 739 F.2d 624 (Fed. Cir. 1984).

ITT EXTRA personal computer versus XTRA intermodal transportation support services;[29]

EXXON gas station versus EXXON ice cream making machines.[30]

On the other hand, where the court finds genuine issues as to the relationship of the goods or services, summary judgment has been denied.[31]

Laches

Summary judgment has been successfully invoked where there is a strong case of laches (delay in pursuit of plaintiff's claims and detrimental reliance by defendant on plaintiff's delay). Laches is less hazy and grayish than likely confusion. Summary judgment on a laches theory is especially appealing where plaintiff has delayed a very long time.[32]

Laches may become even more susceptible to summary judgment where the reasonableness of plaintiff's delay is determined by reference to an analogous statute of limitations. This approach was followed by the Sixth Circuit in the *Tandy* RADIO SHACK case. There, summary judgment for defendant based on a laches claim was reversed. The Appeal Court looked to the three-year tort statute of limitations and held that plaintiff's thirty-two-month delay was prima facie reasonable.[33]

---

29. ITT Corp. v. XTRA Corp., 225 U.S.P.Q. 723 (D. Mass. 1985).
30. Exxon Corp. v. National Foodline Corp., 579 F.2d 1244 (C.C.P.A. 1978).
31. American Int'l Group, Inc. v. London Am. Int'l Corp., 664 F.2d 348 (2d Cir. 1981) (summary judgment reversed).
32. Saratoga Vichy Spring Co. v. Lehman, 625 F.2d 1037 (2d Cir. 1980) (61 years delay); NAACP v. N.A.A.C.P. Legal Defense & Educ. Fund, 753 F.2d 131 (D.C. Cir. 1985) (almost thirteen years' delay). See chapter 8, pp. 153-64, *supra*, on laches.
33. Tandy Corp. v. Malone & Hyde, Inc., 769 F.2d 362 (6th Cir. 1985).

Trademark Validity

Summary judgment has been granted where plaintiff's mark appears inherently generic, descriptive, functional, or lacking in secondary meaning. Examples are:

LIQUID CONTROLS for meters to measure liquid flow	generic[34]
DAMN I'M GOOD for charm bracelets bearing phrase "DAMN I'M GOOD"	functional[35]
Red Heart Design on stuffed bears	descriptive and lacking in secondary meaning (sales of only 5,000 bears)[36]
Tab Design on shoes	no secondary meaning as a matter of law in light of widespread third party use[37]

By the same token, plaintiff's mark may be so "obviously" nondescriptive, that plaintiff will be granted summary judgment.[38]

On the other hand, summary judgment has been denied because of factual issues as to descriptiveness and secondary meaning. For example:

---

34. Liquid Controls, Corp. v. Liquid Control Corp., 802 F.2d 934 (7th Cir. 1986).
35. Damn I'm Good, Inc. v. Sakowitz, Inc., 514 F. Supp. 1357, 1363 (S.D.N.Y. 1981).
36. Wiley v. American Greetings Corp., 762 F.2d 139 (1st Cir. 1985).
37. Genesco, Inc. v. Levi Strauss & Co., 219 U.S.P.Q. 1205 (T.T.A.B. 1983).
38. Jeno's Inc. v. Commissioner of Patents & Trademarks, 227 U.S.P.Q. 227 (D. Minn. 1985) (PIZZA ROLLS suggestive for frozen snacks).

Sesame Crunch Cookie	Effect of third party use on secondary meaning issue of fact[39]
AHS versus AHS healthcare	Secondary meaning and likely confusion issues of fact[40]

Purchaser Sophistication

Summary judgment has been granted where purchaser sophistication and the high cost of the products compelled sufficient consumer care to make confusion unlikely.[41]

Intent

Where bad intent is critical to plaintiff's case, summary judgment is routinely refused.[42] But where infringement is "obvious," for reasons including defendant's intent, summary judgment has been granted.[43]

Res Judicata and Collateral Estoppel

Res judicata and collateral estoppel claims are especially suited to summary judgment since they raise issues of law, not fact. Res judicata means that the same thing cannot be litigated by the same party more than once.

---

39. The Nestle Co., Inc. v. Toyva Corp., 227 U.S.P.Q. 477 (T.T.A.B. 1985).
40. American Hosp. Supply Corp. v. Advanced Health Sys., Inc., 212 U.S.P.Q. 181 (N.D. Ill. 1980).
41. Pignons S.A. de Mecanique de Precision v. Polaroid Corp., 498 F. Supp. 805 (D. Mass. 1980), *aff'd*, 657 F.2d 482 (1st Cir. 1981).
42. Lord Jeff Knitting Co. v. Warnaco, Inc., 225 U.S.P.Q. 671, 672 (S.D.N.Y. 1984).
43. Rolls-Royce Motors, Ltd. v. A & A Fiberglass, Inc., 428 F. Supp. 689 (N.D. Ga. 1977); Vaudable v. Montmartre, Inc., 123 U.S.P.Q. 357, 193 N.Y.S.2d 332 (Sup. Ct. 1959).

One aspect of res judicata, termed "claim preclusion," prohibits a party from bringing the same action under different theories when those theories could have been raised in the first action.

Another aspect of res judicata is "issue preclusion," also known as collateral estoppel.[44] Collateral estoppel is where the identical legal issue has already been decided in prior litigation involving the same parties.[45] For example, in *J.I. Case*, the legal issue of applicant's right to register had already been decided adversely to applicant in a prior opposition proceeding involving essentially the same mark for the same goods. Summary judgment was granted refusing registration on the grounds of collateral estoppel.[46]

One problem with collateral estoppel in trademark cases is that "trademark rights are not static."[47] A mark that has not achieved secondary meaning at one point in time may, after additional years of use, come to achieve secondary meaning.[48]

Market conditions relevant to the issue of likely confusion can also change significantly over time:

> The CCPA decision was based on the likelihood of confusion by consumers in the market as it appeared in the early 1970's. Since that time the markets, consumers, volume of business and advertising of the parties have changed significantly. The CCPA's determination of likelihood of confusion may be totally irrelevant in this new environment. It would be unfair to award summary judgment on collateral estoppel grounds without some findings of fact as to likelihood of confusion at this time.[49]

---

44. *See* Chromalloy Am. Corp. v. Kenneth Gordon, Ltd., 736 F.2d 694, 696-97 (Fed. Cir. 1984).
45. EZ Loader Boat Trailers, Inc. v. Cox Trailers, Inc., 568 F. Supp. 1229, 1230 (N.D. Ill. 1983).
46. J.I. Case Co. v. F.L. Indus., Inc., 229 U.S.P.Q. 697 (T.T.A.B. 1986).
47. *In re* Morton-Norwich Prods., Inc., 671 F.2d 1332, 1344 (C.C.P.A. 1982).
48. Old Grantian Co. v. William Grant & Sons Ltd., 361 F.2d 1018, 1022-23 (1966).
49. Plus Prods. v. Natural Organics, Inc., 223 U.S.P.Q. 27, 28 (S.D.N.Y. 1984).

Generally speaking, the closer in time between the litigations, the more difficult it will be to show a factual change sufficient to avoid collateral estoppel. However, one court has refused to find collateral estoppel where only a few months separated the two actions:

> While a relatively short period of time has expired since the previous litigation, there is no basis to hold that a party is precluded as a matter of law from demonstrating that secondary meaning can be acquired within a few months. Indeed, in this day of modern communications it is frequently the case that a particular product or name becomes familiar to many consumers overnight and the question of whether secondary meaning exists is dependent on a variety of factual questions and determinations.[50]

Dilution

A dilution claim is also a good bet for summary judgment since it is not necessary to prove likely confusion.[51] Whether the issues of distinctiveness and dilution can be decided on summary judgment will depend on what, if any, material facts are in dispute.[52]

Summary

The sampling of summary judgments granted and denied suggests that if your case is strong enough, no single issue will preclude summary relief. And if you have a clear cut claim such as laches or entirely unrelated goods, by all means go for it!

---

50. Metro Kane Imports, Inc. v. Federated Dep't Stores, 625 F. Supp. 313, 315 (S.D.N.Y. 1985), *aff'd*, No. 86-7104, slip op. (2d Cir. Mar. 22, 1986).
51. *See* L.L. Bean, Inc. v. Drake Publishers, Inc., 228 U.S.P.Q. 733 (D. Me. 1986).
52. See chapter 7, pp. 143-46, *supra*, on elements of dilution cause of action.

Offer of Judgment

After a little discovery, defendant may see the handwriting on the wall. But, even though defendant is ready to end the battle, plaintiff will not always accept a reasonable surrender. In this situation, defendant should consider making an offer of judgment. Rule 68 of the Federal Rules of Civil Procedure provides that if the offer made is not accepted and the judgment awarded at the end of trial is not more favorable than the offer, the offeree must pay the costs incurred after the offer. Costs, which may include trial transcripts and expert witness fees, can add up. Even if costs are not significant, the offer may cause the offeree to realistically assess his position before he invests further in the case. And before long, more teeth may be added to the offer of judgment. There is a proposal to change the rule to require the offeree to pay the attorney's fees incurred by the offeror after the offer.

12

Proving the Fundamentals at Trial

Choosing Your Witnesses and Exhibits

A trial is not a mechanical exercise—it is or should be high drama. The object is to persuade the audience (be it judge or jury) of the merits of your case. In order to persuade, you must hold the attention of the audience and your witnesses must be credible.

Trial counsel should interview potential witnesses in advance. The witnesses should have knowledge of the subject matter and exhibit convincing demeanor. The witnesses should not be argumentative or cute. They should believe in their case. Test the ability of the witnesses to stand up to cross-examination before making a final selection.

Also, keep in mind that you are trying to impress the court with the importance of your case. Be sure to have at least one witness who ranks high in the corporate hierarchy. For example, plaintiff's president can testify as to the damage caused by defendant's use.

The right exhibits can go a long way to getting your point across. Pictures have always spoken louder than words. If defendant has copied plaintiff's logo or type style, a blowup comparison or overlay of the two marks will make the point. And by all means, try to place your graphic exhibit where it is visible throughout the trial.

Overall Presentation

In presenting your client's case, anticipate the other side's defense. Do not let defendant make it look like you are hiding an important fact that does not support your case. Let your witness report the good news and put the best face on the bad news.

Place your best foot forward. First impressions count. If key evidence must come from adversary witnesses, call them as part of your own case. Do not save a telling point for cross-examination if it can be made early on. If you wait, the trier of fact may have already formed an unfavorable opinion that could be difficult to change.

Keep it simple. If you have half a dozen theories, choose the strongest one or two. Choose the theory that permits your entire case to hang together. While alternative pleading is permissible under the rules, a consistent story is more believable.

Proving Trademark Ownership

Plaintiff must prove he is the first user of the mark. This can be done through the introduction of documentary material such as purchase orders, invoices, catalogs, advertising, and promotional literature.

Much of this material constitutes records kept in the ordinary course of business and is admissible under the Federal Rules of Evidence as an exception to the hearsay rule. The documentary evidence should be accompanied by live testimony from the custodian of plaintiff's records or "other qualified witness."[1] In addition, there should be testimony by persons familiar with plaintiff's marketplace.

This is also an area where a federal registration earns its keep. The registration provides a presumption that use in commerce was made at least as early as the filing date of the application.[2] The registration also provides a presumption that the registrant owns the mark and has the exclusive right to use the mark on the goods specified in the registration.[3]

1. FED. R. EVID. 803(6); Yamada Int'l v. Hoshino Gakki Co., 231 U.S.P.Q. 926 (T.T.A.B. 1986).
2. Rolley, Inc. v. Younghusband, 204 F.2d 209, 210-11 (9th Cir. 1953).
3. 15 U.S.C. § 1057(b).

Proving Trademark Validity

The owner of an unregistered mark has the burden of proving that his mark is valid. The proof required to carry this burden depends on the type of mark. This brings us back to the arbitrary-suggestive-descriptive-generic classifications.[4]

Arbitrary or fanciful marks (with no relationship to the goods) as well as suggestive marks (requiring imagination to reach a conclusion as to the nature of the goods) are protectable without proof of secondary meaning.[5] Descriptive marks (that immediately convey to the purchaser the nature or use of the goods), require proof of secondary meaning. Generic marks (regarded by purchasers as the common name for the goods) cannot be valid trademarks.[6]

Presumption of Validity

A federal registration creates a presumption of trademark validity that may carry plaintiff's burden of proof. But it would be very risky to rely on the registration alone.

Regardless of how the court is likely to classify his mark, plaintiff should be prepared to introduce evidence of public recognition akin to secondary meaning. This is because: 1) the better known a mark is, the more important it is to plaintiff's business and the easier it will be to show that defendant's use has damaged plaintiff; and 2) the better known a mark is, the stronger it is and the easier it will be to achieve a wide scope of protection.

---

4. Abercrombie & Fitch Co. v. Hunting World, Inc., 537 F.2d 4 (2d Cir. 1976); *see* chapter 2, pp. 17-23, *supra*.
5. Abercrombie & Fitch Co. v. Hunting World, Inc., 537 F.2d 4, 11 (2d Cir. 1976). *See* chapter 2, pp. 17-23, *supra*.
6. C.L.A.S.S. Promotions, Inc. v. D.S. Magazines, Inc., 753 F.2d 14, 16 (2d Cir. 1985).

Proving Secondary Meaning

There are two types of proof of secondary meaning (consumer association of the mark with a single source):

1. proof showing plaintiff's efforts to establish secondary meaning (inferential proof); and
2. proof showing the impact made by plaintiff's efforts (direct proof).

Inferential proof of secondary meaning includes:

- long use;
- extensive sales, *e.g.*, dollars, units, and geographical coverage;
- advertising dollar expenditures;
- sample ads from various media;
- circulation figures for advertising media used;
- trade show and point of purchase displays;
- advertising by customers;
- copying by defendant.[7]

Sometimes courts will rely on inferential proof to find secondary meaning. Sometimes courts look for direct evidence—evidence showing that the public actually does associate the mark with a single source.[8]

Direct evidence of secondary meaning includes:

- unsolicited publicity (*e.g.*, editorial comment or news articles);
- licenses and requests for licenses;
- consumer correspondence;

---

7. For discussions on proving secondary meaning, see Harlequin Enters., Ltd. v. Gulf & Western Corp., 644 F.2d 946, 950 (2d Cir. 1981); Isaly Co. v. Kraft, Inc., 619 F. Supp. 983, 990-91 (M.D. Fla. 1985), *aff'd in part, rev'd in part*, 805 F.2d 974 (11th Cir. 1986).
8. American Footwear Corp. v. General Footwear Co., 609 F.2d 655, 663 (2d Cir. 1979).

- testimony by consumers;
- survey evidence.

Survey evidence on secondary meaning is particularly important in product appearance cases.[9] A court may be initially reluctant to grant trademark protection for product appearance. A survey can go a long way toward persuading a court that consumers associate the appearance of plaintiff's product with a single source.

Proving Likelihood of Confusion

Proof as to likely confusion should be geared to the factors pertinent to this issue.[10] These factors and the type of evidence relevant to each factor are summarized as follows:

Factor: The Strength of the Mark

- derivation of the mark—*e.g.*, its history as a coined or arbitrary word;
- absence of mark from dictionaries;
- advertising and sales figures for products bearing the mark;
- unsolicited publicity referring to the mark;
- consumer correspondence referring to the mark;
- absence of third party use (shown through Nexis search and testimony by others in the field).

Factor: Similarities Between the Marks

- physical samples of the products;

9. Metro Kane Imports, Ltd. v. Rowoco, Inc., 618 F. Supp. 273, 276 (S.D.N.Y. 1985) (survey "highly desirable, if not essential, evidentiary data").
10. For detailed discussion of factors considered by the courts in determining likely confusion, see chapter 7, pp. 117-37, *supra*.

- photos showing defendant's and plaintiff's products interspersed on the shelves;
- promotion of the marks apart from their packaging, *e.g.*, supermarket shelf-talkers, newspaper ads, radio ads;
- correspondence abbreviating or misspelling the marks so as to make them more similar;
- expert testimony as to linguistics or lexicography regarding similarity in appearance, meaning, or sound.[11]

Factor: Proximity and Marketing of the Products

- testimony as to channels of trade and customers;
- displays in same stores or same sections of stores;
- advertising in same media;
- expert testimony re selling environment.[12]

Factor: Likelihood of Bridging the Gap

- plaintiff's plans to expand into defendant's line of business —the more concrete the better (*e.g.*, memos on discussions and actions taken);
- plaintiff's previous activities in defendant's line of business;
- existence of companies that make both plaintiff's and defendant's products.

Factor: Defendant's Bad Faith Adoption

- defendant's knowledge of plaintiff's mark, *e.g.*, through search reports or marketplace;

---

11. Pathfinder Communications Corp. v. Midwest Communications Co., 593 F. Supp. 281, 294 (N.D. Ind. 1984).
12. Playboy Enters., Inc. v. Chuckleberry Publishing, Inc., 486 F. Supp. 414, 429 (S.D.N.Y. 1980).

- defendant's copying of package design, type style, or other elements from plaintiff;
- advertising agency memos regarding association of defendant's mark with plaintiff's well-known mark;
- instructions to designer to imitate plaintiff's package;
- defendant's proceeding after knowledge of plaintiff's objection.

Factor: Quality of Defendant's Products

- expert analysis of parties' products—comparison showing inferiority of defendant's products as to performance, materials, etc.;
- customer complaints regarding defendant's products.

Factor: Consumer Sophistication and Care

- price range of products (inexpensive products subject to "impulse," less careful purchase);
- purchase environment, *e.g.*, studies as to time taken to select product in supermarket;
- characteristics of typical buyer—*e.g.*, education level, professional expertise;
- expert testimony of professionals in field as to care exercised by average consumers.[13]

Factor: Actual Confusion

- testimony by consumers who were confused;
- testimony and documents showing misdirected mail, mistaken purchase orders, misdirected phone calls;
- testimony by investigators who shopped stores and asked for plaintiff's product but were given defendant's product.

13. McGregor-Doniger Inc. v. Drizzle, Inc., 599 F.2d 1126, 1138 (2d Cir. 1979).

Especially where evidence of actual confusion is lacking, plaintiff should consider a survey to demonstrate likely confusion. The judicial attitude toward surveys has moved 180 degrees in the last decade. While many courts used to exclude survey evidence as inadmissible hearsay or give it little weight, surveys are now generally looked on as significant evidence. Some courts have even gone so far as to draw negative inferences from the absence of survey evidence.[14] So let's take a look at how a survey used for litigation should be conducted.

Survey Evidence

Survey Procedure

To be persuasive, a survey must be conducted under rigorous standards. In summary:

1. The survey must be designed by an independent expert, not by the attorneys or client;
2. The relevant "universe" (purchasers and prospective purchasers of the products) must be surveyed;
3. A representative sample of the universe must be selected by some unbiased procedure;
4. The questions asked must be clear, precise, and nonleading;
5. The survey should reflect the consumer environment;
6. The survey should be conducted by trained interviewers who have no knowledge of the litigation or the purpose for which the survey is conducted; and

---

14. Information Clearing House v. Find Magazine, 492 F. Supp. 147, 160 (S.D.N.Y. 1980); Eagle Snacks, Inc. v. Nabisco Brands, Inc., 625 F. Supp. 571, 583 (D.N.J. 1985).

7. The data must be accurately reported and analyzed in accordance with accepted statistical principles.[15]

Some dos and don'ts to keep in mind if you are conducting or attacking a survey are reviewed below.

Hiring an Expert

It is critical that the survey be designed by an independent expert. A survey prepared by the attorney or the client's marketing department is automatically subject to claims of bias.[16] Surveys for litigation are a breed apart and an expert with experience in the design and use of surveys for court proceedings is a must.

The qualified expert will know that he is not setting out to prove likely confusion or no likely confusion—but to test whether there is likelihood of confusion. The qualified expert will also be attuned to the common criticisms of surveys used in litigation and will be equipped to avoid or meet these criticisms.

Remember that the survey expert will be testifying in court and he should be credible, intelligible, and professional. Also, the attorneys' communications with the survey expert will not be protected by attorney-client privilege.

The Relevant Universe

The universe is the portion of the population with certain characteristics pertinent to the question being tested. The relevant universe for the usual trademark survey comprises purchasers and potential purchasers of the products in issue.

The universe may be limited by sex, age, geography, or any other characteristic of the typical purchaser of the goods. A proper

15. *See* MANUAL FOR COMPLEX LITIGATION, 116 (5th ed. 1981); Toys "R" Us, Inc. v. Canarsie Kiddie Shop, Inc., 559 F. Supp. 1189, 1204-05 (E.D.N.Y. 1983).
16. Hershey Foods Corp. v. Cerreta, 195 U.S.P.Q. 246, 256 (T.T.A.B. 1977); Boehringer Ingelheim, GmbH v. Pharmadyne Laboratories, 532 F. Supp. 1040, 1057-58 (D.N.J. 1980).

survey will screen out people who don't display the pertinent characteristics with introductory questions.

Surveys have been criticized where the universe excluded potential purchasers[17] or purchasers of defendant's product.[18]

Sampling the Universe

It is an expensive proposition to test all the prospective purchasers in the relevant universe. Sampling procedures are designed to get a group whose reactions are representative of the universe as a whole.

A truly representative sample may also be prohibitively expensive, especially where the products are nationally distributed consumer items. Accordingly, various sampling procedures whose results cannot be statistically projected to the entire universe are frequently employed.

A common sampling method is the quota-intercept procedure. Here, a specific number of consumers are interviewed at certain locales, *e.g.*, shopping malls. If the locales are distributed geographically (say in three different parts of the country), a sample of 200 consumers per locale should give the court meaningful results.[19]

The Questionnaire

The questionnaire must be devoid of leading questions, *i.e.*, questions that suggest the desired answer. Examples of criticized leading questions are:

> Do you think Manhattan, Inc. magazine might be a regional version of Inc. Magazine?[20]

---

17. Universal City Studios, Inc. v. Nintendo Co., Ltd., 746 F.2d 112, 118 (2d Cir. 1984), *aff'd*, 797 F.2d 70 (2d Cir. 1986).
18. Amstar v. Domino's Pizza, Inc., 615 F.2d 252, 264 (5th Cir. 1980).
19. *See* Scotch Whisky Ass'n v. Consolidated Distilled Prods., Inc., 210 U.S.P.Q. 639, 641 (N.D. Ill. 1981).
20. Inc. Publishing Corp. v. Manhattan Magazine, Inc., 616 F. Supp. 370, 391 (S.D.N.Y. 1985).

> To the best of your knowledge, was the Donkey Kong game made with approval or under the authority of the people who produce the King Kong movies?[21]

These questions were considered leading because the respondents were presented with particular similarities or associations rather than allowed to arrive at them on their own. The court in *Donkey Kong* stated:

> The participants were presented with the Donkey Kong—King Kong connection rather than permitted to make their own associations. When the participants were asked "As far as you know, who makes Donkey Kong?" not one suggested Universal or the makers of the King Kong movies.[22]

The court in *Inc. Magazine* also noted how to avoid leading questions:

> To avoid leading questions in the instant case, the respondents could have been asked to consider a group of magazines, and then asked:
>
> "Do you think there is any relationship between any of these magazines? Which ones? What is the relationship?" The answers to these or comparable questions would have constituted the unconditioned, unfettered opinion of the respondents' minds.[23]

In the *Wuv's* restaurant case, we find these examples:

Leading:	Do you believe that this restaurant is connected or related to any other restaurants?
Nonleading:	What company or person do you believe owns or operates this restaurant?[24]

---

21. Universal City Studios, Inc. v. Nintendo Co., Ltd., 746 F.2d 112, 118 (2d Cir. 1984), *aff'd*, 797 F.2d 70 (2d Cir. 1986).
22. *Id.*
23. Inc. Publishing Corp. v. Manhattan Magazine, Inc., 616 F. Supp. 370, 394 (S.D.N.Y. 1985).
24. Wuv's Int'l, Inc. v. Love's Enters., Inc., 208 U.S.P.Q. 736, 755 (D. Colo. 1980).

The leading question suggested that a connection did exist with another restaurant.

Questions designed to test secondary meaning were discussed in the *Canfield* CHOCOLATE FUDGE case.[25] Defendant attempted to show the absence of secondary meaning in CHOCOLATE FUDGE for a flavored beverage by showing plaintiff's can and asking:

> What do the words "Chocolate Fudge" on this can indicate to you?

The court scorned defendant's approach, stating:

> It is really absurd to show someone a can with the word "Canfield's" (in large bold lettering) cheek-by-jowl with the words "Chocolate Fudge" (in prominent but slightly smaller type), ask the subject what the words "Chocolate Fudge" mean to him or her, and draw a negative inference when the answer does not come back "Canfield's." Surely the interviewee could rationally—indeed would most normally—respond in a manner that did not parrot what was so patent from the exhibited product itself: that the product was produced by (and therefore associated with) Canfield. At a minimum, no probative conclusion whatever can be drawn from the paucity of "Canfield's" answers to survey question 2.[26]

The *Canfield* court offered the following question as an example of the correct approach:

> Do you associate [claimed trademark] with [product identification] of one, or more than one, company?[27]

Questionnaires that call for guessing on the part of the respondent are also subject to criticism. In the *Inc. Magazine* case, the court noted its distrust of the word "might." "'Might' suggests what is *possible* not what is *probable* or *likely*."[28] One way of

25. A.J. Canfield Co. v. Vess Beverages, Inc., 612 F. Supp. 1081, 1092 (N.D. Ill. 1985), *aff'd*, 796 F.2d 903 (7th Cir. 1986).
26. *Id.* 612 F. Supp. at 1092-93.
27. *Id.* 612 F. Supp. at 1093.
28. Inc. Publishing Corp. v. Manhattan Magazine, Inc., 616 F. Supp. 370, 393 (S.D.N.Y. 1985).

avoiding this problem (in addition to avoiding the word "might") is to state in the questionnaire that the respondent should not guess.

Bias may also creep into a survey through the preliminary questions. Where the party's trademark is the correct answer to a preceding question, the respondent may be conditioned to provide this name to the critical question.[29]

The Consumer Environment

The more remote the survey is from actual marketplace conditions, the less persuasive it will be. For example, telephone surveys where the respondent cannot see the products in question eliminate what may be significant stimuli for the consumer.

> The survey was conducted by telephone; consequently the respondents were unable to examine the packages.[30]

While a survey designed to test likelihood of confusion will be more persuasive where respondents are shown the package just as it appears in the marketplace, this does not hold true for a survey designed to test secondary meaning. In a secondary meaning survey, it may be necessary to mask over plaintiff's company name or other cues of origin on plaintiff's package to test if respondents associate the mark by itself with a single source:

> Creating a "prop" for a secondary meaning survey should not be confused with failing to replicate the market place in a likelihood of confusion survey. Deleting plaintiff's name from a product or package is necessary in determining whether or not some other claimed indicia [sic] of origin possesses secondary meaning. By contrast, masking defendant's name in a likelihood of confusion survey eliminates a cue as to the origin of a product which might reduce the level of confusion in an actual purchasing situation.[31]

---

29. Henri's Food Prod. Co. v. Kraft, Inc., 717 F.2d 352, 356-57 (7th Cir. 1983).
30. Thompson Medical Co. v. Pfizer, Inc., 753 F.2d 208, 211 n.2 (2d Cir. 1985).
31. Palladino, *Techniques for Ascertaining If There Is Secondary Meaning*, 73 TRADEMARK REP. 391, 395 (1983) quoted with approval in A.J. Canfield

Reflecting marketplace conditions calls for care as to the survey locale. Surveys done at home may be faulted for not capturing the purchaser in a buying mood.[32] On the other hand, surveys conducted in the store where the respondent can see the product in issue as he is being surveyed have also drawn fire.[33]

Surveys outside the store where the products are sold seem to be a good bet. Just be sure the interviewers do not wander. One survey was criticized in part because an interviewer moved from outside the retail location to a nearby bowling alley.[34]

Professional Unbiased Interviewers

Professional interviewers should be carefully selected and trained.[35] The survey expert should prepare written interviewer instructions, which will be introduced in evidence along with the survey. The interviewers should not deviate from the instructions and should conduct practice interviews so that any improper techniques (*e.g.*, departing from the questionnaire) can be nipped in the bud.

It is vital that the interviewers not know the purpose of the survey or the client sponsoring the survey. The interviewers should be warned not to engage in speculation on the subject.[36]

Co. v. Vess Beverages, Inc., 612 F. Supp. 1081, 1093 (N.D. Ill. 1985); *aff'd*, 796 F.2d 903 (7th Cir. 1986).

32. American Luggage Works v. United States Trunk Co., 158 F. Supp. 50, 53 (D. Mass. 1957), *aff'd*, 259 F.2d 69, 77 (1st Cir. 1958).
33. Marcalus Mfg. Co. v. Watson, 156 F. Supp. 161, 164 (D.D.C. 1957), *aff'd*, 258 F.2d 151 (D.C. Cir. 1958).
34. Toys "R" Us, Inc. v. Canarsie Kiddie Shop, Inc., 559 F. Supp. 1189, 1204 (E.D.N.Y. 1983).
35. Survey conducted by college students condemned in General Motors Corp. v. Cadillac Marine & Boat Co., 226 F. Supp. 716, 734 (W.D. Mich. 1964).
36. Toys "R" Us, Inc. v. Canarsie Kiddie Shop, Inc., 559 F. Supp. 1189, 1204 (E.D.N.Y. 1983).

Accurate Tabulation, Analysis, and Verification

Your survey expert, like your other witnesses, must be credible. His credibility and independence will be suspect if his tabulation and analysis distort the results.[37]

It is important to verify the survey results. This can be accomplished by a supervisor's call backs to a certain percent of respondents to confirm they were in fact interviewed. It is also helpful if a field supervisor or the designer observes a sample of interviews in process so they can testify that the interviewers did follow instructions.

Ideally, the designers, field supervisor, and interviewers will testify in court as to each phase of the survey. Practically, it may only be necessary for the designer to testify at trial. If testimony from other survey personnel is necessary, the parties may stipulate to use deposition testimony to save trial time. Or the parties may stipulate that the testimony of one interviewer reflects the practices of all interviewers.

Assessing the Survey Results

Assuming your survey is properly designed, conducted and analyzed, what results will be considered persuasive?

With regard to secondary meaning, ranges of association with a single source from 30.5 percent and above have been considered sufficient.[38] A 25 percent association with a single source has been held insufficient proof of secondary meaning.[39]

37. A.J. Canfield Co. v. Vess Beverage, Inc., 612 F. Supp. 1081, 1092 (N.D. Ill. 1985), *aff'd*, 796 F.2d 903 (7th Cir. 1986).
38. Henri's Food Prod. Co. v. Kraft, Inc., 717 F.2d 353, 362 n.2 (7th Cir. 1983).
39. Zippo Mfg. Co. v. Rogers Imports, Inc., 216 F. Supp. 670, 689 (S.D.N.Y. 1963).

With regard to likelihood of confusion, ranges from 7.7 percent to 25 percent have been held sufficient to support likely confusion.[40] A 7.6 percent confusion figure has been held to weigh against a finding of infringement.[41]

40. Grotrian, Helfferich, Schulz, Th. Steinweg Nachf v. Steinway & Sons, 365 F. Supp. 707, 716 (S.D.N.Y. 1973) (7.7%, 8.5%); Jockey Int'l, Inc. v. Burkard, 185 U.S.P.Q. 201, 205 (S.D. Cal. 1975) (11.4%); Seven-Up Co. v. Green Mill Beverage Co., 191 F. Supp. 32, 36 (N.D. Ill. 1961) (25%); Humble Oil & Refining Co. v. American Oil Co., 259 F. Supp. 559, 564 (E.D. Mo. 1966) (18%); Simoniz Co. v. Stumpmier, 117 U.S.P.Q. 130, 131 (E.D. Ill. 1957) (18%, 24%); James Burrough Ltd. v. Sign of the Beefeater, Inc., 540 F.2d 266, 278 (7th Cir. 1976) (15%); RJR Foods, Inc. v. White Rock Corp., 201 U.S.P.Q. 578, 581 (S.D.N.Y. 1978), *aff'd*, 603 F.2d 1058, 1061 (2d Cir. 1979) (15-20%).

41. Henri's Food Prod. Co. v. Kraft, Inc., 717 F.2d 352, 359 (7th Cir. 1983).

13

Enforcing Trademark Rights: Available Remedies

Injunctive relief is the traditional remedy for trademark infringement, although in some cases monetary relief will also be awarded. This chapter discusses the circumstances calling for injunctive and monetary relief, as well as other remedies available in trademark actions. Each remedy is treated in a separate section as follows:

1. Injunctive Relief;
2. Monetary Relief;
3. Cancellation of Trademark Registration;
4. Barring Importation;
5. Criminal Penalties; and
6. Declaratory Judgment of Noninfringement.

Injunctive Relief

The beauty of injunctive relief is its flexibility. The Lanham Act provides that the courts "shall have the power to grant injunctions, according to the principles of equity and upon such terms as the court may deem reasonable."[1]

Injunctive relief may take a variety of forms, such as:

1. prohibition against defendant's infringing use;
2. recall of infringing items;
3. disclaimer of association with plaintiff;

1. 15 U.S.C. § 1116.

4. corrective advertising; and
5. contempt order to enforce compliance with injunction.

Injunctions Prohibiting Infringing Use

Injunctions prohibiting defendant's infringing use are a common form of equitable relief. Injunctions may be granted preliminarily (in advance of trial) or permanently (after trial). Preliminary injunctions require proof that plaintiff will suffer irreparable harm (injury not fully compensable in damages) before trial can be held—with the harm to plaintiff outweighing any irreparable harm to defendant—and likely success on the merits.[2]

Permanent injunctions are granted to prevent damage to the trademark owner and to protect the public from confusion. Likelihood of confusion, irreparable harm, plus a balance of equities tipping in favor of plaintiff are the prerequisites for permanent injunctive relief.[3]

The injunction may allow defendant to use up existing stock[4] or require defendant to deliver up and destroy all material bearing his infringing mark.[5] The injunction may prohibit defendant from filling existing orders or even require defendant to notify customers of their right to cancel and receive a refund.[6] The injunction may also direct defendant to request the telephone company to remove defendant's mark from yellow page advertising and business listings.[7]

---

2. See chapter 11, pp. 219-24, *supra*, on standards for granting preliminary injunctive relief.
3. Vitaroz Corp. v. Borden, Inc., 644 F.2d 960, 965-69 (2d Cir. 1981).
4. W.E. Bassett Co. v. Revlon, Inc., 354 F.2d 868, 872 (2d Cir. 1966), *aff'd in part, rev'd in part*, 435 F.2d 656, 660 (2d Cir. 1970).
5. 15 U.S.C. § 1118.
6. Visa Int'l Serv. Ass'n v. Bankcard Holders of Am., 211 U.S.P.Q. 28, 33 (N.D. Cal. 1981).
7. Blue Cross & Blue Shield Ass'n v. Blue Cross Mutual Clinic, Inc., 227 U.S.P.Q. 474, 477 (S.D. Fla. 1985).

It is customary to require defendant to file with the court a written report setting forth the action he has taken to comply with the injunction.

Product Recall

The court may order defendant to recall infringing items that have already been distributed. Product recall is by no means routine, but will be granted when necessary to redress the infringement.

In the *Perfect Fit* case, the District Court ordered defendant to send a letter to his customers requesting return of the infringing merchandise. The Second Circuit held that the recall order was well within the District Court's broad equity powers. The balancing process employed by the Court in ruling on product recall is revealed in the following passage:

> We conclude that this was an appropriate case for the exercise of the court's power to require a recall. The district court found that Acme had intentionally copied Perfect Fit's trade dress, and on appeal we held that, as a matter of law, Acme's trade dress was likely to cause confusion among customers, see 618 F.2d at 954-55. Acme's infringing trade dress was therefore likely to divert customers from Perfect Fit's product to Acme's. Particularly because the first appeal had prolonged the litigation and therefore increased the probable injury to Perfect Fit, the district court was entirely justified in fashioning swift and complete relief for Perfect Fit. The recall procedure would naturally hasten the removal of the offending materials from public view and therefore seek to end quickly the injury to Perfect Fit.
>
> Acme's argument that the recall provision is unduly burdensome is unpersuasive. Of course, a district court should carefully consider the likely burden and expense of a recall before it imposes the remedy. In some circumstances the imposition of a recall may be unduly onerous, as where the defendant's products are widely distributed and particularly expensive to ship. Or the probable benefit to the plaintiff from a recall may not outweigh the burden to the defendant in some cases even if that burden is relatively

light. These are matters to be weighed in the first instance by the district court, and we see no abuse here of the district court's discretion.[8]

Disclaimers of Association

Disclaimers are statements designed to minimize confusion by advising the consumer that defendant's product is not made or authorized by plaintiff.

Disclaimers as a form of relief for trademark infringement are usually confined to situations where defendant has a strong equitable interest in his continued use of the infringing mark. For example, disclaimers have been ordered where:

- The dispute involved the personal name of family members and the court recognized defendant's interest in using his own name;[9]
- Defendant had invested substantial sums in his mark which he had adopted in good faith;[10]
- The parties had adopted a previously abandoned mark within a few days of each other;[11] and
- Plaintiff had delayed in bringing suit.[12]

Courts have rejected disclaimers as a method of preventing confusion where:

8. Perfect Fit Indus., Inc. v. Acme Quilting Co., 646 F.2d 800, 807 (2d Cir. 1981).
9. Taylor Wine Co. v. Bully Hill Vineyards, Inc., 569 F.2d 731, 735 (2d Cir. 1978).
10. Mushroom Makers, Inc. v. R.G. Barry Corp., 441 F. Supp. 1220, 1234 (S.D.N.Y. 1977), *aff'd*, 580 F.2d 44, 49 (2d Cir. 1978), *cert. denied*, 439 U.S. 1116 (1979).
11. Manhattan Indus., Inc. v. Sweater Bee by Banff, Ltd., 627 F.2d 628, 651 (2d Cir. 1980).
12. Grenadier Corp. v. Grenadier Realty Corp., 568 F. Supp. 502, 507 (S.D.N.Y. 1983).

- Only a complete prohibition of defendant's infringing use would sufficiently remedy the wrong;[13]
- The disclaimer would not be noticed;[14]
- The disclaimer would not tell the purchaser which product is the product he is seeking, *e.g.*, which Dobbs hat is "his" Dobbs hat.[15]
- The disclaimer was not permanently affixed to the goods, *i.e.*, it was applied to nonpermanent hang tags;[16]
- Survey evidence showed continued confusion even after the disclaimer was adopted;[17]
- Defendant's use of the disclaimer before suit was filed demonstrated his recognition that confusion was likely.[18]

Corrective Advertising

Corrective advertising is advertising designed to minimize confusion by pointing out there is no relationship between the parties. This kind of advertising can be run by either plaintiff or defendant.

Defendant was ordered to use corrective advertising in the *Hess* case. The District Court injunction permitted defendant to sell HESS women's shoes in the Baltimore area where plaintiff operated HESS shoe stores on condition that: 1) defendant state prominently in all his advertising for the next year that he was not affiliated with the HESS mark owned by plaintiff; and 2) defendant use the same statement on a prominent sign displayed in his show area. The Fourth Circuit upheld the injunction, noting that

---

13. Boston Professional Hockey Ass'n v. Dallas Cab & Emblem Mfg., Inc., 510 F.2d 1004, 1013 (5th Cir. 1975); *see also* Marquis Who's Who, Inc. v. North Am. Advertising Assocs., Inc., 426 F. Supp. 139, 143 n.5 (D.D.C. 1976).
14. Hat Corp. of Am. v. D.L. Davis Corp., 4 F. Supp. 613, 622 (D. Conn. 1933).
15. *Id.*
16. Le Sportsac, Inc. v. K Mart Corp., 754 F.2d 71, 79 (2d Cir. 1985).
17. Wendy's Int'l v. Big Bite, Inc., 576 F. Supp. 816, 825 (S.D. Ohio 1983).
18. Esso, Inc. v. Standard Oil Co., 98 F.2d 1, 7 (8th Cir. 1938).

the Distict Court's wide discretion in fashioning equitable relief includes the right to require corrective advertising.[19]

A plaintiff may also be awarded money to run his own advertising campaign to correct the confusion caused by defendant's use.[20]

Contempt

After getting an injunction, what does plaintiff do if defendant violates it? The answer is: plaintiff moves for contempt. In a civil contempt action, plaintiff must prove by clear and convincing evidence that defendant is in violation of the court order.[21] Plaintiff need not prove that the violation was intentional or willfull.[22] If defendant's contempt is found willful, however, plaintiff is entitled to an award of attorneys' fees.[23] Willfulness has been found where defendant did not make "every possible effort" to obey the court decree.[24]

Civil contempt remedies are intended to restore plaintiff to the position he "would have held had the injunction been obeyed."[25] This may be accomplished by a fine to compensate plaintiff for damages resulting from defendant's violation and to coerce

---

19. N. Hess' Sons v. Hess Apparel, Inc. 738 F.2d 1412 (4th Cir. 1984).
20. See this chapter, pp. 257-65, *infra*, on calculation of monetary damages for corrective advertising.
21. Hart Schaffner & Marx v. Alexander's Dep't Stores, Inc., 341 F.2d 101, 102 (2d Cir. 1965).
22. MCA, Inc. v. Wilson, 425 F. Supp. 457, 459 (S.D.N.Y. 1977).
23. Babee-Tenda Corp. v. Scharco Mfg. Co., 156 F. Supp. 582, 587 (S.D.N.Y. 1957).
24. Aspira of New York, Inc. v. Board of Educ., 423 F. Supp. 647, 651 (S.D.N.Y. 1976).
25. Vuitton et Fils S.A. v. Carousel Handbags, 592 F.2d 126, 130 (2d Cir. 1979).

defendant into future compliance with the court decree.[26] Civil contempt fines, however, may not be imposed as a penalty.[27]

The same acts may justify both civil and criminal contempt. Criminal contempt requires adherence to certain notice procedures, proof beyond a reasonable doubt, and a showing of willfulness. If criminal contempt is proven, fines may be imposed as a penalty.[28]

Monetary Relief

Monetary relief is by no means routinely awarded in trademark infringement actions. Under the Lanham Act, monetary relief, *i.e.*, profits, damages, and costs, shall be awarded "subject to the principles of equity":

> When a violation of any right of the registrant of a mark registered in the Patent and Trademark Office shall have been established in any civil action arising under this Chapter, the plaintiff shall be entitled . . . subject to the principles of equity, to recover (1) defendant's profits, (2) any damages sustained by the plaintiff, and (3) the costs of the action. The court shall assess such profits and damages or cause the same to be assessed under its direction. In assessing profits the plaintiff shall be required to prove defendant's sales only; defendant must prove all elements of cost or deduction claimed. In assessing damages the court may enter judgment, according to the circumstances of the case, for any sum above the amount found as actual damages, not exceeding three times such amount. If the court shall find that the amount of the

26. *See* Sunbeam Corp. v. Golden Rule Appliance Co., 252 F.2d 467, 470-71 (2d Cir. 1958). *See also* Chas. Pfizer & Co. v. Davis-Edwards Pharmacal Corp., 385 F.2d 533, 536 (2d Cir. 1967) (Fine of $5,000 for each future violation of order upheld).
27. Andre Matenciot, Inc. v. David & Dash, Inc., 422 F. Supp. 1199, 1210 (S.D.N.Y. 1976).
28. FED. R. CRIM. P. 42; United States v. United Mine Workers of Am., 330 U.S. 258 (1947). United States *ex rel.* Vuitton et Fils S.A. v. Karen Bags, Inc., 592 F. Supp. 734 (S.D.N.Y. 1984), *aff'd*, 780 F.2d 179 (2d Cir. 1985), *cert. granted* ___ U.S. ___, 106 S. Ct. 3270 (1986).

> recovery based on profits is either inadequate or excessive the court may in its discretion enter judgment for such sum as the court shall find to be just, according to the circumstances of the case. Such sum in either of the above circumstances shall constitute compensation and not a penalty. The court in exceptional cases may award reasonable attorney fees to the prevailing party.[29]

Despite the "shall be entitled" language of the Lanham Act, courts have wide discretion under "the principles of equity". Courts often find that the equities are satisfied by an injunction and that no monetary award is necessary.[30]

When monetary relief is awarded, it may be based on:

- defendant's profits;
- plaintiff's damages (trebled);
- compensation for corrective advertising;
- punitive damages;
- attorneys' fees; and
- costs.

In theory, this relief is cumulative, *i.e.*, plaintiff may recover for each separate element. In practice, the circumstances giving rise to any kind of monetary relief are limited.

Defendant's Profits

Defendant's profits are usually awarded only where defendant is guilty of intentional infringement, *i.e.*, deliberately trading on plaintiff's mark.[31] The profit award is designed to compensate plaintiff for lost sales and to deter deliberate infringement.[32] Defendant should not expect to insulate himself from a finding of

---

29. 15 U.S.C. § 1117.
30. Champion Spark Plug Co. v. Sanders, 331 U.S. 125 (1947).
31. Foxtrap, Inc. v. Foxtrap, Inc., 671 F.2d 636, 640 (D.C. Cir. 1982).
32. Monsanto Chem. Co. v. Perfect Fit Prods. Mfg. Co., 349 F.2d 389, 397 (2d Cir. 1965).

deliberate infringement just because he has relied on advice of counsel.[33]

Arguably, defendant's profits should be awarded only where the goods are competitive since it is only then that defendant's sales divert business directly from plaintiff. However, some courts award profits where goods are not competitive under an unjust enrichment theory. The accounting is not dependent upon injury to plaintiff but on the theory that defendant should not benefit from his deliberate use of plaintiff's mark.[34] Other courts refuse an accounting of profits where the goods are not competitive and there has been no actual damage.[35] Some courts also require proof of actual confusion before imposing a profit award.[36]

In calculating profits, plaintiff must prove defendant's sales and then defendant must prove deductions as well as any portion of the profit not attributable to the infringing use.[37] Deductions from gross sales include overhead, operating expenses, materials, and labor.[38]

Under the Lanham Act, the court may increase or decrease a profit award if the court finds it "is either inadequate or excessive."[39]

Actual Damages

Damages are designed to compensate plaintiff for actual injury caused by defendant's wrongful conduct. Plaintiff does not have to prove that defendant intended to cause damage. But where

33. Wolfe v. National Lead Co., 272 F.2d 867, 871 (9th Cir. 1959).
34. W.E. Bassett Co. v. Revlon, Inc., 435 F.2d 656, 664 (2d Cir. 1970).
35. Raxton Corp. v. Anania Assocs., Inc., 668 F.2d 622, 625 (1st Cir. 1982).
36. Perfect Fit Indus., Inc. v. Acme Quilting Co., 618 F.2d 950, 955 (2d Cir. 1980).
37. 15 U.S.C. § 1117. Mishawaka Mfg. Co. v. Kresge Co., 316 U.S. 203, 205 (1942).
38. W. E. Bassett Co. v. Revlon, Inc., 435 F.2d 656, 665 (2d Cir. 1970).
39. 15 U.S.C. § 1117.

defendant's conduct is not flagrant and the damage is slight, damages have been refused.[40]

Damages may be awarded in addition to defendant's profits, especially if the profit award is not based on plaintiff's lost sales. For example, if the parties are not competitive but defendant has intentionally infringed plaintiff's mark, defendant's profits may be awarded to deter intentional infringement. If, in addition, plaintiff can show actual harm, *e.g.*, damage to his reputation, damages may also be awarded.[41]

There are two major hurdles on the damage track: a) proving the fact of damage; and b) proving the amount of damage.

Proving the Fact of Damage

Damage cannot be based on speculation or feelings.[42] Conclusory allegations will not suffice. Some actual amount of damage must be proven.[43] It is not necessary, however, to show that the illegal act was the only cause of injury. It is enough that the illegal act was a material cause of injury.[44]

Measuring Damage

The courts have adopted the following guides in measuring damages:

40. Champion Spark Plug Co. v. Sanders, 331 U.S. 125, 131-32 (1947); Electronics Corp. of Am. v. Honeywell, Inc., 358 F. Supp. 1230, 1234 (D. Mass.), *aff'd*, 487 F.2d 513 (1st Cir. 1973), *cert. denied*, 415 U.S. 960 (1974).
41. Heaton Distrib. Co. v. Union Tank Car Co., 387 F.2d 477, 486 (8th Cir. 1967).
42. Zirin Laboratories Int'l Inc. v. Mead-Johnson & Co., 208 F. Supp. 633, 636 (E.D. Mich. 1962); Strike It Rich, Inc. v. Jos. Schlitz Brewing Co., 505 F. Supp. 89, 91 (D.C. Cir. 1980).
43. Caesar's World, Inc. v. Venus Lounge, Inc., 520 F.2d 269, 273 (3d Cir. 1975).
44. 2 McCarthy, Trademarks and Unfair Competition 30:27, at 510, 511 (2d ed. 1984).

Plaintiff's Lost Profits: Plaintiff can prove lost profits by showing that the reasonable profits he had forecast were not realized. Defendant can counter plaintiff's proof by showing that acts other than defendant's infringement were responsible for plaintiff's failure to realize his forecast profits.[45]

Reasonable Royalty: Previous negotiations between the parties or custom in the trade can provide the basis for computing a reasonable royalty. If the infringement is willful, however, the reasonable royalty may not be an adequate measure of damages since the infringer will still be making a profit.[46]

Corrective Advertising: The landmark case on corrective advertising is the *Big O* BIGFOOT decision.[47] The giant Goodyear company proceeded to launch a major campaign for its BIGFOOT tires despite the objection of its smaller competitor, Big O, the prior user of BIGFOOT on tires. The jury found that Goodyear was guilty of deliberate infringement and that Goodyear's national advertising campaign had damaged Big O's reputation by making it appear that Big O was the infringer. To correct the misconception that Goodyear was the original source of BIGFOOT tires, Big O was awarded the money required to conduct a corrective advertising campaign. Because Big O did business in only fourteen states, the jury awarded 14/50ths of the $10 million Goodyear had spent on national advertising for BIGFOOT. The award was reduced by the Court of Appeals on the theory that corrective advertising need not be on a dollar for dollar basis. The Court adopted the 25 percent ratio used in FTC cases, which still gave Big O a hefty $700,000—plus punitive damages.

---

45. Borg-Warner Corp. v. York-Shipley, Inc., 136 U.S.P.Q. 255, 259 (N.D. Ill. 1963).
46. Playboy Enters., Inc. v. Baccarat Clothing Co., 692 F.2d 1272, 1274-75 (9th Cir. 1982).
47. Big O Tire Dealers, Inc. v. Goodyear Tire & Rubber, 408 F. Supp. 1219, 1232 (D. Colo. 1976), *aff'd with modification as to amount*, 561 F.2d 1365 (10th Cir. 1977); *see also* Aetna Health Care Sys., Inc. v. Health Care Choice, Inc., 231 U.S.P.Q. 614, 626 (N.D. Okla. 1986).

Trebling Damages

The Lanham Act provides for increasing the award of actual damages to an amount "not exceeding three times" such damages . . . "according to the circumstances of the case."[48] Increased damages "shall constitute compensation and not a penalty."[49]

While an award of increased damages may not be used as a penalty, it may be used to deter willful infringement.[50] Increased damages are also justified where defendant's "stonewalling" on the production of sales records makes it difficult to prove the amount of damages.[51]

Punitive Damages

Punitive damages are not mentioned in the Lanham Act and the courts have held they are not recoverable under that statute.[52]

Punitive damages are recoverable under the laws of many states where the party is guilty of some egregious conduct. In New York, for example, punitive damages are recoverable for:

> tortious acts which involve ingredients of malice, fraud, oppression, insult, wanton or reckless disregard of the plaintiff's rights, or other circumstances of aggravation, as a punishment of the defendant and admonition to others.[53]

Most jurisdictions require a finding of actual damage to support an award of punitive damages. Usually the amount of punitive

48. 15 U.S.C. § 1117.
49. *Id.*
50. Holiday Inns, Inc. v. Airport Holiday Corp., 493 F. Supp. 1025, 1028, *aff'd*, 683 F.2d 931, 933 (5th Cir. 1980).
51. Boston Professional Hockey Ass'n v. Dallas Cap & Emblem Mfg., Inc., 597 F.2d 71, 77 (5th Cir. 1979).
52. Metric & Multistandard Components Corp. v. Metric's, Inc., 635 F.2d 710, 715 (8th Cir. 1980); Caesars World, Inc. v. Venus Lounge, Inc., 520 F.2d 269, 274 (3d Cir. 1975).
53. N.Y. JUR. 2D § 176 (1984); *See* Universal City Studios v. Nintendo Co., Ltd., 615 F. Supp. 838, 863 (S.D.N.Y. 1985), *aff'd*, 797 F.2d 70 (2d Cir. 1986).

damages "should bear some reasonable relation to the harm done" and be sufficient to "smart the offender."[54] Thus, the financial capacity of the accused party and the flagrancy of the conduct are relevant factors.[55]

In the *Universal Studios* DONKEY KONG case, application of the relevant factors resulted in a punitive damage award equal to plaintiff's attorneys' fees.[56] In the *Big O* case, the jury award of six times the actual damages was upheld.[57]

Attorneys' Fees

The Lanham Act provides that the court may award reasonable attorneys' fees to the prevailing party "in exceptional cases."[58] The statutory history indicates that "exceptional" includes cases of deliberate or willful infringement and that "prevailing party" includes defendants as well as plaintiffs.[59]

The courts have implemented the statutory intent by awarding fees where:

- Defendant's conduct was deliberate and willful;[60]
- Defendant's conduct was fraudulent;[61]
- Defendant proceeded to use the mark after requesting and being denied permission;[62]

---

54. Universal City Studios v. Nintendo Co., Ltd., 615 F. Supp. 838, 863 (S.D.N.Y. 1985), *aff'd*, 797 F.2d 70 (2d Cir. 1986).
55. *Id.*
56. *Id.*
57. Big O Tire Dealers, Inc. v. Goodyear Tire & Rubber Co., 408 F. Supp. 1219, 1232 (D. Colo. 1976), *aff'd with modification as to amount*, 561 F. 2d 1365, 1376 (10th Cir. 1977).
58. 15 U.S.C. § 1117.
59. S. REP. NO. 1400, 93d Cong., 2d Sess. (Dec. 17, 1974).
60. Quaker State Oil Ref. Corp. v. Kooltone, Inc., 649 F.2d 94, 95 (2d Cir. 1981).
61. Armstrong Cork Co. v. Armstrong Plastic Covers Co., 434 F. Supp. 860, 873 (E.D. Mo. 1977).
62. Amana Soc'y v. Gemeinde Brau, Inc., 417 F. Supp. 310, 311-12 (N.D. Iowa 1976), *aff'd*, 557 F.2d 638, *cert. denied*, 434 U.S. 967 (1976).

- Plaintiff brought suit in bad faith without an investigation of the merits of his claim;[63]
- Plaintiff's claims had no real substance;[64]
- Plaintiff filed suit as a competitive ploy;[65]
- Plaintiff's conduct in bringing suit 3,000 miles from defendants' home base was contrary to Supreme Court authority on proper venue and amounted to harassment.[66]

The Court in the *Firehouse* case found that something less than bad faith "was sufficient to make a case 'exceptional' ":

> [W]e think "exceptional," as Congress used the word in section 35 of the Lanham Act, is most reasonably read to mean [w]hat the word is generally understood to indicate - uncommon, not run-of-the-mine. On that familiar construction, we regard as "exceptional" Noxell's decision to locate in the District of Columbia its suit against San Francisco firefighter English and the fledgling San Francisco barbeque business English organized and operated.
>
> * * *
>
> We think it altogether "exceptional," indeed, we called it "remarkable," *id.* at 316, for Noxell to launch litigation against Firehouse and English at a place far removed from California when a Supreme Court decision precisely in point *** plainly declared the impropriety of that course.

There has been some dispute as to whether attorneys' fees are available in actions based on unregistered marks under Section 43(a) of the Lanham Act. Attorneys' fees are only specified under Section 35 of the Act, which provides remedies for the infringement of registered marks. The Ninth Circuit originally refused to award fees under Section 43(a), but has reversed itself to join the

63. Viola Sportswear, Inc. v. Minum, 574 F. Supp. 619, 621 (E.D.N.Y. 1983).
64. Mennen v. Gillette Co., 565 F. Supp. 648, 652 (S.D.N.Y. 1983), *aff'd*, 742 F.2d 14 (2d Cir. 1984).
65. Fuddruckers, Inc. v. Doc's D. R. Others, Inc., 227 U.S.P.Q. 408, 524 (D. Ariz. 1985).
66. Noxell Corp. v. Firehouse No. 1 Bar-B-Que Restaurant, 771 F.2d 521, 526-27 (D.C. Cir. 1985).

8th and 11th Circuits.[67] These three Circuits now agree that the availability of fees under Section 43(a) is a necessary deterrent consistent with the overall purpose of the Lanham Act.

Costs

Court costs are recoverable by the prevailing party "as of course . . . unless the court otherwise directs."[68] Costs may include filing fees, court reporter fees for transcripts necessary for use in the case, printing and witness fees, and compensation of court appointed experts.[69]

Cancellation of Trademark Registration

The Statutory Basis

A trademark registration may be cancelled either by the court as the result of a civil action, or by the Patent and Trademark Office as the result of a cancellation proceeding.

The Lanham Act specifically grants the court power to determine:

> [T]he right to registration, order the cancellation of registrations, in whole or in part, restore cancelled registrations, and otherwise rectify the register with respect to the registrations of any party to the action.[70]

The Lanham Act also provides for the initiation of cancellation proceedings on certain specified grounds depending on the age and status of the registration.[71]

---

67. Transgo, Inc. v. Ajac Transmission Parts Corp., 768 F.2d 1001, 1026 (9th Cir. 1985); Metric & Multistandard Components v. Metric's, Inc., 635 F.2d 710, 716 (8th Cir. 1980); Rickard v. Auto Publisher, Inc., 735 F.2d 450, 458 (11th Cir. 1984).
68. FED. R. CIV. P. 54(d).
69. 28 U.S.C. § 1920.
70. 15 U.S.C. § 1119.
71. 15 U.S.C. § 1064.

The Grounds for Cancellation

A registration issued less than five years before the cancellation action can be attacked on the usual grounds of likely confusion with a prior mark, descriptiveness, and/or genericness. However, after five years has elapsed, cancellation is no longer permitted on grounds of priority or descriptiveness.[72]

There is some dispute as to whether the limits placed on Patent and Trademark Office cancellation proceedings also apply to court proceedings. A coherent reading of the statute suggests that the grounds for cancellation should be the same in both forums.[73]

The Prerequisite for Court Jurisdiction

A party seeking to cancel a registration may not bring suit on that ground alone. His recourse in that situation is to apply to the Patent and Trademark Office, thus first exhausting his administrative remedies.[74]

There must be a ground of federal jurisdiction independent of the cancellation claim to support the court action. For example, where plaintiff claims infringement of his registered mark, he may request the court to cancel defendant's registration.[75]

Court Versus Patent and Trademark Office

What happens when one party brings a cancellation proceeding in the Patent and Trademark Office and the adverse party files suit? Usually one of the actions will be stayed while the other proceeds to judgment.

---

72. 15 U.S.C. § 1064. For further details on cancellation proceedings in the Patent and Trademark Office, see chapter 14, pp. 301-08, *infra*.
73. D.M. & Antique Import Corp. v. Royal Saxe Corp., 311 F. Supp. 1261, 1268 (S.D.N.Y. 1970); Fletcher, *Incontestability and Constructive Notice: A Quarter Century of Adjudication*, 63 TRADEMARK REP. 71, 93 (1973).
74. Universal Sewing Mach. Co. v. Standard Sewing Equip. Corp., 185 F. Supp. 257, 259 (S.D.N.Y. 1960).
75. *Id.*

The practice of the Trademark Trial and Appeal Board has traditionally been to stay the proceeding before it.[76] The theory is that the court action is more inclusive (involving right to use and register) and will be determinative of the action before the Board.[77] Sometimes, however, a court will defer to the expertise of the Board and will stay the action before it.[78] The decision as to whether the court or Board action is stayed could turn on how far along either proceeding is, the need for preliminary relief, and the presence of additional issues in the court action.[79]

Barring Importation from Abroad

Recording a Trademark Registration with Customs

The Effect of Recordal

The owner of a U.S. registration may obtain valuable protection by recording his registration with U.S. Customs. The effect of the deposit is to bar importation of goods bearing an infringing mark.[80]

Customs acts as the policing official for the trademark owner, inspecting shipments and seizing merchandise deemed to violate the registration. Where the seized goods bear a counterfeit mark,[81]

76. *See* T.M.R.P. 2.117(a). This practice applies equally to cancellation and opposition proceedings.
77. Other Tel. Co. v. Connecticut Nat'l Tel. Co., 181 U.S.P.Q. 779, 782 (Comm'r Pat. 1974).
78. Driving Force, Inc. v. Manpower, Inc., 498 F. Supp. 21, 25 (E.D. Pa. 1980).
79. Sonora Cosmetics, Inc. v. L'Oreal S.A., 631 F. Supp. 626 (S.D.N.Y. 1986); Tuvache, Inc. v. Emilio Pucci Perfumes Int'l, Inc., 263 F. Supp. 104, 106 (S.D.N.Y. 1967).
80. 15 U.S.C. § 1124. See also pp. 270-76, *infra*, on rights of U.S. owner to bar gray market goods under Section 526 of the Tariff Act.
81. Counterfeit is defined by reference to the Lanham Act definition as "a spurious mark which is identical with or substantially indistinguishable from a registered mark." 15 U.S.C. § 1127.

they are forfeited by the importer to be disposed of by destruction or gift to charity after removal of the mark.[82]

Where the seized goods bear an infringing mark (*i.e.*, a mark likely to cause confusion), they may be sent back to the place of origin or enter the United States after removal of the mark.[83]

If the trademark owner gives his consent, goods bearing either a counterfeit mark or an infringing mark may be released for entry into the United States.[84]

Recordal Procedure

Recordation with Customs is initiated by filing an application, which may take several months to process. The application must contain the following information:

1. the name, business address, and citizenship (state of incorporation) of the trademark owner;
2. the places of manufacture of goods bearing the recorded trademark;
3. the name and principal business address of each foreign person or business authorized or licensed to use the trademark and a statement as to the use authorized.
4. the identity of any parent or subsidiary company or other foreign company under common ownership or control that uses the trademark abroad;
5. a certified status copy of the Patent and Trademark Office certificate of registration that shows title to be in the name of the applicant for recordation.
6. five copies of the certificate or of a U.S. Patent and Trademark Office facsimile for distribution to ports of entry—the copies may be privately reproduced and shall be approximately 8 x 10½ inches in size;

82. 19 C.F.R. § 133.52(c).
83. 19 C.F.R. § 133.51(b)(1)(2). Where goods previously released are found to infringe a recorded mark, a redelivery notice may be issued. As to goods not redelivered, a liquidated damage claim lies. § 133.24.
84. 19 C.F.R. § 133.23(a), 133.21(c).

7. a filing fee for each trademark and each class of goods for which recordation is desired.[85]

Recordation is for the same period that the registration is in effect. Renewal of the registration, however, will not automatically renew the Customs recordation. A separate application to renew the Customs recordation must be filed.[86]

Trade names may also be recorded with Customs after they have been used for six months.[87] The information required for trade name recordal is set forth in the regulations.[88] Unlike trademark registrations that have already been subject to opposition, trade name recordation may be opposed.[89]

Enlisting the Aid of Customs: Action Beyond Recordation

Once recordation is accomplished, Customs will theoretically bar merchandise bearing an infringing mark. But if Customs has thousands of registered marks on deposit, how can the field personnel at the ports of entry be aware of all these marks? The answer is: they can't. But, the trademark owner can help call attention to his mark as well as alert Customs personnel to suspected importers and exporters of infringing merchandise.

One way to enlist the aid of Customs is for the trademark owner's representative to visit ports where infringing goods are most likely to enter. Customs personnel in charge of the class of goods of interest should be contacted. Samples or pictures of the trademark owner's product can be provided. Anything that will cause the mark to be remembered will help.

Where foreign sources of infringing goods are known, the trademark owner should supply the names to Customs. Ditto for

85. 19 C.F.R. § 133.2, 133.3.
86. 19 C.F.R. § 133.7.
87. 19 C.F.R. § 133.12, 133.13.
88. *Id.*
89. 19 C.F.R. § 133.14.

the names of importers. This will help pinpoint shipments that can be given more than the usual spot check.

When Customs makes a seizure, the trademark owner should publicize it (taking care to be sure all statements are truthful). Word spreads fast in an industry and the hassle of detained goods, or the loss of forfeited goods, can be a strong deterrent.

Challenging Customs Decisions

To challenge a Customs decision on the issue of infringement, administrative remedies must first be exhausted by appeal to the Commissioner of Customs. Review of that decision may be had by the federal district court.[90]

The Agency determination can be overturned where it is "arbitrary, capricious, an abuse of discretion or otherwise not in accordance with law."[91]

Excluding Genuine Goods under Section 526 of the Tariff Act

By recording his registration with Customs, a U.S. trademark owner may bar the importation of foreign goods bearing the same mark even though the foreign goods originate from the same source as the U.S. owner's goods. The right to bar genuine foreign goods is accorded to U.S. owners under Section 526 of the Tariff Act (19 U.S.C. § 1526).

Section 526 places no conditions on the U.S. owner's right to exclude genuine foreign goods bearing an identical mark. But Customs has interpreted the statute to permit the entry of genuine foreign goods where the U.S. trademark owner is owned or controlled by the foreign owner of the mark.

---

90. Montres, Rolex, S.A. v. Snyder, 718 F.2d 524, 526 (2d Cir. 1983).
91. 5 U.S.C. § 706(2)(A) (1982). Montres, Rolex, S.A. v. Snyder, 718 F.2d 524, 530 (2d Cir. 1983).

The history of Section 526, the dispute over Customs' efforts to limit the statute, and recent case law will be reviewed in this section. But first, a brief overview of the problem.

The Parallel Import/Gray Goods Problem

Typically, the U.S. trademark owner is the exclusive U.S. distributor of the foreign goods and owns the U.S. mark as a result of assignment from the foreign manufacturer. The problem arises when third parties purchase the foreign manufacturer's goods abroad and seek to import them into the United States without authorization from the U.S. trademark owner.

The unauthorized imports are referred to as "parallel imports" or "gray market" goods. The imports are "parallel" in the sense that they are made by the same manufacturer who makes the U.S. trademark owner's goods. They are "gray market" goods since they are legitimately sold abroad, but are not authorized by the U.S. trademark owner for sale in this country.

U.S. trademark owners point to Section 526 as plainly prohibiting unauthorized imports. They also argue that the parallel imports infringe the U.S. owner's mark because they are not subject to the U.S. owner's quality control and are taking a free ride on the goodwill of the U.S. business.

Parallel importers argue that the limitation imposed by Customs on Section 526 is proper and that they are providing increased competition, frequently underselling the exclusive U.S. distributor.

Section 526: Its Language and History

Section 526 provides:

> "it shall be unlawful to import into the United States any merchandise of foreign manufacture if such merchandise, or the label, sign, print, package, wrapper, or receptacle, bears a trademark owned by a citizen of, or by a corporation or association created or organized within, the United States, and registered in the Patent and Trademark Office by a person domiciled in the United

States . . . and if a copy of the certificate of registration of such trademark is filed with the Secretary of the Treasury . . . unless written consent of the owner of such trademark is produced at the time of making entry." [19 U.S.C. § 1526(a)].

There was minimal floor debate on Section 526, and the case law draws differing conclusions as to the light this debate sheds on the Congressional intent.[92] It is clear, however, that Section 526 was a reaction to the Second Circuit's decision in *Bourjois v. Katzel.* There, a U.S. distributor of JAVA face powder purchased rights to the JAVA mark in the United States from the French manufacturer. The U.S. owner invested considerable sums in developing the U.S. market. A third party (Katzel) purchased the powder sold abroad by the French manufacturer and imported it into the United States in competition with the U.S. owner. The District Court enjoined Katzel's importation of JAVA. The Second Circuit reversed, holding that Katzel's use of JAVA on "the same genuine goods" was not an infringement:

> [I]f the claimed infringing goods were the same genuine goods the plaintiff sold under the trademark, "the rights of the owner of the trademark are not infringed."[93]

In response to the inequities it perceived in *Katzel,* Congress passed Section 526. After Section 526 was enacted, the Supreme Court reversed *Katzel,* but made no mention of Section 526. In finding Katzel's use to be an infringement, the Supreme Court recognized the U.S. trademark owner's investment in the promotion and quality of the products he sold in this country:

> [P]laintiff "uses care in selecting colors suitable for the American market, in packing and in keeping up the standard, and has spent

92. *See* Vivitar Corp. v. United States, 593 F. Supp. 420 (Ct. Int'l Trade 1984), *aff'd on other grounds,* 761 F.2d 1552 (Fed. Cir. 1985); Coalition to Preserve the Integrity of American Trademarks v. United States, 790 F.2d 903 (D.C. Cir. 1986), *cert. granted,* __ U.S. __, 107 S. Ct. 642 (1986) [hereinafter *COPIAT*].

93. A. Bourjois & Co. v. Katzel, 275 F. 539, 543 (2d Cir. 1923), *rev'd,* 260 U.S. 689 (1921).

much money in advertising, etc., so that . . . the labels have come to be understood by the public here as meaning goods coming from the plaintiff.[94]

Efforts to Narrow Section 526

The Customs Regulations: Initially, the Customs regulations followed the broad language of Section 526 and prohibited the importation of genuine goods regardless of the relationship between the U.S. trademark owner and the foreign trademark owner. Beginning in 1936, however, Customs adopted various regulations that permitted importation of genuine goods as a result of the foreign owner's relationship with the U.S. owner.[95]

The consistency of the various Customs regulations prior to 1972 has been the subject of considerable debate. According to some courts, the series of regulations from 1936 to 1972 are inconsistent and vacillating. According to Customs, the regulations reflect its consistent position that genuine goods manufactured by the foreign parent or subsidiary of the U.S. trademark owner should not be excluded under Section 526.[96]

In 1972, the Customs regulations were revised to their current form. Customs will not bar merchandise under Section 526 where:

(1) Both the foreign and the U.S. trademark or trade name are owned by the same person or business entity;

(2) The foreign and domestic trademark or trade name owners are parent and subsidiary companies or are otherwise subject to common ownership or control (see §§ 133.2(d) and 133.12(d);

---

94. 260 U.S. at 691. The Supreme Court Bourjois v. Katzel decision is frequently cited as support for the territorial principle of trademark rights: the trademark identifies the local business goodwill of the domestic owner.

95. For a detailed history of the Customs regulations see Vivitar Corp. v. United States, 761 F.2d 1552 (Fed. Cir. 1985).

96. Vivitar Corp. v. United States, 593 F. Supp. 420, 430, (Ct. Int'l Trade 1984), *aff'd on other grounds*, 761 F.2d 1552, 1568 (Fed. Cir. 1985); *COPIAT*, *supra* note 92, 790 F.2d at 916.

(3) The articles of foreign manufacture bear a recorded trademark or trade name applied under authorization of the U.S. owner.[97]

The Antitrust Theory: Until recently, Customs asserted that the 1972 regulations were based on the 1956 *Guerlain* case.[98] In *Guerlain*, the government filed suit alleging antitrust violations against several American toiletry companies. The District Court held that use of Section 526 by the American part of a "single international enterprise" to bar genuine goods sold abroad by the foreign part of the same enterprise monopolized trade in the trademarked goods in violation of Section 2 of the Sherman Act. However, the case was dismissed by the government while on appeal. Apparently the government recognized that Section 526 on its face gave the U.S. owner the right to bar genuine foreign goods and believed that change was required by legislative rather than court action.[99] Following the government dismissal of *Guerlain*, a bill was introduced to preclude relief under Section 526 where the trademark owner was affiliated with or controlled by the foreign manufacturer. But the bill never passed.

The antitrust theory abandoned by the government in *Guerlain* surfaced again over two decades later as a defense to suits brought by U.S. trademark owners to halt parallel imports. The theory has not fared well.[100]

---

97. 19 C.F.R § 133.21(c). "Common ownership" under the regulations is defined as: "individual or aggregate ownership of more than 50 percent of the business entity," and "common control" as "effective control in policy and operations." Such control is not "necessarily synonymous with common ownership." 19 C.F.R. § 133.2(d)(1)(2).

98. United States v. Guerlain, Inc., 155 F. Supp. 77 (S.D.N.Y. 1957), *vacated and remanded*, 358 U.S. 915 (1958), *action dismissed*, 172 F. Supp. 107 (S.D.N.Y. 1959).

99. Osawa & Co. v. Bell & Howell Photo, 589 F. Supp. 1163, 1176 (S.D.N.Y. 1984).

100. *Id.* at 1177-78; *see also COPIAT*, *supra* note 92, 790 F.2d at 916, (antitrust doctrine has changed significantly since the *Guerlain* era).

Recent Law

The 1980s have witnessed an eruption of litigation over the exclusion of genuine foreign goods. As the value of the U.S. dollar rose against foreign currency, parallel imports burgeoned, and so did attempts to halt them. The decisions seem to fall into the following camps:

1. The Customs regulations are invalid. Section 526 means what it says and the U.S. trademark owner is entitled to bar importation of products bearing the identical mark regardless of the U.S. company's relationship to the foreign manufacturer.[101]
2. The Customs regulations are not invalid, but are not controlling with respect to the scope of protection of Section 526. The U.S. owner may file suit to enjoin the sale of parallel imports as a violation of Section 526 even though the Customs regulations did not bar importation.[102]
3. Trademarks have a territorial foundation, and the goodwill of the U.S. owner, established through quality control, advertising, selection of retailers, provision of repair services, warranties, etc., should be protected. Parallel imports that infringe on this domestic goodwill may be enjoined.[103]

---

101. *COPIAT*, *supra* note 92.
102. Vivitar Corp. v. United States, 761 F.2d 1552 (Fed. Cir. 1985); Olympus Corp. v. United States, 792 F.2d 315 (2d Cir. 1986).
103. Weil Ceramics & Glass, Inc. v. Dash, 618 F. Supp. 700 (D.N.J. 1985); Osawa & Co. v. Bell & Howell Photo, 589 F. Supp. 1163 (S.D.N.Y. 1984); Bell & Howell: Mamiya Co. v. Masel Supply Co., 548 F. Supp. 1063 (E.D.N.Y. 1982), *vacated on other grounds*, 719 F.2d 42 (2d Cir. 1983); Premiere Dental Prods. Co. v. Darby Dental Supply Co., 794 F.2d 850 (3rd Cir. 1986).

4. There can be no infringement where the goods are genuine, *i.e.*, originally from the same foreign source and are of equal quality.[104]

As this book goes to press, the question of parallel imports remains a disputed one—with a direct conflict in the circuits that is due to be resolved by the Supreme Court or new legislation.

Proceedings Before the ITC

Scope

The International Trade Commission (ITC) is another vehicle for protecting against unfair competition from abroad. Section 337 of the Tariff Act prohibits unfair methods of competition or unfair acts in the importation of articles into the United States.[105]

It is not necessary to own a registered mark to bring an ITC action; unfair acts include infringement of registered and unregistered marks and false advertising.[106] The ITC follows the federal court standards in determining trademark validity and likely confusion.

An additional requirement for an ITC action is proof that the accused imports tend to destroy or substantially injure the relevant domestic industry. The domestic industry must also be efficiently and economically operated. The fact that the U.S. company is

---

104. Bell & Howell: Mamiya Co. v. Masel Supply Co., 719 F.2d 42, 45 (2d Cir. 1983) (Dictum); Monte Carlo Shirt, Inc. v. Daewoo Int'l (America) Corp., 707 F.2d 1054 (9th Cir. 1986); but note El Greco Leather Prods. Co. v. Shoe World, Inc., 806 F.2d 392 (2d Cir. 1986) (absence of quality control by U.S. owner precludes finding that the foreign manufactured goods are genuine. If the goods are not genuine they are infringing under 15 U.S.C. Section 1114).

105. 19 U.S.C. § 1337.

106. *In re* Certain Airtight Cast-Iron Stoves, 215 U.S.P.Q. 963, 969 (U.S. Int. Tr. Comm. 1980).

wholly owned by a foreign company will not defeat ITC jurisdiction, so long as the U.S. company adds significant domestic value to the product.[107]

A major advantage to an ITC proceeding is that relief can be in rem—against the product itself, regardless of whether all manufacturers are known at the time of the proceeding.[108]

Procedure

Another major advantage to an ITC proceeding is its speed. The statute requires that the case be concluded within twelve months. Time for completion may be extended to eighteen months for complicated cases. Preliminary relief is also available.

An ITC proceeding is initiated by the submission of a complaint to the Commission. Prior to its formal submission, meetings with Commission staff are routinely held to review the complaint and assure compliance with Commission procedures.

The ITC has its own rules on motion practice and discovery—all within a very compressed time frame. The Commission participates as a third party and normally undertakes its own discovery.[109]

The hearing and prehearing conferences are before an Administrative Law Judge who recommends a decision to the Commission. The Commission decision may be vetoed within sixty days by the President of the United States based on its economic and political impact on foreign relations.[110] Absent Presidential veto, the Commission decision may be appealed to the Court of Appeals for the Federal Circuit.[111]

---

107. *Id.* at 968. Legislation to eliminate the injury and domestic industry requirements is pending. S. 539.
108. 19 U.S.C. § 1337(d).
109. 19 C.F.R. § 210.4(b).
110. 19 U.S.C. § 1337(g).
111. 19 C.F.R. § 210.71.

Res Judicata Effect of ITC Ruling on District Court

Trademark owners who choose the ITC forum should not expect to circumvent an adverse ITC ruling by filing the same action in a district court. In *Union Mfg. v. Han Baek*, the ITC held that defendant's copy of plaintiff's vacuum bottle did not constitute trademark infringement or false designation of origin under Section 43(a). Plaintiff filed essentially the same claim in the New York District Court where a jury ruled for plaintiff on the false designation of origin claim. The Second Circuit Court of Appeals held that res judicata bars the relitigation of the claim in federal court.

> [It is not] apparent why the policies underlying the doctrine of res judicata should not require Union, having chosen to initiate an administrative adjudication, to take the exclusive avenue of appeal afforded by law—review of ITC decisions by the Court of Appeals for the Federal Circuit, 19 U.S.C. § 1337(c); 28 U.S.C. § 1295(a)(b) (1982). At least when the issues raised and the procedures available in the ITC proceeding are in all important respects the same as those in the District Court, *** res judicata should bar the relitigation of the claim in federal court. To hold otherwise would undermine the legitimacy of the ITC proceeding; the party losing the administrative adjudication could simply file an identical action in a federal district court and thereby avoid the strict standard of review [*i.e.*, substantial evidence test] governing appeal of ITC determinations in the Federal Circuit. Litigants should not be able to circumvent the decisional authority of the ITC and the reviewing authority of the Federal Circuit by filing in a district court what amounts to a collateral attack on the ITC determination.[112]

---

112. Union Mfg. Co. v. Han Baek Trading Co., 763 F.2d 42, 45 (2d Cir. 1985). For a definition and discussion of res judicata see chapter 11, pp. 230-32, *supra*.

Criminal Penalties

Prior to the passage of the Counterfeiting Act of 1984, criminal penalties were only a gleam in the eye of trademark owners. The gleam has now materialized in the case of counterfeits, with the new Act providing substantial fines and prison terms.[113] Now the problem is to persuade the government prosecutors that their limited manpower should be expended on criminal proceedings to halt the sale of counterfeit merchandise. One solution to the manpower shortage is the appointment of the trademark owner's attorney as a special prosecutor in criminal contempt actions. This practice has received mixed reviews depending on the circuit and is under study by the Supreme Court.[114]

Declaratory Judgment of Noninfringement

Just as the first user may bring a court action to seek relief from an infringing use, the second user may bring a court action to seek relief from threats of infringement. This action by the second user is called a declaratory judgment action. The second user asks the court to declare that his use does not infringe the first user's mark.

The sine qua non for declaratory relief is the presence of an "actual controversy."[115] If the second user has been threatened with suit, an actual controversy clearly exists. It is not so clear whether the filing of a notice of opposition or cancellation in the Patent and Trademark Office amounts to an actual controversy.

---

113. See chapter 7, *supra*, p. 138, on criminal penalties under the Counterfeiting Act.
114. *Compare* Polo Fashions, Inc. v. Stock Buyers Int'l, Inc., 760 F.2d 698, 704 (6th Cir. 1985) (appointment disapproved) *with* United States *ex rel.* Vuitton et Fils S.A. v. Klayminc, 780 F.2d 179 (2d Cir. 1985) (appointment approved); *cert. granted*, __ U.S. __ 106 S. Ct. 3270 (1986).
115. 28 U.S.C. § 2201; Public Service Comm'n v. Wycoff, 344 U.S. 237, 241 (1952).

Recent case law indicates it does if accompanied by threatening correspondence.[116]

Declaratory relief is particularly useful for a company at an early stage of a name change, before significant investment has been made in advertising, literature, etc.[117]

The declaratory judgment action also has the advantage of allowing the accused infringer to select the forum. In addition, the Federal Rules provide that declaratory judgment actions be given "preference," which should result in a shortened time to trial.[118]

Appeals from the District Court

Many crucial issues in trademark law can be viewed differently by different judges. For example, a mark that is descriptive to one judge may be suggestive to another. Or marks that appear similar to one judge may not appear so similar to another.[119] Because trademark law is more subjective than other areas of law, trademark appeals generally stand a better chance than other appeals.

The appellant's chances are further enhanced in those circuits where likelihood of confusion is considered a question of law, rather than a question of fact. Under Rule 52(a) of the Federal Rules of Civil Procedure, the district court findings of fact cannot be reversed unless they are "clearly erroneous." Legal questions, however, are judged by the less stringent standard of plain "error."

The current rundown on the standard for likely confusion in the different circuits is as follows: Likely confusion is a question of fact, subject to the clearly erroneous standard in the:

---

116. Manufacturers Hanover Corp. v. Maine Sav. Bank, 225 U.S.P.Q. 525, 526-27 (S.D.N.Y. 1985).

117. Armstrong Cork Co. v. World Carpets, Inc., 597 F.2d 496, 499 (5th Cir. 1979).

118. FED. R. CIV. P. 57.

119. See Ambrit, Inc. v. Kraft, Inc., 805 F.2d 974, 983 (11th Cir. 1986) referring to the "subjective eyeball test" for judging similarity in design marks.

- First Circuit[120]
- Fourth Circuit[121]
- Fifth Circuit[122]
- Seventh Circuit[123]
- Eighth Circuit[124]
- Ninth Circuit[125]
- Tenth Circuit[126]
- Eleventh Circuit[127]

Likely confusion is an ultimate question of law and the underlying factors are questions of fact in the:

- Second Circuit[128]
- Third Circuit[129]
- Sixth Circuit[130]
- Federal Circuit[131]

Some circuits have recently changed their position on the treatment of likely confusion, and litigants should be alert for further changes in this area.

---

120. Purolator, Inc. v. EFRA Distribs., Inc., 687 F.2d 554, 559 (1st Cir. 1982).
121. Pizzeria Uno Corp. v. Temple, 747 F.2d 1522, 1526 (4th Cir. 1984).
122. Sun Banks of Fla., Inc. v. Sun Fed. S. & L. Ass'n, 651 F.2d 311, 314 (5th Cir. 1981).
123. WSM, Inc. v. Hilton, 724 F.2d 1320, 1326 (8th Cir. 1984).
124. Scandia Down Corp. v. Euroquilt, Inc., 772 F.2d 1423, 1427-29 (7th Cir. 1985).
125. Levi Strauss & Co. v. Blue Bell, Inc., 778 F.2d 1352, 1355 (9th Cir. 1985).
126. J.M. Huber Corp. v. Lowery Wellheads, Inc., 778 F.2d 1467, 1470-71 (10th Cir. 1985).
127. John H. Harland Co. v. Clarke Checks, Inc., 711 F.2d 966, 973 (11th Cir. 1983).
128. Plus Prods. v. Plus Discount Foods, Inc., 722 F.2d 999, 1004-05 (2d Cir. 1983).
129. Surgical Supply Serv., Inc. v. Adler, 321 F.2d 536, 539 (3d Cir. 1963).
130. Frisch's Restaurant, Inc. v. Shoney's Inc., 759 F.2d 1261, 1264 (6th Cir. 1985).
131. Kimberly-Clark Corp. v. H. Douglas Enters., 774 F.2d 1144, 1146 (Fed. Cir. 1985).

14

Patent and Trademark Office Inter Partes Proceedings

Opposition Proceedings

Publication in Official Gazette

After a trademark application has passed muster in the U.S. Patent and Trademark Office, it is published for opposition in the Official Gazette.[1] The Gazette is organized by classes of goods and contains basic data, such as: the mark (including any design elements), the applicant's name and location, the goods, the dates of first use, the application filing date and claims to distinctiveness (Section 2f).

Only marks entitled to registration on the Principal Register are subject to opposition. There is no opposition proceeding for marks allowed on the Supplemental Register. Action against registrations on the Supplemental Register can only be by way of cancellation.[2]

Any party who believes he would be damaged by the registration on the Principal Register has thirty days after publication in the Official Gazette to take action. It is common practice to request an extension of time to oppose during this initial thirty-day period. The extension provides an opportunity to investigate the application and contact the other side to discuss settlement. Extensions up to ninety days may be granted without consent by the adverse party.

1. See chapter 5, pp. 89-97, *supra*, on examination procedure prior to publication.
2. See this chapter, pp. 307-08, *infra*, on proceedings to cancel marks on Supplemental Register.

There are a number of ways to monitor the Official Gazette for the publication of conflicting marks. The monitoring task can be assigned to employees familiar with the company's trademarks, outside trademark counsel or "watching" services. With important marks, all three methods may be used. If a potential conflict is missed, action can still be taken by way of cancellation or court proceedings.[3]

Basis for Opposition

The "Damage" Requirement for Standing

An opposition may be filed by "any person who believes that he would be damaged by the registration of a mark."[4] The standing requirement is liberally interpreted. Standing exists where the opposer has "a personal interest in the outcome beyond that of the general public."[5] For example, in order to challenge a mark as generic or merely descriptive, opposer should have an interest in using the mark generically or descriptively. In other words, opposer must be commercially involved with goods that could be described by the alleged mark.[6]

Substantive Grounds for Opposition

The common grounds for opposition include:

1. likely confusion with opposer's previously used or registered mark;
2. descriptiveness and genericness;
3. misdescriptiveness and deceptiveness; and
4. fraud.

---

3. See this chapter, pp. 301-08, *infra*, on cancellation proceedings.
4. 15 U.S.C. § 1063.
5. Lipton Indus., Inc. v. Ralston Purina Co., 670 F.2d 1024, 1028 (C.C.P.A. 1982).
6. C.R. Bard, Inc. v. Willy Rusch K.G., 172 U.S.P.Q. 250 (T.T.A.B. 1971).

Likelihood of Confusion and Priority:

1. Special Rules in Judging Likely Confusion: Generally speaking, the factors considered in judging likely confusion in an opposition proceeding are the same as in a court infringement action.[7] There are, however, a few rules peculiar to opposition practice. For example:

> Applicant's goods in issue are determined by the goods as defined in the application.[8]

This means that the description used in the application controls, even if applicant's use is narrower or broader.

> Applicant's goods are presumed to travel in the normal channels of trade for such goods.[9]

This means that applicant's men's cologne, even if sold only through specialized shops and hair stylists, is presumed sold in all retail outlets that normally carry men's cologne, *e.g.*, drugstores, department stores. Applicant cannot assert a limitation in trade channels unless the limitation is spelled out in applicant's description of goods.

> Unless the application and opposer's registration show the marks in special form, applicant cannot rely on distinctions in format as avoiding confusion.[10]

This means that applicant's mark presented in typed letter form is presumed to cover all the available styles of print. Applicant cannot assert a difference with opposer's mark based on difference in print styles.

---

7. See chapter 7, pp. 118-37, *supra*, on factors to consider in determining likely confusion.
8. Chase Manhattan Bank, N.A. v. Life Care Servs. Corp., 227 U.S.P.Q. 389, 392 (T.T.A.B. 1985).
9. Wella Corp. v. California Concept Corp., 558 F.2d 1019, 1021-22 (C.C.P.A. 1977).
10. Squirtco v. Tomy Corp., 697 F.2d 1038, 1041-42 (Fed. Cir. 1983); *In re* Fisher Tool Co., Inc., 224 U.S.P.Q. 796, 797 (T.T.A.B. 1984).

> Opposer's rights will be defined as broadly as the mark and goods listed in the registration, even if his use is narrower.[11]

This means that if opposer's registration covers toy balloons, but opposer's use is limited to balloons for promoting soft drinks, applicant cannot assert a difference in goods based on opposer's limited use. This does not mean that opposer's rights are restricted to his registration. He may also rely on use beyond the goods described in his registration.[12]

2. Prior Use and Prior Registration: Prior use in an opposition proceeding is determined by the same rules used to determine prior use in a court proceeding.[13] Prior use may be based on public use as a trademark, trade name, or in advertising.[14] It is not necessary that the prior use qualify as "technical" trademark use, *i.e.*, use in connection with the goods transported in commerce.[15]

Prior use, however, does not always determine the outcome of an opposition. If opposer owns a registration, applicant cannot succeed on the basis of use prior to opposer's registration. Applicant's remedy lies in a counterclaim to cancel opposer's registration.[16]

Descriptiveness and Genericness: The Lanham Act prohibits registration of terms that are "merely descriptive" or "the common descriptive name" of the goods.[17] The term "merely descriptive" refers to marks that describe the nature, or other qualities of the goods and cannot serve as trademarks without proof of secondary meaning.[18] The term "common descriptive name" is the

11. Squirtco v. Tomy Corp., 697 F.2d 1038, 1042-43 (Fed. Cir. 1983).
12. Burger Chef Sys., Inc. v. Burger Man, Inc., 492 F.2d 1398, 1399 (C.C.P.A. 1974).
13. *See* chapter 4, pp. 61-68, *supra*.
14. Otto Roth & Co. v. Universal Foods Corp., 640 F.2d 1317, 1320 (C.C.P.A. 1981), *on remand* 215 U.S.P.Q. 1140 (T.T.A.B. 1982).
15. Bourns, Inc. v International Resistance Co., 341 F.2d 146, 147 (C.C.P.A. 1965).
16. Liberty & Co. v. Liberty Trouser Co., 216 U.S.P.Q. 65, 68 (T.T.A.B. 1982).
17. 15 U.S.C. §§ 1052(e)(1), 1064(c).
18. See chapter 2, pp. 19-21, *supra*, for case law on descriptiveness.

equivalent of the "generic name" for the goods. A common descriptive name cannot be registered even if secondary meaning is established.[19] Functional configurations, like generic terms, are incapable of trademark significance and are unregistrable.[20]

To be entitled to raise the claims of descriptiveness or genericness, opposer must have an interest in using the claimed mark, *e.g.*, sell the goods that the mark describes.[21]

Misdescriptiveness and Deceptiveness: The Lanham Act prohibits the registration of marks that are deceptively misdescriptive, geographically misdescriptive, or deceptive as applied to applicant's goods.[22] Parties who deal in goods competitive with applicant's goods have standing to oppose applications to register misdescriptive or deceptive marks.[23] The test for deceptiveness is: 1) does the mark misdescribe the goods; 2) is anyone likely to believe the misrepresentation; and 3) will the misrepresentation materially affect the decision to purchase the goods.[24] If the misrepresentation materially affects the decision to purchase, then the mark is deceptive. If not, the mark is deceptively misdescriptive and can be registered with proof of distinctiveness.

Fraud: Fraud in the filing of an application is a recognized ground for opposition, although the burden of proof is a heavy one.[25] Fraud charges typically involve applicant's statement in the

19. See chapter 2, pp. 18-19, *supra*, for case law on genericness.
20. Best Lock Corp. v. Schlage Lock Co., 413 F.2d 1195 (C.C.P.A. 1969).
21. C.R. Bard, Inc. v. Willy Rusch K.G., 172 U.S.P.Q. 250, 251 (T.T.A.B. 1971).
22. 15 U.S.C. § 1052(e), (a).
23. Otard, Inc. v. Italian Swiss Colony, 141 F.2d 706, 707 (C.C.P.A. 1944) (distributors from COGNAC region may oppose CALOGNAC brandy not from COGNAC region).
24. *In re* Shapeley, Inc., 231 U.S.P.Q. 73 (T.T.A.B. 1986) (SILKEASE for women's clothing deceptive). See also chapter 2, pp. 32-33, *supra*, for case law on deceptiveness.
25. W.D. Byron & Sons v. Stein Bros. Mfg. Co., 377 F.2d 1001, 1004 (C.C.P.A. 1967) Alabama Bd. of Trustees v. BAMA-Werke Curt Baumann, 231 U.S.P.Q. 408, 412 (T.T.A.B. 1986) (fraud must be "proven to the hilt").

application that he knows of no other company that has the right to use the mark. Where applicant is aware of other uses of the same mark, he may be accused of fraud in making this statement. Applicant has successfully defended against this charge based on his belief that his rights are superior or that there is no conflict.[26]

Improper Grounds

Certain causes of action available in court proceedings are not available in opposition proceedings. Claims of unfair competition, dilution, and false advertising will not be heard in proceedings before the Patent and Trademark Office.[27] This is an important factor to consider in deciding whether to voice a protest by way of opposition or court action.

Defenses to Opposition

Many of the same defenses available to defendant in federal court infringement proceedings are available to applicant in opposition proceedings.[28] The list includes absence of likely confusion, laches, acquiescence, estoppel, abandonment, fraud, and unclean hands. Defenses based on trademark misuse, unfair competition, and violation of the antitrust laws, however, which may be asserted in court, may not be asserted in an opposition.

A number of special rules apply to the defense of Patent and Trademark Office proceedings. They are discussed below.

---

26. *See* Money Store v. Harriscorp Fin., Inc., 212 U.S.P.Q. 583 (N.D. Ill. 1981), *vacated*, 689 F.2d 666 (7th Cir. 1982). See chapter 8, pp. 180-84, *supra*, for further discussion and case law on fraud.
27. Coca-Cola Co. v. Seven-Up Co., 178 U.S.P.Q. 309, *aff'd*, 497 F.2d 1351 (C.C.P.A. 1973); Wright Line, Inc. v. Data Safe Servs. Corp., 229 U.S.P.Q. 769 n.3 (T.T.A.B. 1985).
28. See chapter 8, *supra*, on defenses to infringement proceedings.

The Requirement Regarding Counterclaims

> An attack against opposer's registration will not be entertained in the absence of a counterclaim to cancel the registration.[29]

This means that defenses such as abandonment and fraud will not be heard unless applicant files a counterclaim to cancel opposer's registration. However, there is one situation where fraud will be considered in the absence of a counterclaim, *i.e.*, where it is raised as an unclean hands defense.[30] If successful, this unclean hands defense will preclude opposer from relying on his registration, although the registration remains on the register.[31]

A counterclaim to cancel opposer's registration is compulsory.[32] If grounds to support the counterclaim exist at the time of the opposition, the counterclaim must be brought as part of the opposition proceeding or it is waived.[33]

Laches, Acquiescence, and Estoppel

Theoretically, laches, acquiescence, and estoppel apply to inter partes proceedings before the Patent and Trademark Office. Indeed, the Lanham Act specifically says so:

> In all inter partes proceedings equitable principles of laches, estoppel, and acquiescence where applicable may be considered and applied.[34]

The rub is that no matter how long opposer has known of applicant's use, opposer could not object to applicant's registration until the mark was published for opposition.

The impact of a laches defense may depend on the extent to which use and registration coincide. For example, if applicant's

---

29. Cosmetically Yours, Inc. v. Clairol, Inc., 424 F.2d 1385, 1387 (C.C.P.A. 1970).
30. Duffy-Mott Co. v. Cumberland Packing Co., 424 F.2d 1095, 1099 (C.C.P.A. 1970).
31. *Id.*
32. T.M.R.P. 2.106(b), 2.114(b).
33. T.M.R.P. 2.106(b), 2.114(b).
34. 15 U.S.C. § 1069.

use is geographically limited, the nationwide registration would be enlarging applicant's rights. Opposer's past delay in protesting a limited use should not be interpreted as approval of the expanded rights accorded by federal registration.

On the other hand, where the grant of registration is consistent with applicant's right to use, there is a strong argument that laches as to applicant's use should protect applicant's right to register.[35]

The Trademark Trial and Appeal Board appears to have taken a middle ground on the laches issue. The Board has adopted the general rule that:

> Laches is a defense where likelihood of confusion is reasonably debatable. Laches is not a defense where likelihood of confusion is inevitable.[36]

This means that if the confusion issue is close, opposer's laches will swing the decision in favor of applicant.

Laches is not, however, a defense to claims of descriptiveness or genericness.[37] For one thing, until applicant applies for registration, it may not be clear that he is asserting trademark rights. For another, the strong public policy against monopolizing descriptive or generic terms outweighs any equitable interest applicant may have developed as a result of opposer's laches.

Applicant's Prior Registration of Similar Mark for Similar Goods

Where applicant owns a prior registration for essentially the same mark on the same goods, opposer cannot be "damaged" by the issuance of the second registration.[38] The question here is what

35. Hitachi Metals Int'l, Ltd. v. Yamakyu Chain Kabushiki Kaisha, 209 U.S.P.Q. 1057, 1066-67 (T.T.A.B. 1981).
36. *Id.* at 1067, 1069.
37. Care Corp. v. Nursecare Int'l, Inc., 216 U.S.P.Q. 993, 995 (T.T.A.B. 1982) (descriptive); Yankee, Inc. v. Geiger, 216 U.S.P.Q. 996, 1000 (T.T.A.B. 1982) (generic).
38. Morehouse Mfg. Corp. v. J. Strickland & Co., 407 F.2d 881, 883-84 (C.C.P.A. 1969).

constitutes the same mark and the same goods—will the elimination of a design element or the addition of another item to a broad list of goods make the difference? Maybe yes, maybe no.[39]

Procedure in Inter Partes Patent and Trademark Office Proceedings

The procedure in Patent and Trademark Office inter partes proceedings is quite different from federal court actions. This section will summarize:

1. the evidentiary presumptions and rules that should guide the attorney in preparing his case before the Trademark Trial and Appeal Board; and
2. the step-by-step process of pleading, discovery, motion practice, testimony, briefing, and oral argument that goes into making a case before the Board.

For ease of reference, the Patent and Trademark Office procedure is described in terms of an opposition, although the same rules apply to cancellation, interference, and concurrent use proceedings.

Evidentiary Presumptions and Rules

Because Patent and Trademark Office proceedings routinely involve a pending application or an existing registration, the practitioner must deal with certain evidentiary presumptions. These include:

- Applicant's use is presumed to date back to the filing date of the subject application.[40]

---

39. Haggar Co. v. Hugger Corp., 172 U.S.P.Q. 253, 254 (T.T.A.B. 1971); Continental Specialties Corp. v. Continental Connector Corp., 192 U.S.P.Q. 449, 451-52 (T.T.A.B. 1976).
40. J.C. Hall Co. v. Hallmark Cards, Inc., 340 F.2d 960, 962 (C.C.P.A. 1965).

- Use prior to the filing date must be proven and use prior to the first use alleged in the application must be proven by clear and convincing evidence.[41]
- Registrant's use is presumed to date back to the filing date of his application in the absence of testimony establishing earlier use.[42]
- A registered mark is presumed in continuous use from the application filing date to the present.[43]

Other evidentiary principles frequently encountered are:

- Applicant cannot amend his description of goods after opposition has been filed without opposer's consent.[44]
- Opposer cannot withdraw his opposition "without prejudice" after applicant has answered, unless applicant consents to the withdrawal.[45]
- Discovery depositions can only be offered in evidence by an adverse party, unless the deponent is unavailable for certain reasons, *e.g.*, death, illness, etc.[46] The adverse party may submit additional portions for clarification.[47]
- Only the party taking discovery by way of interrogatories or admissions can initially rely on the responses. Of course, the responding party can introduce other portions for purposes of clarification.[48]

---

41. George Putnam Co., Inc. v. Hydro-Dynamics, Inc., 228 U.S.P.Q. 951, 953 (T.T.A.B. 1986).
42. Harvey Aluminum, Inc. v. American Screen Prods. Co., 305 F.2d 479, 481 (C.C.P.A. 1962).
43. J.C. Hall Co. v. Hallmark Cards, Inc., 340 F.2d 960, 962-63 (C.C.P.A. 1965).
44. T.M.R.P. 2.133.
45. T.M.R.P. 2.106(c), 2.114(c).
46. T.M.R.P. 2.120(j)(1), (2).
47. T.M.R.P. 2.120(j)(4).
48. *Id.* Chesebrough-Pond's, Inc. v. Soulful Days, Inc., 228 U.S.P.Q. 954, 955 n.4 (T.T.A.B. 1985).

- Certain material is automatically in evidence, *e.g.*, the file of the subject application and registrations under attack.[49] The specimens from such files, however, are not automatically in evidence.[50]
- Certain material may be introduced by way of a notice of reliance: official Patent and Trademark Office records, *e.g.*, registrations,[51] publications in general circulation,[52] and discovery from the adverse party.[53]
- Evidence directed to likelihood of confusion is admissible up through the testimony phase of the proceeding (corresponding to the trial phase of court litigation).[54]
- Evidence as to descriptiveness must date from before the subject application was filed.[55]
- Rulings on objections to testimony and other evidence are reserved until the final hearing. Such objections are waived unless renewed in the briefs.[56]
- Documents attached to pleadings and briefs will not be received in evidence.[57]

The Course of Proceedings

The Pleadings

While the Notice of Opposition corresponds generally to a civil complaint, there are strict rules as to the time for filing. Filing

49. T.M.R.P. 2.122(b).
50. T.M.R.P. 2.122(b)(2).
51. T.M.R.P. 2.122(d)(2).
52. T.M.R.P. 2.122(e).
53. T.M.R.P. 2.120(j).
54. R.J. Reynolds Tobacco Co. v. American Brands, Inc., 493 F.2d 1235, 1238 (C.C.P.A. 1974).
55. De Walt, Inc. v. Magna Power Tool Corp., 289 F.2d 656, 659-60 (C.C.P.A. 1961).
56. Volkswagenwerk Ag. v. Clement Wheel Co. Inc., 204 U.S.P.Q. 76, 82-83 (T.T.A.B. 1979).
57. OPTOmechanisms, Inc. v. Optoelectronics, Inc., 175 U.S.P.Q. 246, 247 n.2 (T.T.A.B. 1972).

must take place within the initial thirty-day period following publication in the Official Gazette or subsequent extensions of the period approved by the Trademark Trial and Appeal Board. The Board will conduct the trial of the opposition.

Two copies of the Notice of Opposition must be filed with the Board. The Board attends to service on applicant and sets the time to answer, usually forty days from the date of service.

The answer, like the answer to a complaint, must admit, deny, or plead lack of knowledge as to each allegation. The answer shall also contain any affirmative defenses and counterclaims. It bears repeating that a claim to cancel any registration relied on by the adverse party is a compulsory counterclaim to the opposition.[58]

Discovery

Timing: Following service of the answer, the Board sets time periods for discovery and the taking of testimony.[59] Discovery may begin at any time following the service of the answer. The initial notice setting dates provides for a discovery close—usually ninety days following the mailing of the notice. The discovery and testimony periods can be extended by agreement or for good cause.[60]

Scope and Methods: The Federal Rules of Civil Procedure apply to the scope and methods of discovery unless "otherwise provided" by the Trademark Rules of Practice.[61] An example of "otherwise provided" is the special provision in the Trademark Rules that only the inquiring party can rely on requests for admissions.[62]

The scope of discovery is governed by Rule 26 of the Federal Rules of Civil Procedure. Rule 26 permits inquiries "reasonably calculated to lead to the discovery of admissible evidence." Insofar

---

58. T.M.R.P. 2.106. See this chapter, p. 289, *supra*, on counterclaims.
59. T.M.R.P. 2.120, 2.121.
60. T.M.R.P. 2.121(a)(1).
61. T.M.R.P. 2.120.
62. T.M.R.P. 2.120(j)(5).

as the issues before the Board are narrower than the issues before a court, the scope of discovery will also be narrower.

All the usual discovery methods available in court are available in the Patent and Trademark Office, *i.e.*, interrogatories, document requests, depositions, and requests for admissions.[63] All of this material, with the exception of documents, may be introduced by the inquiring party by way of a notice of reliance filed during that party's testimony period.[64]

1. Interrogatories: The Board has disapproved "boiler-plate" interrogatories and the practice of objecting to your opponent's interrogatories as harassing, while serving the identical interrogatories on your opponent.[65] If you duplicate your opponent's interrogatories, you will be held to vouch for their reasonableness.

2. Document Requests: A frequent document request in Office proceedings calls for advertising, labels, and invoices relating to the mark in issue. The Board has ruled that a request for "all" such documents is satisfied by the production of representative samples.[66] Other proper subjects for discovery are annual sales and advertising figures.[67] The Board has also ruled that search reports are discoverable, but the attorney's opinion as to the search is privileged attorney-client material.[68] Customer lists may also be privileged and protected from production on grounds of business confidence.[69] But a party should not expect to introduce at trial any material he refused to produce in discovery.

---

63. See chapter 10, pp. 214-17, *supra*, for discussion of the procedure and strategy regarding various discovery methods.
64. T.M.R.P. 2.120(j)(3).
65. C.H. Stuart Inc. v. S.S. Sarna, Inc., 212 U.S.P.Q. 386 (T.T.A.B. 1980); Sentrol, Inc. v. Sentex Sys., Inc., 231 U.S.P.Q. 666 (T.T.A.B. 1986).
66. Procter & Gamble Co. v. Keystone Auto. Warehouse, 191 U.S.P.Q. 468, 471 (T.T.A.B. 1976).
67. Sunkist Growers, Inc. v. Benjamin Ansehl Co., 229 U.S.P.Q. 147, 149 (T.T.A.B. 1985).
68. Fisons Ltd. v. Capability Brown Ltd., 209 U.S.P.Q. 167, 170-71 (T.T.A.B. 1980).
69. Cool Ray, Inc. v. Eye Care, Inc., 183 U.S.P.Q. 618, 621 (T.T.A.B. 1974).

Documents produced in discovery cannot simply be introduced by a notice of reliance. They may be introduced by:

1. the trial testimony of a witness having knowledge of the documents;[70]
2. notice of reliance on a response to a request for admission admitting genuineness of the documents;[71]
3. identification by a witness during a discovery deposition, plus an offer in evidence made during the deposition and a notice of reliance on the documents along with the deposition.[72]

Documents are to be produced where they are usually maintained, where the parties agree, or where the Board orders.[73]

*3. **Discovery Depositions:*** Discovery depositions are taken in the district where the deponent resides or is regularly employed.[74] Depositions of nonparty witnesses can be compelled by a subpoena issued by the district court where the witness resides.[75] The discovery deposition of a nonparty cannot be introduced by notice of reliance, unless the other side consents.[76] There is a required format for deposition transcripts taken in Patent and Trademark Office proceedings that the court reporter should be instructed to follow.[77]

Sanctions: Disputes over discovery are resolved by motion practice before the Trademark Trial and Appeal Board. Like most

---

70. Harvey Hubbell, Inc. v. Red Rope Indus., Inc., 191 U.S.P.Q. 119, 121 n.1 (T.T.A.B. 1976).
71. Rice, *Making Documents Obtained During Discovery and Third-Party Registrations of Record*, 67 TRADEMARK REP. 54 (1977).
72. Johnson & Johnson, Inc. v. American Hosp. Supply Corp., 187 U.S.P.Q. 478, 479 (T.T.A.B. 1975).
73. Sunkist Growers, Inc. v. Benjamin Ansehl Co., 229 U.S.P.Q. 147, 148 (T.T.A.B. 1985).
74. T.M.R.P. 2.120(b).
75. 35 U.S.C. § 24.
76. T.M.R.P. 2.120(j)(2).
77. T.M.R.P. 2.123(g).

district courts, the Board requires the parties to certify that they have made a good faith effort to settle the dispute but were unable to do so prior to making a motion.[78] Procedures are available for telephone conferences.[79]

Sanctions for failure to comply with discovery orders correspond to those provided by the Federal Rules, including dismissal of the opposition.[80] However, the Trademark Trial and Appeal Board is not empowered to award attorneys' fees.[81]

Motion Practice

Motion practice before the Board accords generally with the Federal Rules. There are a few motions peculiar to Patent and Trademark Office proceedings, such as motions to dismiss for failure to introduce testimony or any other evidence.[82] A similar motion also lies where plaintiff has introduced only Patent and Trademark Office records.[83]

Summary judgment motions may be made under the traditional standards applied by federal courts.[84] The motion must be made before the opening of opposer's testimony period. The Court of Appeals for the Federal Circuit has suggested that summary judgment should be used more often for disposing of cases before the Board.[85]

---

78. T.M.R.P. 2.120(e).
79. T.M.R.P. 2.120(i).
80. T.M.R.P. 2.120(g), (e).
81. T.M.R.P. 2.120(g).
82. T.M.R.P. 2.132(a).
83. T.M.R.P. 2.132(b).
84. FED. R. CIV. P. 56. See chapter 11, pp. 224-32, *supra*, on summary judgment.
85. Pure Gold, Inc. v. Syntex (U.S.A.), Inc., 739 F.2d 624, 626 n.2 (Fed. Cir. 1984).

Motions to strike are appropriate where opposer alleges grounds clearly improper under Patent and Trademark Office proceedings, *e.g.*, dilution and unfair competition.[86]

Motions must be responded to within fifteen days after service.[87] Where no response is filed, the motion will be treated as conceded.[88] A reply to a response is not provided for by the rules.

Trial Testimony

The Paper Record: Trial testimony is intended to correspond with the trial phase of a court proceeding. But there is one major difference: no judge presides over the trial in the Patent and Trademark Office. The testimony is transcribed by a court reporter and the transcript, along with other evidence, is submitted to a panel of three members of the Trademark Trial and Appeal Board for decision. It is essentially a "paper" record.

Objections as to admissibility of evidence are decided when the Board reads the parties' briefs. The objections must be renewed in the briefs or they are waived.[89]

Timing: The testimony period, like Gaul, is divided into three parts. The party in the position of plaintiff (opposer or cancellation petitioner) leads off with a thirty-day period during which testimony can be taken. This testimony period is usually set to begin thirty days after the close of discovery.

The testimony period of the party in the position of defendant (applicant in an opposition or registrant in a cancellation) also lasts thirty days. It is set to begin thirty days after the close of plaintiff's testimony period.

---

86. *See* Coca-Cola Co. v. Seven-Up Co., 178 U.S.P.Q. 309, *aff'd*, 497 F.2d 1351 (C.C.P.A. 1973); Wright Line, Inc. v. Data Safe Servs. Corp., 229 U.S.P.Q. 769, n.3 (T.T.A.B. 1985).
87. T.M.R.P. 2.127(a).
88. *Id.*
89. Volkswagenwerk Ag. v. Clement Wheel Co., 204 U.S.P.Q. 76, 82 (T.T.A.B. 1979).

The third phase of testimony is the rebuttal period. It begins thirty days after the close of the preceding period, but lasts only for fifteen days.

A typical notice of testimony mailed, for example, on November 18, 1986 will read:

Discovery close	February 18, 1987
Testimony period for party in position of plaintiff closes (opening 30 days prior thereto)	April 18, 1987
Testimony period for party in position of defendant closes (opening 30 days prior thereto)	June 18, 1987
Rebuttal period to close (opening 15 days prior thereto)	August 4, 1987

It is up to the parties to calculate the opening dates. These periods can be extended by stipulation or by motion for good cause.[90]

Form of Testimony: Admissible evidence includes testimony by deposition as well as notice of reliance on discovery, Patent and Trademark Office records and documents in circulation to the general public.[91] Testimony can also be submitted by way of affidavit or stipulation if the other side agrees.[92]

When trial testimony is taken by deposition, a notice of taking testimony must be served on the other side. The notice identifies the witnesses to be called, the time and place of testimony and invites the adverse party to attend and cross-examine.[93]

90. T.M.R.P. 2.121(d).
91. T.M.R.P. 2.120(j), 2.122(d), (e).
92. T.M.R.P. 2.123(b).
93. T.M.R.P. 2.123(c), 2.123(e)(3).

Testimony can also be taken by way of written questions. This is the required method for testimony taken outside the United States.[94]

The rebuttal period cannot be used to introduce overlooked evidence which properly belongs to the case-in-chief. Such testimony will be stricken as improper rebuttal.[95]

Service and Filing of the Record: Copies of all material introduced during the testimony period must be served on the adverse party. A copy of the transcript of testimony along with exhibits must be served within thirty days after completion of the testimony and shall be filed promptly.[96] The exhibits must be properly marked with the number and title of the case and the name of the offering party.[97]

Briefs and Oral Hearings

A briefing schedule is also set by the Trademark Trial and Appeal Board. The timing is:

Brief of party in position of plaintiff	Due sixty days after close of rebuttal testimony
Brief of party in position of defendant	Due thirty days after due date of plaintiff's brief
Reply brief of party in position of plaintiff	Due fifteen days after due date of defendant's brief[98]

94. T.M.R.P. 2.123(a)(2).
95. American Meat Inst. v. Horace W. Longacre, Inc., 211 U.S.P.Q. 712, 719 (T.T.A.B. 1981).
96. T.M.R.P. 2.125.
97. T.M.R.P. 2.123(g)(2).
98. T.M.R.P. 2.128(a)(1).

The briefs are similar to post-trial briefs in court proceedings. There are specific rules regarding the number of copies filed, format, and length.[99]

An oral hearing will be granted upon request by either party. The request must be filed within ten days after the due date of the reply brief.[100] The hearing takes place at the Trademark Trial and Appeal Board in Crystal City, Virginia, before a three member panel of the Board.

Reconsideration and Appeal

Reconsideration may be sought by a petition filed within thirty days of the Board's decision.[101]

Appeal may be had to the Court of Appeals for the Federal Circuit or review may be sought by a federal district court. The pros and cons of each alternative are reviewed later in this chapter.[102]

Cancellation Proceedings

Procedure

Cancellation proceedings are brought to cancel existing registrations. The procedure is similar to opposition proceedings. The pleadings consist of a petition to cancel filed in duplicate with the Board and served by the Board on the registrant. An answer is required forty days later. The owner of the registration sought to be cancelled is in the position of defendant and is referred to as the respondent. The party seeking cancellation is in the position of plaintiff and is referred to as petitioner.

---

99. T.M.R.P. 2.128(b).
100. T.M.R.P. 2.129.
101. T.M.R.P. 2.129(c).
102. *See* this chapter, pp. 314-18, *infra*.

The same evidentiary rules and course of proceedings set forth at pages 291-301 of this chapter apply generally to cancellation proceedings.

Burden of Proof

There was a time when the burden of proof in a cancellation proceeding was considered heavier than in an opposition. This is no longer the law. The burden in both actions is the same: plaintiff must prove his case by a preponderance of the evidence.[103]

Still, where the registered mark has been in use for sometime after issuance, it may be harder for plaintiff to sustain his burden against defenses such as no likely confusion, laches, etc. There are also some grounds of attack that are not available against registrations over five years old.[104]

The All or Nothing Rule

A registration will be either cancelled completely or not at all.[105] No limitations, *e.g.*, deletion of goods from a class, can be made in a cancellation action by the Trademark Trial and Appeal Board, although a federal court does have this power.[106]

The "Damage" Requirement for Standing

The requirement for standing in a cancellation action is similar to that in an opposition: petitioner must believe he is damaged by the existence of the registration sought to be cancelled.[107] Allegations sufficient to support standing include likelihood of confusion

---

103. Massey Junior College, Inc. v. Fashion Inst. of Technology, 492 F.2d 1399, 1402-04 (C.C.P.A. 1974).
104. *See* this chapter, p. 306, *infra*.
105. Selfway, Inc. v. Travelers Petroleum, Inc., 579 F.2d 75, 80-81 (C.C.P.A. 1978).
106. 15 U.S.C. § 1119.
107. 15 U.S.C. § 1064.

and rejection of petitioner's application on the basis of the challenged registration.[108]

In the case of a cancellation action attacking the registered mark as generic or descriptive, petitioner must have an interest in using the challenged mark.[109]

Petitioner does not have standing solely because the registrant has brought suit or filed opposition against petitioner based on the challenged registration.[110]

Grounds for Cancellation

Before the Five-Year Limit

For the first five years of a registration, cancellation may be brought on all the grounds available in an opposition proceeding.[111]

The available grounds during the initial five years include:

1. likelihood of confusion with petitioner's previously used or registered mark;
2. descriptiveness and genericness;
3. misdescriptiveness and deceptiveness;
4. fraud; and
5. abandonment.[112]

Grounds onc through four above are generally the same as those discussed in the preceding section relating to oppositions. However, there is a significant difference in the affect of a prior registration in an opposition and in a cancellation proceeding. In

108. Lipton Indus., Inc. v. Ralston Purina Co., 670 F.2d 1024, 1029 (C.C.P.A. 1982).
109. Golomb v. Wadsworth, 592 F.2d 1184, 1185-86 (C.C.P.A. 1979).
110. Yard-Man, Inc. v. Getz Exterminators, Inc., 157 U.S.P.Q. 100, 105 (T.T.A.B. 1968).
111. 15 U.S.C. § 1064. See this chapter, pp. 304-06, *infra*, for discussion of grounds after five-year limit.
112. Abandonment is discussed in chapter 8, pp. 164-72, *supra*.

an opposition, opposer's prior registration will prevail against applicant's prior use in the absence of a counterclaim to cancel opposer's registration. In a cancellation proceeding, where both petitioner and respondent own registrations, priority of use controls.[113]

The grounds for cancellation do not include trademark misuse, unfair competition or violation of the antitrust laws.[114]

Grounds for Cancellation after Five-Year Limit

A registration more than five years old cannot be cancelled because of 1) likely confusion with petitioner's prior use or registration, or 2) descriptiveness of the registered mark.

Cancellation of a registration over five years old is limited to the grounds that:

1. The mark is generic;
2. The mark has been abandoned;
3. The registration was obtained by fraud;
4. The mark comprises immoral, scandalous, or deceptive matter;
5. The mark comprises national insignia;
6. The mark comprises the names of living individuals or U.S. presidents;
7. The mark is an improperly used collective or certification mark;
8. The mark disparages or falsely suggests a connection with persons, institutions, beliefs, or national symbols;
9. The mark is used to misrepresent source of the goods.[115]

---

113. Scoa Indus., Inc. v. Kennedy & Cohen, Inc., 188 U.S.P.Q. 411, 413 (T.T.A.B. 1975), *appeal dismissed*, 530 F.2d 953 (C.C.P.A. 1975).

114. Knickerbocker Toy Co., Inc. v. Faultless Starch Co., 467 F.2d 501, 509 (C.C.P.A. 1972).

115. 15 U.S.C. § 1064, incorporating 15 U.S.C. § 1052(a), (b), (c).

Grounds one through four are discussed in detail elsewhere in this book.[116] Grounds five through seven are very specialized.

Grounds eight and nine, false suggestion and misrepresentation of source, have been the subject of some controversy, particularly as to their possible duplication of the likelihood of confusion ground. Since likelihood of confusion has been ruled out as a ground for attack against a registration over five years old, something more than likelihood of confusion is needed to successfully plead a claim of false suggestion or misrepresentation of source.

Falsely Suggesting a Connection: Marks that "falsely suggest a connection" with persons or institutions may be cancelled at any time.[117] Originally this provision was designed to protect the right of privacy and publicity.[118] Not surprisingly, efforts were made to use this section to circumvent the protection accorded five-year old registrations from charges based on confusion. To prevent this result, some decisions required intent to trade on the senior party's goodwill as a necessary element.[119] Recently, however, the elements of a pleading under this section have been refined and intention to trade is no longer required. The elements that must be pleaded are:

1. that defendant's mark is the same or a close approximation of plaintiff's previously used name or identity;
2. that defendant's mark would be recognized as such;
3. that plaintiff is not connected with the activities performed by defendant under the mark; and

116. For genericness, see chapter 8, pp. 179-80, *supra*; for abandonment see chapter 8, pp. 164-72, *supra*; for fraud see chapter 8, pp. 180-83, *supra*; for deceptive matter see chapter 2, pp. 32-33, *supra*.

117. 15 U.S.C. § 1064 incorporating 15 U.S.C. § 1052(a).

118. University of Notre Dame Du Lac v. J.C. Gourmet Food Imports Co., 703 F.2d 1372 (Fed. Cir. 1983).

119. Dynachem Corp. v. Dexter Corp. 203 U.S.P.Q. 218, 220 (T.T.A.B. 1979); Signature Guardian Sys., Inc. v. Lee, 209 U.S.P.Q. 81, 87 n.4 (T.T.A.B. 1980).

4. that plaintiff's name or identity is of sufficient fame or reputation that when defendant's mark is used on defendant's goods or services, a connection with plaintiff would be presumed.[120]

An example of a mark falsely suggesting a connection with an institution is WESTPOINT for rifles. The institution—of course—is the U.S. Military Academy a/k/a/ West Point.[121]

Misrepresentation of Source: Section 14(c) of the Lanham Act allows cancellation at any time if the registered mark is being used "to misrepresent the source of the goods or services in connection with which the mark is used."[122] Misrepresentation of source means something more than likelihood of confusion. A claim under Section 14(c) requires "blatant misuse of the mark . . . in a manner calculated to trade on the goodwill and reputation of petitioner."[123] An allegation of "willful adoption of a colorable imitation of petitioner's mark" will not suffice.[124]

Defenses

Defenses to cancellation proceedings include the same defenses available in oppositions,[125] except as to those registrations over five years old. It bears repeating that registrations in existence over five years cannot be cancelled on the basis of likely confusion or descriptiveness.

---

120. Consolidated Natural Gas Co. v. CNG Fuel Sys., 228 U.S.P.Q. 752, 754 (T.T.A.B. 1985).
121. *In re* Cotter & Co., 228 U.S.P.Q. 202 (T.T.A.B. 1985).
122. 15 U.S.C. § 1064(c).
123. McDonnell Douglas Corp. v. National Data Corp., 228 U.S.P.Q. 45, 47 (T.T.A.B. 1985).
124. *Id.*
125. *See* this chapter, pp. 288-91, *supra*.

Cancellation of a Supplemental Registration

Registrations on the Supplemental Register are not subject to opposition, but they are subject to cancellation.

Procedure and Standing

The procedure for cancelling a registration on the Supplemental Register is generally the same as the procedure for cancelling a registration on the Principal Register. The requirement for standing is also similar for both proceedings.[126]

Grounds for Cancellation

There is no time limitation on bringing an action to cancel a Supplemental Registration. The grounds for cancellation, however, are limited to the following:

1. The registrant was not entitled to register the mark at the time of his application; and
2. The mark is not used by the registrant or has been abandoned.[127]

Under the first ground, the Supplemental Registration may be cancelled if:

a. The registered mark is likely to be confused with petitioner's previously used or registered mark;[128]
b. The registered mark is deceptive, consists of national insignia, or the name of a living individual who has not given his consent;[129]
c. The registered mark was or has become generic;[130]

---

126. *See* this chapter, pp. 302-03, *supra*.
127. 15 U.S.C. § 1092.
128. 15 U.S.C. §§ 1091, 1052(d).
129. 15 U.S.C. §§ 1091, 1052 (a),(b),(c).
130. Harvey Hubbell, Inc. v. Dynamic Instrument Corp., 165 U.S.P.Q. 412 (T.T.A.B. 1970). *In re* Thunderbird Prods. Corp., 406 F.2d 1389, 1391 (C.C.P.A. 1969).

d. Registrant was not entitled to register the mark at the time of his application because he did not have exclusive use during the year preceding the filing of his application.[131]

The second ground permits cancellation where the mark is "not used" or "has been abandoned" by the registrant. The difference between nonuse and abandonment is not clear.

Since a mark on the Supplemental Register is by definition descriptive, descriptiveness is not a ground for cancellation.[132]

Concurrent Use Proceedings

The object of concurrent use proceedings is to provide separate registrations to different parties based on a division of trading areas. Concurrent registrations may be issued as a result of proceedings before the Trademark Trial and Appeal Board or by order of the court.[133]

Conditions for Concurrent Use Registration

The basic condition for a concurrent use registration is that the marks are used in different territories so as not to cause likely confusion. It is the division of territories that is critical. Other elements that might prevent likely confusion such as difference in

---

131. 15 U.S.C. § 1092. Kwick-Kopy Franchise Corp. v. Dimensional Lithographers, 173 U.S.P.Q. 378, 381 (T.T.A.B. 1972) (registration cancelled because of petitioner's use during the one-year period of registrant's claimed "exclusive" use prior to filing).

132. Registration on the Supplemental Register is not, however, a binding admission that the mark did not have secondary meaning at the time of registration. California Cooler, Inc. v. Loretto Winery, Ltd., 774 F.2d 1451, 1454 (9th Cir. 1985).

133. 15 U.S.C. § 1052(d).

goods, marks, etc., do not entitle the parties to concurrent registration.

The Lanham Act also specifies that the applicant for concurrent registration must have used his mark in commerce prior to the filing date of the other party's pending application or registration. There is legislation pending that would eliminate this "jurisdictional" requirement in those cases where the first applicant consents to concurrent registration.[134]

Initiation of Proceedings

Concurrent use proceedings may be initiated by a trademark application containing the usual elements, plus an identification of:

1. the extent of the concurrent use by others, *i.e.*, the specific territories;
2. the applications or registrations filed by others;
3. the goods bearing the mark used by others;
4. the time period of use by others; and
5. the area, goods, and method of use of the mark by applicant.[135]

Once the application has passed the opposition period, notices are sent by the Board to the parties identified in the application. The notice provides a period of forty days to answer. An applicant or registrant, however, need not formally answer.[136] A nonapplicant, nonregistrant party, on the other hand, must answer, or judgment will be entered preventing that party from claiming rights more extensive than those set forth in the application.[137]

134. S. 1002.
135. T.M.R.P. 2.42.
136. T.M.R.P. 2.99(g).
137. T.M.R.P. 2.99(d)(3).

The applicant for concurrent use is in the position of plaintiff.[138] Generally, the course of proceedings for concurrent use registrations are governed by the same rules as other Patent and Trademark Office inter partes proceedings.[139]

General Rules

Nationwide Registration Accorded to the First User

Where neither party has a registration, the first user is generally entitled to a nationwide registration, subject to the second user's area of use.[140] Thus the first user has rights under his registration even where he is not using the mark. The second user is confined to his area of use.[141] The leading case of *Beatrice Foods* laid down three exceptions to this rule:

1. The parties themselves can agree to leave an open area where neither party has rights.
2. Where the second user is first to register, the second user may retain the nationwide registration subject to the first user's territory. This promotes the policy of encouraging registration.
3. Open areas may be preserved if necessary to insure against likely confusion.[142]

Agreements Between the Parties Normally Accepted as Reasonable Trade Area Division

The parties may work out an agreement dividing the trade areas under certain conditions. Unless the agreement was made in bad faith or does not prevent likely confusion, it should be

138. T.M.R.P. 2.99(e), 2.116(b).
139. *See* this chapter, pp. 291-301, *supra*.
140. The first use required for concurrent use proceedings is use of any kind, *e.g.*, intrastate use, not necessarily use in commerce. Tie Rack Enters., Inc. v. Tie Rak Stores, 168 U.S.P.Q. 441, 443 (T.T.A.B. 1970).
141. *In re* Beatrice Foods Co., 429 F.2d 466 (C.C.P.A. 1970).
142. *Id.* at 474.

accepted.[143] If the Trademark Trial and Appeal Board does not believe the agreement will prevent likely confusion, it may suggest additional conditions. For example, in the *Purple Cow* case, the Board rejected the original agreement of the parties because it permitted advertising by each party to spill over into the other party's territory.[144] The parties revised the agreement, incorporating the Board's suggestion that any likely spillover advertising be accompanied by a disclaimer of association. The revised agreement was accepted by the Board.

Allowing Second User's Good Faith Expansion vis-à-vis Static First User

If the first user has made no effort to expand for some period of time, the second user may expand even though he has knowledge of the first user.[145] But if the second user's expansion is undertaken in bad faith, *e.g.*, in a deliberate effort to box in the first user, the first user's rights will not be limited.[146]

Remember the Equities

The objective of concurrent use proceedings is to resolve the conflict between parties seeking registration for confusing marks that are used in different territories.[147] The general rules recited above are just that—general rules. The Court of Customs and Patent Appeals has specifically rejected any "mechanical approach", *e.g.*, inflexible deference to the first to register, and

---

143. *Id.*
144. Meijer, Inc. v. Purple Cow Pancake House, 226 U.S.P.Q. 280, 282 (T.T.A.B. 1985).
145. Weiner King, Inc. v. Wiener King Corp., 615 F.2d 512, 523 (C.C.P.A. 1980).
146. Tie Rack Enters., Inc. v. Tie Rak Stores, 168 U.S.P.Q. 441, 446-47 (T.T.A.B. 1970).
147. *In re* Beatrice Foods Co., 429 F.2d 466 (C.C.P.A. 1970).

stressed the importance of balancing the rights of the parties and the public in light of all the equities.[148]

Interference Proceedings

Interference proceedings are nearly obsolete—so we won't spend too much time on the subject.

The Issue of Priority

The basic issue in an interference is priority of use. Unlike an opposition or cancellation proceeding, which is initiated by a party who believes he is being damaged, an interference is declared by the Commissioner of Patents and Trademarks "upon petition showing extraordinary circumstances." An interference may be declared between two conflicting applications or between an application and a conflicting registration that has not yet become incontestable.[149] The Lanham Act provides:

> Upon petition showing extraordinary circumstances, the Commissioner may declare that an interference exists when application is made for the registration of a mark which so resembles a mark previously registered by another, or for the registration of which another has previously made application, as to be likely when applied to the goods or when used in connection with the services of the applicant to cause confusion or mistake or to deceive. No interference shall be declared between an application and the registration of a mark the right to the use of which has become incontestable.[150]

148. Weiner King, Inc. v. Wiener King Corp., 615 F.2d 512, 525 (C.C.P.A. 1980).
149. 15 U.S.C. § 1066 *as amended.*
150. *Id.*

The Requirement of Extraordinary Circumstances

The Lanham Act was amended in 1983 to require a showing of "extraordinary circumstances" as the prerequisite for an interference. This amendment was a codification of what had been the practice for the last decade. This practice recognized that normally priority was most efficiently decided by way of a cancellation or opposition. For an interference to be granted, there must be a showing that, absent an interference, a party will be unduly prejudiced.[151] In other words, there must be a showing that the issue could not be most efficiently determined in an opposition or cancellation action. An example of the rare situation amounting to "extraordinary circumstances" is a multiparty conflict between petitioner's application and five other pending applications. Because resolution of the priority issue would require successive oppositions, an interference is the most efficient procedure.[152]

Procedure

The party in the position of plaintiff in an interference is the party with the latest filing date. This party is known as the junior party and has the burden of proof.[153]

The party in the position of defendant is the party with the earliest filing date. This party is known as the senior party.

The procedure and evidence for proving priority in an interference is generally the same as in an opposition or cancellation action.[154]

Registrations on the Supplemental Register and registrations that have become incontestable are not subject to interference.[155]

---

151. *See* T.M.R.P. 2.91(a).
152. *In re* Family Inns of Am., Inc., 180 U.S.P.Q. 332, 333 (Comm'r Pat. 1974).
153. T.M.R.P. 2.96.
154. *See* this chapter, pp. 283-301, *supra*.
155. T.M.R.P. 2.91(b).

Review of Trademark Trial and Appeal Board Decisions

Two Routes of Review

There are two routes of review from decisions of the Trademark Trial and Appeal Board:

1. appeal to the Court of Appeals for the Federal Circuit (CAFC);
2. review by a federal district court.[156]

The party seeking review makes the initial choice of routes by filing either a notice of appeal to the CAFC or a civil action within sixty days of the Board decision.[157]

If the party seeking review chooses the CAFC, the adverse party can veto this route. The adverse party has twenty days after notice of appeal to the CAFC to elect review by a federal district court.[158]

When the adverse party elects federal court review, the party seeking review has thirty days to file the civil action.[159] If the party seeking review chooses the district court route, this choice controls. In other words, either party can insist on review by the district court.

Trial De Novo in the District Court

There are significant differences in the two routes of review. The district court route provides for trial de novo—allowing for the introduction of new evidence. In the CAFC, the record on appeal will be confined to the record before the Trademark Trial and Appeal Board. New evidence is not permitted.

---

156. 15 U.S.C. § 1071(a), (b).
157. 15 U.S.C. § 1071(a)(2), (b).
158. 15 U.S.C. § 1071(a)(1).
159. *Id.*

Review by the district court also permits the parties to seek injunctive relief for infringement by way of the complaint or counterclaim.[160] The CAFC appeal will be confined to deciding the issue of right to registration.

While review by the district court broadens the litigation, this does not mean that new legal issues that could have been raised below can be raised for the first time on appeal.[161]

Review by the district court also permits one more bite of the apple—further appeal to the Circuit Court of Appeals. In contrast, the CAFC route is the last stop before the Supreme Court.

Effect of the Trademark Trial and Appeal Board Decision

Will it be any easier to overturn a Trademark Trial and Appeal Board decision in a district court than in the CAFC? The answer to this question turns on a number of factors, including:

1. the different legal standards of review;
2. the availability of new evidence;
3. the pertinent precedent in the district court forum compared with the CAFC; and
4. the presence of equitable considerations that will weigh heavily with a district court if an injunction is requested.

Legal Standards of Review

The CAFC will not overturn findings of fact by the Trademark Trial and Appeal Board unless they are clearly erroneous.[162] The

160. 15 U.S.C. § 1071(a), T.M.R.P. 2.145(a); Fuller Prods. Co. v. Fuller Brush Co., 299 F.2d 772, 774, *cert. denied*, 370 U.S. 923 (1962); Johnson & Johnson v. Colgate-Palmolive Co., 345 F. Supp. 1216 (D.N.J. 1972).
161. Lantech, Inc. v. Mossinghoff, 228 U.S.P.Q. 775, 777 (W.D. Ky 1985).
162. Joseph & Feiss Co. v. Joseph Kanner Hat Co., 337 F.2d 1014, 1015 (C.C.P.A. 1964).

issue of likely confusion, however, is considered an issue of law by the CAFC.[163]

In most district courts the findings of the Trademark Trial and Appeal Board will control "unless the contrary is established by evidence which in character and amount carries thorough conviction."[164]

The "thorough conviction" test is used both where the Trademark Trial and Appeal Board decision is reviewed by the district court and where a separate infringement action follows a Trademark Trial and Appeal Board decision that was not appealed.[165] There is some authority, however, rejecting the "thorough conviction" rule in favor of the "clearly erroneous" rule where new evidence is not introduced in the district court.[166]

The Availability of New Evidence

There will almost always be areas of proof that have been overlooked, considered unnecessary at the time or recently discovered. Evidence deliberately withheld from the Trademark Trial and Appeal Board, however will not be readily accepted in a trial de novo.[167]

One fertile area for new evidence is survey data. With the hindsight of an adverse decision, it may be possible to design a

---

163. Kimberly-Clark Corp. v. H. Douglas Enters., 774 F.2d 1144, 1146 (Fed. Cir. 1985).

164. Morgan v. Daniels, 153 U.S. 120 (1894); Johnson & Johnson, Inc. v. Colgate-Palmolive Co., 345 F. Supp. 1216, 1221 (D.N.J. 1972). There may be some variation of this rule in a particular district so be sure to check the standard in your forum.

165. Freedom S. & L. Ass'n v. Way, 757 F.2d 1176, 1180-81 (11th Cir. 1985).

166. Sarah Coventry, Inc. v. T. Sardelli & Sons, Inc., 392 F. Supp. 347, 354 (D.R.I. 1975).

167. Aqua-Chem, Inc. v. Baldwin-Lima-Hamilton Corp., 167 U.S.P.Q. 257, 259 (N.D. Ill. 1970) (patent interference).

survey that will persuade the court of the "error" of the Trademark Trial and Appeal Board.[168] Needless to say, the more significant the new evidence, the freer the district court will feel to reverse the Trademark Trial and Appeal Board.

Location for District Court Trial

In choosing the route of review, another factor is the location (venue) of the district court. The general venue statute controls, requiring suit to be brought where all defendants reside or where the claim arose.[169] The winning party before the Board is the defendant in the district court, and the district court trial will more than likely be held in defendant's home court.[170] Thus the party seeking review would do well to consider the applicable precedent in defendant's home circuit.

Remember the Equities

While principles of equity shall be considered in all proceedings under the Lanham Act,[171] different equities may come into play when injunctive relief is in issue. It is one thing for the Board and CAFC to deny registration to applicant with a substantial investment at stake—it is quite another for the district court to enjoin applicant's use.

A request for injunctive relief at the district court level will also alter some of the rules of the game. Elements of proof such as package appearance, use of company name, etc., which are not considered in a proceeding restricted to registration rights, are very much a factor in district court injunction proceedings. These additional factors make it all the easier for the district court to depart from the Board holding based on the court's view of the equities.

168. For discussion of surveys, see chapter 12, pp. 242-50, *supra*.

169. 28 U.S.C. § 1391(b), (c).

170. See chapter 10, pp. 205-07, *supra*, on importance of defendant's convenience to determination of "where claim arose."

171. 15 U.S.C. §§ 1069, 1116.

Looking Further Down the Road

It is useful to look down the road to the standard to be applied on any appeal from the district court to the circuit court. The decision of the district court will not be reversed unless it is clearly erroneous. To be more precise, the question is whether the district court was clearly erroneous in ruling that the evidence supporting its ruling carried thorough conviction.[172]

Litigants should also consider the affect of the CAFC decision. As a court created under article III of the U.S. Constitution, the CAFC findings on likelihood of confusion are barred from relitigation between the same parties under the doctrine of collateral estoppel.[173] A losing party in the Trademark Trial and Appeal Board may be better off with no appeal than a loss in the CAFC. The victor in a CAFC proceeding may decide to go for an injunction in the district court where the issue of likely confusion cannot be relitigated.

In summary, the losing party may have a lot more to lose on appeal than he did in the Trademark Trial and Appeal Board decision below.

---

172. Freedom S. & L. Ass'n v. Way, 757 F.2d 1176, 1182 (11th Cir.), *cert. denied,* 106 S. Ct. 134 (1985).

173. Flavor Corp. of Am. v. Kemin Indus., Inc., 493 F.2d 275, 281 (8th Cir. 1974). See chapter 11, pp. 230-32, *supra*, for discussion of collateral estoppel and res judicata.

15

Licensing a Trademark

Introduction

"License" means permission. As James Bond fans know, 007 was "licensed to kill." In the less violent world of trademarks, the licensee is licensed to use. The licensee is permitted by the licensor (trademark owner) to use the mark under certain conditions. These conditions are usually spelled out in a License Agreement.

The Requirement of Quality Control

The indispensable condition of a valid trademark license is that the licensor control the nature and quality of the goods or services sold under the mark. Control by the licensor is necessary to insure that the licensee's products are of equal quality to the products previously associated with the licensor's mark.

Quality assurance and protection of the public is a central purpose of trademark law. If licensees could deviate willy nilly from the quality standards established by the licensor, the mark would no longer signify a certain standard of quality and the public would be deceived.[1]

> Courts have long imposed upon trademark licensors a duty to oversee the quality of licensees' products [citations omitted]. The rationale for this requirement is that marks are treated by purchasers as an indication that the trademark owner is associated with the product. Customers rely upon the owner's reputation when they

1. Kentucky Fried Chicken v. Diversified Packaging, 549 F.2d 368, 387 (5th Cir. 1977).

select the trademarked goods. If a trademark owner allows licensees to depart from its quality standards, the public will be misled, and the trademark will cease to have utility as an informational device. A trademark owner who allows this to occur loses its right to use the mark.[2]

The Consequences of Failure to Control Quality

The penalty for failure to control quality is a harsh one. The license is deemed a "naked" license and the licensor's mark is deemed "abandoned."

The Lanham Act defines a mark as "abandoned":

> (b) when any course of conduct of the registrant, including acts of omission as well as commission, causes the mark to lose its significance as an indication of origin.[3]

Where the licensor's failure to control (act of omission) causes the mark to lose its significance as an indication of origin, it is abandoned. The question is: how extensive is the abandonment? Are all the owner's rights in the mark forfeited—or just his rights to the specific products and/or geographical area covered by the naked license?

In *Sheila's Shine*, one of the few cases finding abandonment because of the lack of adequate control, the court preserved the licensor's rights in the geographic area where abandonment had not been proven.[4]

The Heavy Burden of Proof

Considering the dire consequences of trademark abandonment, it is not surprising that absence of quality control is tough to prove.

2. *Id.*
3. 15 U.S.C. § 1127(b).
4. Sheila's Shine Prods., Inc. v. Sheila Shine, Inc., 486 F.2d 114, 125-26 (5th Cir. 1973).

The party alleging insufficient control must meet a high burden of proof.[5] In *Sheila's Shine*, the court tolerated three to six years of benign neglect by the licensor, but it drew the line at eleven years.[6] In *Kentucky Fried Chicken*, the court required "only minimal quality control."[7] In *House of Hunan*, the fact that one of plaintiff's licensees did "not enjoy as fine a reputation as [plaintiff]" did not "demonstrate the kind of naked licensing necessary to establish an abandonment."[8]

Methods of Quality Control

The judicial reluctance to find abandonment is reflected not only by the heavy burden of proof, but also by the acceptance of diverse methods of exercising control. These methods run the gamut from written contract, to oral contract, to no contract. In other words, quality control may be implemented through provisions agreed to in writing, through provisions agreed to orally, or through the actual exercise of control even though there is no written or oral contract. Some courts even allow the licensor to sit back and rely on the licensee's quality control.

Written Contract

The written contract providing for quality control is called a trademark license agreement. Typical trademark license provisions, including quality control provisions, are:

---

5. United States Jaycees v. Philadelphia Jaycees, 639 F.2d 134, 140 (3d Cir. 1981).
6. Sheila's Shine Prods., Inc. v. Sheila Shine, Inc., 486 F.2d 114, 123-25 (5th Cir. 1973).
7. Kentucky Fried Chicken v. Diversified Packaging, 549 F.2d 368, 387 (5th Cir. 1977).
8. House of Hunan, Inc. v. Hunan Art Pavilion, 227 U.S.P.Q. 803, 807 (D.D.C. 1985).

- Licensee's acknowledgement of Licensor's right to control quality.
- Licensee's agreement to quality standards established by Licensor. Standards may vary from the specific, *e.g.*, adherence to a certain formula, to the general, *e.g.*, adherence to the quality of sample products approved by Licensor.
- Licensor's right to inspect Licensee's premises to observe the manufacturing process.
- Licensee's provision of samples to Licensor on a regular basis, *e.g.*, every six months, or when requested by Licensor.
- Licensor's approval of Licensee's packaging, advertising, and manner of trademark use.
- Licensee's agreement that his use inures to benefit of Licensor.
- Licensee's agreement that his use will cease upon termination of License with all rights reverting to Licensor.
- Licensee's acknowledgement of validity of mark, ownership by Licensor, and agreement not to challenge ownership or validity.[9]

In addition, the license will usually define the products or services to be licensed, the geographical territory, the exclusive or nonexclusive nature of the grant, the royalty payments (if any), the ability to assign or sublicense, the methods of termination, and the applicable law.

While a written agreement is certainly advisable, it may not be enough. To many courts, the important point is whether control is, in fact, exercised, not just whether there is an acknowledged right to control.[10]

---

9. See this chapter, pp. 327-28, *infra*, on Licensee Estoppel.
10. Dawn Donut Co. v. Hart's Food Stores, Inc., 267 F.2d 358, 368 (2d Cir. 1959).

Oral Contract

A trademark license can be oral as well as written.[11] Of course, written licenses are preferable because their existence and specific provisions are easier to prove in court. Oral licenses are least likely to run into trouble where a parent company licenses its subsidiary. Control by the parent over the quality of the wholly owned subsidiaries' products may be assumed because of the corporate structure.[12] But where the subsidiary owns the mark and licenses it to the parent, control by the subsidiary is not so readily assumed. Control is not automatic just because both companies have the same directors, officers, and locations.[13]

Control in Absence of Contract

The absence of a contract, written or oral, is not fatal to the trademark license. The test is whether quality control was, in fact, exercised:

> The absence, however, of an express contract right to inspect and supervise a licensee's operations does not mean that the plaintiff's method of licensing failed to comply with the requirements of the Lanham Act. Plaintiff may in fact have exercised control in spite of the absence of any express grant by licensees of the right to inspect and supervise.
>
> The question, then, with respect to both plaintiff's contract and non-contract licensees, is whether the plaintiff in fact exercised sufficient control.[14]

Sufficient quality control to defeat a claim of abandonment may be exercised through the licensor's reasonable inspection of

---

11. Council of Better Business Bureaus, Inc. v. Better Business Bureau, 200 U.S.P.Q. 282, 289 (S.D. Fla. 1978).
12. T.M.E.P. 1201.03(b).
13. L & C Hardtmuth, Inc. v. Fabrique Suisse de Crayons Caran D'Ache S.A., 123 U.S.P.Q. 546, 547 (T.T.A.B. 1959).
14. Dawn Donut Co. v. Hart's Food Stores, Inc., 267 F.2d 358, 368 (2d Cir. 1959).

the licensee's goods.[15] One court refused to grant summary judgment on the theory of inadequate control where the licensor inspected the licensee's goods by viewing and purchasing them in the marketplace.[16]

Control by Reasonable Reliance on Licensee

A number of courts have found sufficient quality control where the licensor reasonably relied on his licensee's quality control.[17] In the *Land O'Lakes* case, the contract required the licensee to use his "best efforts to preserve the high standard and goodwill" of the mark.[18] The licensor did no product testing of his own, but relied on the control exercised by the licensee. The licensee did not manufacture the goods (canned vegetables) but applied his label to goods supplied by various companies.

The District Court in *Land O'Lakes* noted that it was incumbent on the licensee to handle quality merchandise to safeguard his market as well as his contractual right to use the mark. The Appeal Court deemed the licensor's reliance on his licensee's quality control "the taking of reasonable measures to protect the quality of the goods bearing the mark."[19]

In affirming the District Court, the Seventh Circuit pointed to the absence of complaints about quality during the forty years of the license arrangement. The Appeal Court also referred to the presence of the licensor's name on the licensee's label. Since customers could send complaints directly to the licensor, the licensor presumably would hear about any quality problems.

15. Carl Zeiss Stiftung v. V.E.B. Carl Zeiss, Jena, 293 F. Supp. 892, 918 (S.D.N.Y. 1968).
16. Weber-Stephen Prods. Co. v. North Am. Prods., Inc., No. 82C6542, slip. op. (N.D. Ill. 1983).
17. Land O'Lakes Creameries, Inc. v. Oconomowoc Canning Co., 221 F. Supp. 576, 581 (E.D. Wis. 1963), *aff'd*, 330 F.2d 667, 670 (7th Cir. 1964).
18. *Id.*, 221 F. Supp. at 581.
19. *Id.*

While use of the licensor's name on the licensee's label was noted in finding that the licensor exercised quality control in *Land O'Lakes*, this is not a requirement for a valid license.[20]

The reasonableness of the licensor's reliance on the licensee may depend on the licensee's past experience with the product, the licensee's expertise and reputation, and the fact that quality was maintained.[21] The proof in these cases is very much in the pudding. The argument goes like this: if, in fact, quality has been maintained, there has been no deception, the mark has not lost its significance as an indication of origin, and there has been no abandonment.[22]

Appointment of Quality Control Agent

It is perfectly proper for the licensor to designate a third party as his agent for performing quality control inspection and testing. An agent will not, of course, set the standards. He will only determine if the licensee's products meet the standards set by the licensor.

Too Much of a Good Thing

Even a good thing like quality control can be overdone. Some methods of control may run afoul of the antitrust laws. The classic case of *Siegel v. Chicken Delight, Inc.* found the requirement that the licensee purchase supplies such as paper plates, cups, and spices from the licensor a prohibited tie-in.[23] The court noted that there are acceptable alternatives for controlling quality of supplies

20. Pneutek, Inc. v. Scherr, 211 U.S.P.Q. 824 (T.T.A.B. 1981).
21. Transgo, Inc. v. Ajac Transmission Parts Corp., 768 F.2d 1001, 1017-18 (9th Cir. 1985); Syntex Laboratories, Inc. v. Norwich Pharmacal Co., 315 F. Supp. 45, 56 (S.D.N.Y. 1970), *aff'd on other grounds*, 437 F.2d 566 (2d Cir. 1971); Winnebago Indus., Inc. v. Oliver & Winston, Inc., 207 U.S.P.Q. 335, 340-41 (T.T.A.B. 1980); Edwin K. Williams & Co. v. Edwin K. Williams & Co.-East, 542 F.2d 1053, 1059-60 (9th Cir. 1976).
22. 15 U.S.C. § 1127(b).
23. Siegel v. Chicken Delight, Inc., 448 F.2d 43 (9th Cir. 1971).

that do not unduly restrict competition such as the setting of quality specifications.

Cases decided some years after *Siegel v. Chicken Delight* have clarified what is not an illegal tie-in. In *Baskin-Robbins*, the license required the licensee to purchase ice cream from the licensor. The court noted that the mark (BASKIN-ROBBINS) and the product (ice cream) are "inextricably interrelated in the mind of the consumer."[24] Because the trademark serves to identify the quality of the product, the trademark and the product are not separate items for tie-in purposes.[25]

Patent and Trademark Office Procedure Regarding Licensing

Use by Related Company

The licensor may rely on use by the licensee to support his trademark application. This is known as use by a "related company." Use by a related company "shall inure to the benefit of the registrant or applicant for registration."[26]

"Related company" is defined by the Lanham Act as follows:

> The term "related company" means any person who legitimately controls or is controlled by the registrant or applicant for registration in respect to the nature and quality of the goods or services in connection with which the mark is used.[27]

Disclosure of Related Company Use in Application

The applicant licensor relying solely on the licensee's use should recite in the application that use is by a related company.[28] The

24. Krehl v. Baskin-Robbins Ice Cream Co., 664 F.2d 1348, 1354 (9th Cir. 1982).
25. *Id.*
26. 15 U.S.C. § 1055.
27. 15 U.S.C. § 1127.
28. T.M.R.P. 2.38(b).

applicant should also be prepared to explain to the Trademark Examiner how control is exercised.[29] For example, applicant may be required to furnish excerpts from the license agreement pertaining to quality control. However, the entire license agreement need not be filed and the licensee need not be identified.[30]

Licensee Estoppel

The doctrine of licensee estoppel precludes the licensee from challenging the ownership and validity of the licensor's mark.[31] The theory is that the licensee who benefits from the use of the mark should not be allowed to have his cake and eat it too:

> In any case the fact that Soft Water entered into this franchise agreement with Union, thereby recognizing the validity of the trademarks at least for the purposes of the contract, estops it from now claiming that the trademarks are not valid. Defendant cannot on the one hand acknowledge the validity of the trademark and on the other hand [when it becomes convenient] claim that the trademark is not valid and cannot be enforced because of abandonment. The contract itself is enough reason that this defense cannot be allowed.[32]

There is some question as to the duration of the estoppel. A number of courts have held that the estoppel applies only to facts arising during the licensed use. In other words, if thc factual basis for the licensee's challenge occurs after termination of the license, licensee estoppel does not apply:

> [A]fter expiration of the license, a former trademark licensee may challenge the licensor's title on facts which arose after the contract has expired. Callmann, *supra* at 454; *Medd v. Boyd Wagner*, 132 F. Supp. 399 (N.D. Ohio 1955). Thus a licensee affirms his

29. T.M.R.P. 2.38(b).
30. T.M.E.P. 1201.03(d).
31. Union Tank Car Co. v. Lindsay Soft Water Corp., 257 F. Supp. 510, 516 (D. Neb. 1966).
32. *Id.*

> licensor's ownership of the mark by entering into the agreement, but the straightjacket effect does not last interminably. In the present case, however, the facts upon which Bankers relies arose during the course of its ten-year agreement with the PGA, so it is estopped to argue abandonment.[33]

The licensor may try to guard against his licensee's challenge based on facts arising after termination of the license by a specific contract provision. For example, the license can provide that the licensee will *never* challenge licensor's ownership and validity of the mark.[34]

---

33. Professional Golfers Ass'n of Am. v. Bankers Life & Casualty Co., 514 F.2d 665, 671 (5th Cir. 1975).
34. *See* Beer Nuts, Inc. v. King Nut Co., 477 F.2d 326, 328 (6th Cir. 1973) (enforcing contract provision that licensee would never challenge mark on grounds of descriptiveness).

16

Assigning a Trademark

Introduction

A trademark assignment is a transfer of ownership. The trademark owner (assignor) gives up all rights to the mark. These rights are acquired by the assignee who stands in the shoes of the assignor.[1] The assignee not only succeeds to all of the assignor's rights, *e.g.*, date of first use, but also to all defenses available against the assignor. For example, the assignor's unreasonable delay in challenging an infringing use (laches) may bar the assignee from challenging that use.[2]

Methods of Assignment

Trademarks, like other forms of property, can be transferred orally or in writing. An oral assignment may be proven by the clear and uncontradicted testimony of a person with knowledge.[3] For ease of proof, of course, you are much better off with a written assignment.

Trademarks may also be transferred as part of the sale of an ongoing business, even though not specifically mentioned in the

1. Johanna Farms, Inc. v. Citrus Bowl, Inc., 468 F. Supp. 866, 874-75 (E.D.N.Y. 1978).
2. Pepsico, Inc. v. Grapette Co., 416 F.2d 285, 286-87 (8th Cir. 1969).
3. Diebold, Inc. v. Multra-Guard, Inc., 189 U.S.P.Q. 119, 124 (T.T.A.B. 1975); Old Swiss House, Inc. v. Anheuser-Busch, Inc., 569 F.2d 1130, 1132 (C.C.P.A. 1978).

sale documents.[4] The same principle applies to the involuntary sale of a business in bankruptcy—trademarks pass to the purchaser of the business even if the marks are not mentioned in the sale documents.[5]

Requirement for Valid Assignment

The Transfer of Goodwill

The cardinal rule of a valid trademark assignment is: the mark must be assigned with the goodwill of the business.

We learned in chapter one that a trademark stands for a certain standard of quality. The goodwill of the mark symbolizes that level of quality that the public has come to associate with products bearing the mark. The assignee must be sure he has the implements necessary to maintain this quality. If he does not, the mark becomes separated from the goodwill. The result of this separation is that the assignee will be unable to rely on the assignor's rights and may even lose the mark altogether.

Goodwill must be assigned with the trademark in order to protect consumers from deception and confusion:

> The cases cited by both sides of this controversy are consistent with the underlying purpose of why a transfer of goodwill is required in order for an assignment of a mark to be effective. The cases all seek to protect customers from deception and confusion.[6]

The Indicia of Goodwill

It may not be enough to recite the transfer of goodwill in an assignment document[7] (although this magic language should by

---

4. President Suspender Co. v. Macwilliam, 238 F. 159, 162 (2d Cir. 1916), *cert. denied*, 243 U.S. 636 (1916).
5. American Dirigold Corp. v. Dirigold Metals Corp., 125 F.2d 446, 453 (6th Cir. 1942).
6. Money Store v. Harriscorp Fin., Inc., 689 F.2d 666, 678 (7th Cir. 1982).
7. *Id.*

all means be used). In deciding whether goodwill has in fact accompanied the mark, a useful touchstone is: has the assignee obtained what he needs to carry on the business of the assignor?[8] Evidence on this point consists of: a) the transfer of tangible assets, *e.g.*, machinery, secret formula, and customer lists; b) the substantial similarity of the assignee's goods to the assignor's goods; and c) the business status of the assignor after the assignment.

The Transfer of Tangible Assets

Where an entire business, *i.e.*, machinery, formula, customer lists, etc. is purchased, it is easy to conclude that goodwill was transferred.[9]

This is not to say, however, that failure to transfer tangible assets means goodwill was not transferred. The importance of the assets to the continuity of the business must be examined. Where the product is the result of a secret formula, the formula is critical to the goodwill symbolized by the mark.[10] However, where the assignee is able to duplicate the product formula and knows who the customers are, there is no need for the assignor's written formula or customer list to be transferred to the assignee.[11]

The Similarity Between the Assignor's and Assignee's Goods

In deciding if goodwill has been transferred, courts focus on the similarities of the assignee's product to the assignor's:

> Inherent in the rules involving the assignment of a trademark is the recognition of protection against consumer deception. Basic to this concept is the proposition that any assignment of a trademark

8. Merry Hull & Co. v. Hi-Line Co., 243 F. Supp. 45, 51-52 (S.D.N.Y. 1965).
9. Oklahoma Beverage Co. v. Dr. Pepper Love Bottling Co., 565 F.2d 629, 632 (10th Cir. 1977).
10. Mulhens & Kropff, Inc. v. Ferd. Muelhens, Inc., 43 F.2d 937, 939 (2d Cir.), *cert. denied*, 282 U.S. 881 (1930).
11. Sterling Brewers, Inc. v. Schenley Indus., Inc., 441 F.2d 675, 680 (C.C.P.A. 1971); Syntex Laboratories, Inc. v. Norwich Pharmacal Co., 315 F. Supp. 45, 55 (S.D.N.Y. 1970), *aff'd*, 437 F.2d 566 (2d Cir. 1971).

> and its goodwill . . . requires that the mark itself be used by the assignee on a product having substantially the same characteristics.[12]

The same principle applies to the assignment of a service mark:

> [T]he transfer of goodwill requires only that the services be sufficiently similar to prevent consumers of the service offered under the mark from being "misled from established associations with the mark."[13]

Product changes that were fatal to the assignment include:

change from cola flavor syrup to pepper flavor;[14]

change from alum baking powder to phosphate;[15]

change in formula of cologne (secret formula not assigned).[16]

Product changes that were nonfatal to the assignment include:

change in type of sugar;[17]

change in wheat component of flour;[18] and

change in type of breeding chick.[19]

In deciding if the assignee's change causes deception, the decisive factor is the significance of the change to the purchasers—will the change materially affect the purchaser's established associations with the mark.

Assignor's Retention of Business

Just because the assignor retains a part of the business does not invalidate the assignment. A trademark may be assigned along

12. Pepsico, Inc. v. Grapette Co., 416 F.2d 285, 288 (8th Cir. 1969).
13. Visa, U.S.A., Inc. v. Birmingham Trust Nat'l Bank, 696 F.2d 1371, 1376 (Fed. Cir. 1982).
14. Pepsico, Inc. v. Grapette Co., 416 F.2d 285 (9th Cir. 1969).
15. Independent Baking Powder Co. v. Boorman, 175 F. 448 (C.C.N.J. 1910).
16. Mulhens & Kropff, Inc. v. Ferd. Muelhens, Inc., 38 F.2d 287 (S.D.N.Y. 1929), *rev'd*, 43 F.2d 937 (2d Cir.), *cert. denied*, 282 U.S. 881 (1930).
17. White Satin Mills Corp. v. Woodward, 34 F.2d 158 (D. Minn.), *aff'd*, 42 F.2d 987 (9th Cir. 1929).
18. Royal Milling Co. v. J.F. Imbs Milling Co., 44 U.S. App. D.C. 207 (1915).
19. Hy-Cross Hatchery, Inc. v. Osborne, 303 F.2d 947 (C.C.P.A. 1962).

with the particular portion of the business it symbolizes.[20] But suppose the assignee receives no assets at all and the assignor continues producing the same product under a different mark? The facts must be examined to see if the assignor's retention of assets prevented the assignee from carrying on the business of the assignee.[21]

Consequences of Invalid Assignment

Where goodwill does not accompany the mark, the assignment may be called an assignment in gross or a naked assignment. Whatever it is called, an assignment without goodwill is invalid, and the assignee cannot rely on the assignor's rights. For example, the assignee cannot tack on the assignor's period of use. Inability to rely on the assignor's use could be critical to the outcome of an infringement action where the assignor's use is needed to establish priority. When the priority rug is pulled out from under the assignee because of an invalid assignment, the assignee may find himself branded as the infringer.[22]

An invalid assignment is not usually fatal where the infringer's use postdates the assignee's own use.[23] However, there have been some extreme cases where the court refused to protect an assignee who made a deceptive use on a "highly inferior or wholly different product":

> [A] variation in formula resulting in a highly inferior or wholly different product which is palmed off on the public in place of that

20. The Lanham Act specifically recognizes the assignability of trademarks with that portion of the business symbolized by the mark. 15 U.S.C. § 1060.
21. See this chapter, pp. 330-31, *supra*.
22. Hiland Potato Chip Co. v. Culbro Corp., 671 F.2d 1190 (8th Cir. 1982).
23. Merry Hull & Co. v. Hi-Line Co., 243 F. Supp. 45, 52 (S.D.N.Y. 1965).

> upon which the good will has been established would not justify the continued protection of the trade-mark.[24]

As a result of the assignee's deceptive use on a "highly inferior or wholly different product," a court may find the assignee has abandoned his rights. In the words of the Lanham Act section on abandonment, the assignee has "caused the mark to lose its significance as an indication of origin."[25]

Assignment Provisions

Every assignment document should transfer the mark along with the goodwill of the business symbolized by the mark.

The Lanham Act section pertaining to trademark assignments should be consulted for appropriate language to use in the assignment document. Typical language used to transfer the mark along with the goodwill is:

> The assignor hereby assigns all right, title, and interest to the mark together with the goodwill of the business in which the mark is used and symbolized by the mark
>
> or
>
> together with that part of the goodwill of the business connected with the use of and symbolized by the mark.[26]

The assignment should identify any trademark registrations or pending applications for the assigned mark and recite the receipt of valuable consideration by the assignor.

The assignment should specify the geographical area of the rights assigned, *e.g.*, throughout the United States, or for the United States and throughout the rest of the world.

24. Mulhens & Kropff, Inc. v. Ferd. Muelhens, Inc., 38 F.2d 287, 295 (S.D.N.Y. 1929), *rev'd*, 43 F.2d 937 (2d Cir.), *cert. denied*, 282 U.S. 881 (1930).
25. 15 U.S.C. § 1127(b). See also chapter 8, pp. 164-72, *supra*, on abandonment.
26. 15 U.S.C. § 1060.

In addition, rights to sue and recover damages for past infringements must be expressly assigned. These rights do not automatically pass with rights to the mark.[27]

Finally, the assignor should be required to provide any materials within his control necessary to establish the validity of the assignment.[28]

Recordal of Assignment with Patent and Trademark Office

The assignment of a registered mark or a pending application should be recorded with the Patent and Trademark Office. While recordal is not mandatory, it has several advantages:

1. The assigned registration will show title in the assignee and will be presumed valid and owned by the assignee.[29]
2. The recorded assignment will be valid as against a subsequent bona fide purchaser.[30]
3. The assignee will be able to take all necessary action to maintain the registration.[31]

Special Situations

Assignment disputes are frequently encountered where:

1. The assigned mark is the personal name of the assignor;
2. The assignor uses the mark to secure a debt;

27. H & J Foods, Inc. v. Reeder, 477 F.2d 1053, 1056 (9th Cir.), *cert. denied*, 414 U.S. 859 (1973).
28. A sample trademark assignment form is contained in Appendix 6 (Trademark Assignment Form).
29. Sonic Distribs., Inc. v. International Battery, Inc., 175 U.S.P.Q. 255, 256 (T.T.A.B. 1972).
30. 15 U.S.C. § 1060.
31. T.M.R.P. 2.186.

3. The assignor is bankrupt or insolvent.

Points to watch for in these special situations are highlighted below.

Assignment of Personal Name

A personal name can be assigned just like any other mark. But unlike other marks, a personal name can sometimes be used by the assignor in a limited fashion after the assignment. For example, even though the assignor has parted with the rights to his name as a trademark or trade name, he may be able to use his name in advertising his association with a new business.[32]

To safeguard against the assignor selling his cake and eating it too, the sale contract should prohibit the assignor from using his name in any way in association with a business similar to the assignee's.

Assignment of Trademark as Security Interest

A trademark may be assigned as security for a debt. If the debtor-assignor defaults, then the mark passes to the creditor-assignee. As is the case with all assignments, the critical element is transfer of the goodwill along with the mark.

The security interest assignment differs from an ordinary assignment in that goodwill need not pass when the assignment is executed. The security interest is conditional in nature, with the transfer of the mark only taking effect upon default. Hence, goodwill need only pass at the time the transfer takes effect, *i.e.*, if and when default occurs.[33]

While it is not necessary for the goodwill to pass at execution of the assignment, it is necessary to structure the assignment so that goodwill is included. The leading decision on this subject is the

32. Madrigal Audio Laboratories, Inc. v. Cello, Ltd., 799 F.2d 814 (2d Cir. 1986).

33. Li'l Red Barn, Inc. v. Red Barn Sys., Inc., 322 F. Supp. 98, 106-07 (N.D. Ind. 1970), *aff'd* per curiam, 174 U.S.P.Q. 193 (7th Cir. 1972).

Haymaker case.[34] There the assignment was collateral for a debt owed to attorneys. The assignment was to the escrowees who were supposed to assign the mark to the attorneys upon default. The escrowees recorded the assignment in the U. S. Patent and Trademark Office in their names.[35] The assignor went out of business and default occurred. Subsequently, a stockholder of the assignor paid off the debt and the escrowees assigned the mark to the stockholder.

The Court held the assignment to the escrowees invalid because the goodwill never passed to the escrowees. This result could be avoided by assigning with the mark a security interest in the business identified by the mark, which business passes to the creditor along with the mark upon default.[36]

Assignments in Bankruptcy

Trademarks may be assigned as part of a bankrupt business—just as they may be assigned as part of a going concern. Once again, the sine qua non of a valid assignment is the transfer of goodwill.

The tricky area with bankruptcy proceedings is the tendency to disperse the assets in different directions. It is not unusual for machinery to be sold to one bidder, inventory to another, and secret formula to a third. Just remember, that if the trademark is severed from the goodwill of the business, the trademark assignment will not be valid.[37]

---

34. Haymaker Sports, Inc. v. Turian, 581 F.2d 257, 260-61 (C.C.P.A. 1978).
35. 15 U.S.C. § 1060 provides for recordal of assignments of federal applications or registrations. For a discussion of recordal of assignments as security interest under the Uniform Commercial Code, see 2 McCarthy Trademarks and Unfair Competition, § 18:1, at 797-99 (2d ed. 1984).
36. *See In re* Roman Cleanser Co., 802 F.2d 207 (6th Cir. 1986) holding that security interest in trademark, formulas, and customer lists, but not machinery, satisfies the statutory requirement that the trademark be assigned with the goodwill of the business.
37. Johanna Farms, Inc. v. Citrus Bowl, Inc., 468 F. Supp. 866, 879 (E.D.N.Y. 1978).

As with other assignments, the assignee of a mark associated with a bankrupt business should obtain the assets needed to continue that business. The assets that are needed are those that permit the assignee to "go on in real continuity" with the past business of the assignor.[38]

38. Merry Hull & Co. v. Hi-Line Co., 243 F. Supp. 45, 51 (S.D.N.Y. 1965), *quoting* Mutual Life Ins. Co. v. Menin, 115 F.2d 975 (2d Cir. 1940).

17

Expanding Trademark Rights

Trademark owners may seek to expand their business through two routes: territorial expansion and product line expansion. Each route is beset by difficulties when a second user enters what the first user regards as his zone of expansion. The common law doctrines and statutory provisions designed to deal with these conflicting uses are the subject of this final chapter.

Territorial Expansion

Conflict over territorial rights can be grouped under four different fact patterns:

1. The second user adopts a mark in a remote area without knowledge of the first party's use in a different area; neither party owns a federal registration.
2. The second user adopts a mark in a remote area after the first user obtains federal registration.
3. The second user adopts a mark in a remote area before the first user obtains federal registration.
4. The remote area second user is the first to obtain federal registration.

Each of these fact patterns is explored below.

Remote Area Good Faith Adoption

Common Law Rule

In this scenario, the parties adopt the same or similar marks in different areas of the country. Neither party owns a federal registration. At the time the second user adopts his mark, he has no knowledge of the first user. The problem arises when the first user (plaintiff) tries to enjoin the second user's (defendant's) mark.

The general rule at common law is that the plaintiff first user will not be able to enjoin defendant's good faith second use in a remote geographical area.[1] Nor will the first user be able to expand into the territory of the second user.[2] Each party is confined to his own area of use.

Beating the Remote Area Defense

The remote area defense will not succeed if: 1) the plaintiff first user has established a reputation in the remote area before defendant adopted his mark; 2) the plaintiff first user can naturally be expected to expand to the remote area; or 3) the defendant second user adopted his mark with knowledge of the plaintiff first user.

Presence via Reputation: The remote area defense presumes that at the time the second user adopted his mark, the first user's mark was not known in the second user's territory. The remote area defense does not apply where the first user has established a reputation in the second user's territory before the second user's adoption. In this case, the second user will be enjoined because his use is likely to cause confusion.

The first user may show the presence of his reputation in the second user's area through:

---

1. Hanover Star Milling Co. v. Metcalf, 240 U.S. 403, 412 (1916); United Drug Co. v. Theodore Rectanus Co., 248 U.S. 90, 100 (1918).
2. Food Fair Stores, Inc. v. Square Deal Market Co., 206 F.2d 482 (D.C. Cir. 1953).

- sales of more than a de minimis nature;[3]
- extensive advertising;[4] and
- mobility of purchasers.[5]

Certain businesses are particularly prone to widespread reputation as a result of their mobile purchasers, *e.g.*, hotels, motels, restaurants, and gas stations.[6]

Natural Zone of Expansion: Another theoretical inroad into the remote area defense is the natural zone of expansion doctrine. In theory, if the first user can prove that the second user's area is within the zone of the first user's natural expansion, the second user will be enjoined. In practice, courts are reluctant to grant relief under this theory, probably because of its harsh result on the good faith second user. In fact, one Court of Appeals has rejected the doctrine outright, noting that the first user could have avoided the problem by obtaining a federal registration.[7]

In those jurisdictions where the natural expansion doctrine still applies, the relevant factors include: the nature and size of the first user's business; his history of expansion; and the relationship of his current business to his claimed zone of expansion, *i.e.*, is the expansion a logical step.[8] The "mere hope" for expansion is not sufficient.[9]

The Good Faith Element: The good faith prong of the remote area defense requires that the second user have no knowledge of

---

3. Sweetarts v. Sunline, Inc. 436 F.2d 705, 710 (8th Cir. 1971).
4. Stork Restaurant v. Sahati, 166 F.2d 348, 356 (9th Cir. 1948); Brooks Bros. v. Brooks Clothing, 60 F. Supp. 442, 453 (D. Cal. 1945).
5. Gastown, Inc. v. Gastown, Inc., 331 F. Supp. 626, 632 (D. Conn. 1971).
6. *Id.*
7. Raxton Corp. v. Anania Assocs., Inc. 635 F.2d 924, 930-31 (1st Cir. 1980); *see* this chapter, pp. 342-43, *infra.*
8. 2 McCarthy, Trademarks and Unfair Competition, § 26.8, at 304-05 (2d ed. 1984).
9. Blue Ribbon Feed Co. v. Farmers Union Cent. Exch., 731 F.2d 415, 422 (7th Cir. 1984).

the first user's mark at the time of adoption.[10] This does not mean, however, that the second user is barred from expanding after learning of the first user.[11] The best way for the first user to preclude the second user's claim of good faith adoption is to obtain a federal registration—more about this in the next section.

If You Can't Beat It, Limit It

If the remote area, good faith defense succeeds, the next question is: how big an area will the second user get? The general rule is that small local businesses will get small local areas. McCarthy's treatise cites case law limiting local eateries to a variety of ranges from three to thirty-six miles.[12]

Remote Area Second User's Adoption After Issuance of Federal Registration

Constructive Notice Provision of the Lanham Act

The Lanham Act sought to solve the uncertainty of the remote area use by providing that registration is "constructive notice of the registrant's claim of ownership."[13] This provision eliminated the defense of good faith where the second user adopted the mark after the first user obtained registration.[14]

The *Dawn Donut* Rule

The hitch in the constructive notice approach is that the registrant will only be able to exercise his right to enjoin the second use at the time he is likely to enter the second user's trade area. This

10. Money Store v. Harriscorp Fin., Inc., 689 F.2d 666, 674-75 (7th Cir. 1982).
11. Weiner King, Inc. v. Wiener King Corp., 615 F.2d 512, 522-23 n.6 (C.C.P.A. 1980).
12. 2 McCarthy, Trademarks and Unfair Competition, § 26:12, at 312 (2d ed. 1984) and cases cited.
13. 15 U.S.C. § 1072.
14. Dawn Donut Co. v. Hart's Food Stores, Inc., 267 F.2d 358, 362 (2d Cir. 1959).

limitation on the federal registrant's nationwide right is known as the *Dawn Donut* rule from the case bearing that name.[15] The reason behind the rule is that likely confusion will presumably not occur unless the registrant intends to move into the second user's area.[16] Until the registrant shows his entry is real, present, and impending, no injunction will issue.[17]

The Hole in the Donut

The problem with the *Dawn Donut* rule is that it permits the second user to continue his use for however long the registrant takes to enter. Of course, this puts the second user's investment completely at risk. Moreover, if the second user's reputation is not consistent with the registrant's, the second user may so tarnish the mark as to make it worthless to the registrant. What's more, the longer the second user's tenure, the more confusing it will be to the public when the registrant finally moves in.

Nevertheless, as things now stand, the registrant can only hope to persuade the second user to make a voluntary change before the registrant's entry is imminent enough for court intervention.

Remote Area Second User's Adoption Before Issuance of Federal Registration

This third fact pattern posits a second user who has begun his use before the first user obtains federal registration. The second user has intervened between plaintiff's first use and plaintiff's federal registration.

---

15. *Id.*
16. Comidas Exquisitos, Inc. v. O'Malley & McGee's, Inc., 775 F.2d 260, 262 (8th Cir. 1985).
17. Mister Donut of Am., Inc. v. Mr. Donut, Inc., 418 F.2d 838, 844 (9th Cir. 1969).

Defense to Incontestable Registration

Where plaintiff's federal registration has become incontestable, the Lanham Act provides a limited defense for the second user.

> If the right to use the registered mark has become incontestable under § 15 hereof, the registration shall be conclusive evidence of the registrant's exclusive right to use the registered mark in commerce . . . except when one of the following defenses or defects is established: . . . (5) That the mark whose use by a party is charged as an infringement was adopted without knowledge of the registrant's prior use and has been continuously used by such party or those in privity with him from a date prior to registration of the mark under this Act . . . : Provided, however, that this defense or defect shall apply only for the area in which such continuous prior use is proved.[18]

This defense is known as the limited area defense because the second user's territory is limited to his area of use existing at the time of the registration.[19] Any expansion by the second user after the registration will be cut back, although the second user can modernize within his limited area.[20] The elements of the limited area defense are:

- the second user's adoption without knowledge of the first user's mark;
- the second user's use before the first user's registration; and
- the second user's continuous use in his area following issuance of the first user's registration.[21]

18. 15 U.S.C. § 1115(b).
19. Burger King of Fla., Inc. v. Hoots, 403 F.2d 904, 906-07 (7th Cir. 1968).
20. Safeway Stores, Inc. v. Safeway Quality Foods, Inc., 433 F.2d 99, 104 (7th Cir. 1970).
21. Foxtrap, Inc. v. Foxtrap, Inc., 671 F.2d 636, 640 (D.C. Cir. 1982).

Continuous use is usage without significant interruptions. Gaps of a year or sixteen months do not meet the continuous use requirement.[22]

Like other defenses to incontestability, the limited area defense is considered to be a defense to a charge of infringement, although according to the strict language of the statute, the defense only reduces the incontestable registration to a contestable one.[23]

Defense to Contestable Registration

What if the registration is not incontestable? Some courts have suggested that a defense to an incontestable registration is a fortiori available against a contestable registration.[24] Another view is that the incontestable defense is basically a codification of the common law remote area good faith adoption defense. Hence, this is an equitable defense equally available against the assertion of a contestable registration under the Lanham Act.[25]

Under either theory, the remote area second user's adoption in good faith prior to the issuance of the first user's registration should protect the second user's rights in his limited area.

Remote Area Second User First to Obtain Registration

The final scene in the territorial battle has the remote area second user as the first party to obtain a federal registration. Here, we see two conflicting policies at work. The general rule that the

---

22. Casual Corner Assocs., Inc. v. Casual Stores of Nevada, Inc., 493 F.2d 709, 712 (9th Cir. 1974); Decatur Fed. Sav. v. Peach State Fed. Sav., 203 U.S.P.Q. 406, 415 (N.D. Ga. 1978).
23. 2 McCarthy, Trademarks and Unfair Competition, § 26:18, at 328 (2d ed. 1984). See chapter 6 pp. 105-11, *supra*, on incontestability.
24. Value House v. Phillips Mercantile Co., 523 F.2d 424, 429 (10th Cir. 1975); Matador Motor Inns, Inc. v. Matador Motel, Inc., 376 F. Supp. 385, 388 (D.N.J. 1974).
25. 15 U.S.C. § 1115(a) preserves the right to prove "any legal or equitable defense or defect which might have been asserted if such mark had not been registered."

first user has priority versus the concept of federal registration as solidifying the registrant's claim.

Both policies are recognized by allowing the first user to continue his use in his specific area, while providing the second user with rights in the rest of the country.

This territorial division applies whether the federal registration owned by the second user is contestable or incontestable. Where the second user owns a contestable registration and the first user can prove exclusive rights in his territory, the first user is entitled to a concurrent registration.[26] Where the second user owns an incontestable registration, the Lanham Act provides a specific defense to incontestability. This defense preserves the first user's rights in his limited area where:

> the use of a mark registered on the principal register infringes a valid right acquired under the law of any State or Territory by use of a mark or trade name continuing from a date prior to the date of registration under this Act of such registered mark.[27]

Thus, the first user nonregistrant is entitled to continue his use made prior to the issuance of the incontestable registration. As in the case of the limited area defense,[28] the territory accorded to the nonregistrant is fixed by his use as of the date of registration.[29]

Product Expansion

Reference to the "doctrine of natural expansion" also surfaces in product expansion cases. The typical fact pattern has a first user for certain goods seeking to bar use of the mark on "related"

---

26. Weiner King, Inc. v. Wiener King Corp., 615 F.2d 512, 523-25 (C.C.P.A. 1980). See chapter 14, pp. 308-12, *supra*, on concurrent use proceedings.
27. 15 U.S.C. § 1065.
28. 15 U.S.C. § 1115(b); *See* this chapter, pp. 344-45, *supra*.
29. Wrist-Rocket Mfg. Co. v. Saunders Archery Co., 578 F.2d 727, 730 (8th Cir. 1978).

goods. The first user complains that the second user's activity will preempt the first user's "right" to expand into a related field.

Some cases appear to treat the doctrine of natural expansion as a right separate from the right to prevent likely confusion. When the cases are closely examined, however, it is clear that the first user's so-called zone of expansion extends no further than his basic right to prevent confusion.

The products that fall within the first user's zone of expansion are those products that the consumer is likely to associate with the first user. In other words, if the consumer believes the second user's products are made or sponsored by the first user, the second user will be enjoined. This is not because there is a mythical zone of expansion accorded to the first user—it is because the second user's activity is likely to cause confusion. As McCarthy puts it:

> The "natural expansion" thesis seems to be nothing more than an unnecessarily complicated application of the likelihood of confusion of source or sponsorship test to a particular fact situation.[30]

Thus the test for natural expansion is simply a restatement of the basic test for trademark infringement: likelihood of confusion.

30. 2 McCarthy, Trademarks and Unfair Competition, § 24:5, at 180 (2d ed. 1984).

Appendix 1—Trademark Application Form

In the United States Patent and Trademark Office

Mark:

Class:

Trademark Application

Honorable Commissioner of
Patents and Trademarks
Washington, D.C. 20231

Applicant: [Insert applicant's name]

Business Address and Situs: [Insert address and state of incorporation or citizenship]

The above identified applicant has adopted and is using the trademark shown in the accompanying drawing for:

[Insert description of goods]

and requests that said mark be registered in the United States Patent and Trademark Office on the Principal Register established by the Trademark Act of July 5, 1946.

The trademark was first used on the goods at least as early as __________; was first used on the goods in interstate commerce at least as early as __________; and is now in use in such commerce.

The mark is used by applying it to the goods, labels, tags and/or containers for the goods, and/or displays associated with the goods and five specimens showing the mark as actually used are presented herewith.

[Insert name of party executing application] declares that: he is the [Insert title] of applicant corporation and is authorized to execute this Declaration on behalf of said corporation; he believes said corporation to be the owner of the mark sought to be registered; to the best of his knowledge and belief, no other person, firm, corporation, or association has the right to use said mark in commerce, either in the identical form or in such near resemblance thereto as to be likely when applied to the goods of such other person, firm, corporation, or association, to cause confusion, or to cause mistake, or to deceive; that all statements made on information and belief are believed to be true; and further, that these statements were made with the knowledge that willful false statements and the like so made are punishable by fine or imprisonment, or both, under Section 1001 of Title 18 of the United States Code and that such willful false statements may jeopardize the validity of the application or any registration resulting therefrom.

The undersigned hereby appoints the following individuals as its attorneys with full power of substitution, association, and revocation, to prosecute this application, to transact all business in the United States Patent and Trademark Office and to receive the Certificate of Registration: [Insert names of attorneys, state of admission to bar, and business address]. All communications to be held with [Insert name of individual attorney handling case].

Applicant's Name

____
Signature

____
Title

____
Date

Drawing Page

Applicant:

Business Address
and Situs:

First Use:

In Commerce:

Goods:

[Insert typed or pen and ink drawing. Pen and ink drawing can be no larger than four inches by four inches.]

Specimen Page

Applicant:

Mark:

Class:

[Affix Five Specimens]

Appendix 2—Trademark Fees[*]

(a)	For filing an application, per class	$200.00
(b)	For filing an application for renewal of a registration per class	300.00
(c)	For filing to publish a mark under section 12 (c), per class	100.00
(d)	For issuing a new certificate of registration upon request of assignee	100.00
(e)	For a certificate of correction of registrant's error	100.00
(f)	For filing a disclaimer to a registration	100.00
(g)	For filing an amendment to a registration	100.00
(h)	For filing an affidavit under section 8 of the Act, per class	100.00
(i)	For filing an affidavit under section 15 of the Act, per class	100.00
(j)	For filing a combined affidavit under sections 8 and 15 of the Act, per class	200.00
(k)	For petitions to the Commissioner	100.00
(l)	For filing petition to cancel or notice of opposition, per class	200.00
(m)	For ex parte appeal to the Trademark Trial and Appeal Board, per class	100.00
(n)	For printed copy of registered Mark	
	Copy only	1.50
	Copy showing title and/or status	6.50
(o)	For certifying trademark records, per certificate	3.50

[*] TMRP 2.6 rev. August 26, 1986.

(p) For expedited handling of such certification, per record requested 25.00

(q) For photocopies or other reproductions of records, drawings, or printed material, per page of the material copied 0.30

(r) For recording trademark assignments and agreements or other papers relating to the property in a registration or application, per document 100.00

For each mark in addition to one assigned in the same document 20.00

(s) For abstracts of title to each registration or application, including the search 12.00

(t) For special service handling of late filed fees in connection with a renewal 100.00

(u) For items and services that the Commissioner finds may be supplied, for which fees are not specified, such charges as may be determined by the Commissioner with respect to each such item or service . . . . actual cost.

Appendix 3—Declaration of Use Form

In the United States Patent and Trademark Office

Mark:

Reg. No.:

Class:

Declaration of Use Under Section 8

[Insert Registrant's name and state of incorporation or citizenship] owns Registration No. __________ registered [Insert date of Registration] as shown by records in the United States Patent and Trademark Office; the mark shown therein is still in use in [Insert type of commerce] as evidenced by the specimen attached hereto showing one manner of use of said mark.

The registrant by [Insert name of party executing Declaration], its [Insert title], declares: that all statements made herein of his knowledge are true and that all statements made on information and belief are believed to be true; and, further, that these statements were made with the knowledge that willful false statements and the like so made are punishable by fine or imprisonment, or both, under Section 1001 of Title 18 of the United States Code and that such willful false statements may jeopardize the validity of the declaration or of the registration.

The undersigned hereby appoints the following individuals as its attorneys with full power of substitution, association and revocation, to file this declaration and to transact all business in the United States Patent and Trademark Office in connection therewith and with said Registration No. __________: [Insert names of attorneys, state of admission to bar and business address]. All communications be held with [Insert name of individual attorney handling case].

Registrant's Name

____
Signature

____
Title

____
Date

Specimen Page

Registrant:

Mark:

Reg. No.:

Class:

[Affix Single Specimen]

Appendix 4—Declaration of Use and Incontestability Form

In the United States Patent and Trademark Office

Mark:

Reg. No.:

Class:

Combined Declaration Under Sections 8 and 15

[Insert Registrant's name and state of incorporation or citizenship] owns Registration Number __________ registered [Insert date of Registration], as shown by records in the United States Patent and Trademark Office; the mark shown therein has been in continuous use in [Insert type of commerce] for more than five consecutive years from [Insert date of Registration] to the date hereof, subsequent to the date of the registration on or in connection with the following:

[Insert goods from Registration meeting requirement of five consecutive years use]

recited in the registration; the mark is still in use in such commerce on or in connection with said goods as evidenced by the specimen attached hereto showing one manner of use of said mark; there has been no final decision adverse to registrant's claim of ownership of such mark for such goods, or his right to register the same, or keep the same on the register; and there is no proceeding involving any of said rights pending in the United States Patent and Trademark Office or in a court and not finally disposed of.

The registrant, by [Insert name of party executing Declaration], its [Insert title], declares: that all statements made herein of his own knowledge are true and that all statements made on information and belief are believed to be true; and further that these statements were made with the knowledge that willful false statements and the like so made are punishable by fine or imprisonment, or both, under Section 1001 of Title 18 of the United States Code and that such willful false statements may jeopardize the validity of the declaration or of the registration.

The undersigned hereby appoints the following individuals as its attorneys with full power of substitution, association, and revocation, to file this Declaration and transact all business in the United States Patent and Trademark Office in connection therewith and with said Registration No. __________: [Insert names of attorneys, state of admission to bar and business address]. All communications to be held with [Insert name of individual attorney handling case].

Registrant's Name

____

Signature

____

Title

____

Date

Specimen Page

Registrant:

Mark:

Reg. No.:

Class:

[Affix Single Specimen]

Appendix 5—Trademark Renewal Form

In the United States Patent and Trademark Office

Mark:

Reg. No.:

Class:

Renewal Application

Honorable Commissioner of
Patents and Trademarks
Washington, D.C. 20231

Registrant: [Insert current Registrant's name]

Business Address and Situs: [Insert address and state of incorporation or citizenship]

The above identified registrant requests that Registration No. ____________ granted to [Insert name of original registrant] on [Insert date of issuance] and which registrant now owns as shown by records in the Patent and Trademark Office, be renewed in accordance with the provisions of Section 9 of the Act of July 5, 1946.

The renewal fee of $ _______ is presented herewith.

[Insert name of party executing application] declares that: he is the [Insert title] of applicant corporation and is authorized to execute this declaration on behalf of said corporation; that [Insert name of current registrant] owns Registration No. ____________; that the mark shown therein is in use in [Insert type of commerce] on the following goods recited in the registration:

[Insert goods from Registration currently in use]

that the attached specimen shows the mark as currently used; that all statements made herein of his knowledge are true and that all statements made on information and belief are believed to be true; and further that these statements were made with the knowledge that willful false statements and the like so made are punishable by fine or imprisonment, or both, under Section 1001 of Title 18 of the United States Code and that such willful false statements may jeopardize the validity of the registration.

The undersigned hereby appoints the following individuals as its attorneys with full power of substitution, association, and revocation, to transact all business in the United States Patent and Trademark Office in connection therewith and to receive the Certificate of Renewal: [Insert names of attorneys, state of admission to bar and business address]. All communications to be held with [Insert name of individual attorney handling case].

Applicant's Name

____
Signature

____
Title

____
Date

NOTE—For Foreign Renewal Applicants:

Be sure to include a Designation of Domestic Representative if current attorneys did **not** handle prior filings in support of the registration.

Specimen Page

Registrant:

Mark:

Reg. No.:

Class:

[Affix Single Specimen]

Appendix 6—Trademark Assignment Form

Assignment of Trademark

WHEREAS, [Insert Assignor's name, state of incorporation (or citizenship), and business address] (hereinafter "Assignor") has used the trademark [Insert mark] (hereinafter referred to as "the said mark"), registered in the United States Patent and Trademark Office as set forth on the attached Schedule A; and

WHEREAS, [Insert Assignee's name, state of incorporation (or citizenship), and business address] (hereinafter "Assignee") is desirous of acquiring any and all rights that Assignor may have in and to the said mark and the registration therefor, together with the goodwill of the business in connection with which the said mark is used and which is symbolized by the said mark, along with the right to recover for damages and profits for past infringements thereof;

NOW, THEREFORE, for good and valuable consideration, receipt of which is hereby acknowledged, Assignor does hereby assign unto Assignee all right, title and interest in and to the said mark and the registration therefor, together with the goodwill of the business in connection with which the said mark is used and which is symbolized by the said mark, along with the right to recover for damages and profits for past infringements thereof;

Assignor agrees to execute and deliver at the request of the Assignee, all papers, instruments, and assignments, and to perform any other reasonable acts the Assignee may require in order to vest all Assignor's rights, title, and interest in and to the said mark in the Assignee and/or to provide evidence to support any of the foregoing in the event such evidence is deemed necessary by the Assignee, to the extent such evidence is in the possession or control of Assignor.

Assignor

[Affix Corporate Seal]

By ______________________________

Corporate Acknowledgment Form

STATE OF)
) ss.:
COUNTY OF)

On this ______ day of ____________, 19__, before me personally came [Insert name of party executing Assignment] to me known, who being by me duly sworn did depose and say that he is the [Insert title] of [Insert Assignor's company name], the corporation described in and which executed the foregoing instrument; that he knows the corporate seal of said corporation; that the seal affixed to said instrument is such corporate seal; that it was so affixed by order of the Board of Directors of said corporation, and that he signed his name thereto by like order.

____
Notary Public

[Affix notary stamp
and notary seal]

Individual Acknowledgment Form

STATE OF)
) ss.:
COUNTY OF)

On this ______ day of ____________, 19__, before me personally came [Insert name of party executing Assignment] to me known to be the person described in the foregoing instrument, who signed the foregoing instrument in my presence and declared the same to be of his free act and deed, on the day and year last above written.

____

Notary Public

[Affix notary stamp
and notary seal]

Schedule A

Registrant:

Reg. No.:

Reg. Date:

Mark:

Tables of Authorities

Cases

A

B

D

E

F

G

H

I

J

K

L

M

N

O

P

Q

R

S

T

U

W

X

Y

Z

Code of Federal Regulations

SECTION

Federal Rules of Civil Procedure

RULE

Federal Rules of Evidence

RULE

State Statutes

Trademark Manual of Examining Procedure

Trademark Rules of Practice

United States Code

Title 15

SECTION

Title 18

SECTION

Title 19

SECTION

Title 28

Title 35

United States Constitution

Index

Index

D

E

G

H

I

J

S

Index

About the Author

SIEGRUN D. KANE, a partner in the New York City law firm of Kane, Dalsimer, Kane, Sullivan and Kurucz, received her B.A. (cum laude) from Mount Holyoke College in 1960 and her J.D. from Harvard University in 1963. She has specialized in trademark, copyright, and unfair competition law for twenty-four years and is a frequent lecturer for the Practising Law Institute, the American Bar Association, and other continuing legal education organizations.